SOUTH HADLEY IN 1750

In Old South Hadley (MA)

Sophie E. Eastman

HERITAGE BOOKS
2008

HERITAGE BOOKS
AN IMPRINT OF HERITAGE BOOKS, INC.

Books, CDs, and more—Worldwide

For our listing of thousands of titles see our website
at
www.HeritageBooks.com

Published 2008 by
HERITAGE BOOKS, INC.
Publishing Division
100 Railroad Ave. #104
Westminster, Maryland 21157

Copyright © 1912 Sophie E. Eastman

All rights reserved. No part of this book may be reproduced or transmitted in any form or by any means, electronic or mechanical, including photocopying, recording or by any information storage and retrieval system without written permission from the author, except for the inclusion of brief quotations in a review.

International Standard Book Numbers
Paperbound: 978-0-7884-2221-8
Clothbound: 978-0-7884-7053-0

To my sister, who has been my help and inspiration in collecting materials for the present volume, and whose patient research has made possible the verification of its facts, this book is affectionately dedicated.

For the assistance rendered by Mr. A. W. Fiske, and other kind friends, in looking up ancient records and in recalling past events, they merit and receive my sincere gratitude.

THIS volume does not assume to be, in any sense, a history. The author has merely tried to gather up and preserve some of the facts and incidents connected with the Early Life of our town. This information was derived, in a great measure, from old Letters and Diaries; Account Books ranging from 1732 to 1820; Town, Church and State Records; Ancient Deeds, Wills and Inventories, and the too-often-forgotten Proprietor's Book.

The truth of every statement has been carefully sifted, and some old manuscripts recently brought to light have yielded new and interesting facts. It is a matter of regret that many items which might have been of interest have necessarily been omitted for the lack of space.

CHAPTER INDEX

PAGE

CHAPTER FIRST
The Origin of the Town.................................... 1

CHAPTER SECOND
Early Life in South Hadley................................ 21

CHAPTER THIRD
Early Life in South Hadley (Concluded)....................... 35

CHAPTER FOURTH
From Dame School to College................................. 48

CHAPTER FIFTH
From Dame School to College (Concluded)...................... 70

CHAPTER SIXTH
The Evolution of a Church................................... 94

CHAPTER SEVENTH
The Indians.. 121

CHAPTER EIGHTH
South Hadley in the Revolution.............................. 136

CHAPTER NINTH
South Hadley After the Revolution........................... 165

CHAPTER TENTH
In the Chimney Corner....................................... 186

CHAPTER ELEVENTH
South Hadley Falls.. 201

INDEX TO ILLUSTRATIONS

	PAGE
South Hadley in 1750	Frontispiece
The Angel of Hadley, 1675	6
In the Bow of Stony Brook	10
Present View from "Bare Hill"	12
Husking for a Neighbor	18
"The Place of General Resort"	22
The Noontide Meal	26
Reading the Bible to the Haymakers	28
The Gaylord Library	32
The Pump	38
The Old Oaken Bucket	40
The Rudiments of Arithmetic	50
Teaching Arithmetic	54
Woodbridge School	70
Autograph of Mary Lyon	76
Third Parsonage	78
Prospect Hill	82
Mt. Holyoke Seminary, the Original Building	84
The Domestic Hall	86
Seminary and College Building, Destroyed by Fire, September, 1896	88
Mary Lyon's Grave	92
The First Parsonage	96
Rev. John Woodbridge	108
Brick Oven	110
Second Meeting House	116
Third Meeting House	118
The Oxbow	122
Island in the Connecticut	124
The Granby Church	128
The Drive	134
Col. Ruggles Woodbridge	140
The Second Parsonage	146
Lake Nonotuck, South Hadley	154
The Grove	164
South Hadley in 1850	170
Doctor Dwight's House	176
College Street	180
Fourth Meeting House, Destroyed by Fire, 1895	184
Ferry at the foot of Mount Holyoke	188
The First Meeting House, Now Used as a Dwelling	190
The First Mountain House on Mount Holyoke	194
"The Old Sleigh"	196
Pass of Thermopylæ	198
The Franklin Stove	198
Drawing in the Back-log	200
The Canal Village	202
Decoration Day at South Hadley Falls	220
The Present Million-Dollar Dam	214
The Carew Mill	216

IN OLD SOUTH HADLEY
BY SOPHIE E. EASTMAN

CHAPTER FIRST
THE ORIGIN OF THE TOWN

CAESAR'S reply, when questioned in regard to his lineage, "I commence an ancestry," might well have been echoed by the pioneers of Hadley. Most of them were fugitives from England, fleeing to this country in order to escape the persecution of Archbishop Laud. They had seen their friends imprisoned and publicly whipped in the market-place simply for seeking a higher standard of purity in the church.

Part of them came in 1632 in the good ship Lyon. They were four weeks in fighting their way from London to Lands End, and two months more in crossing the stormy Atlantic. For five days they were enveloped in a dense fog, not daring to move in either direction; a weary time for the sixteen children and their seventy-three elders, who clustered despairingly about the deck. But happily they escaped disaster. The most notable among the passengers was William Goodwin, a man destined to become of such influence in both church and state that the town still delights to do him honor.

During the following year more of Hadley's early settlers came over in the Griffin, and the tedium of the two months' voyage was beguiled by listening to one hundred and twenty sermons, two being preached on each week-day and three on Sunday.

Among the passengers were three divines, eminent both for learning and piety—the Rev. John Cotton, Thomas Hooker, and Samuel Stone. Only the latter, however, dared to show himself on deck until they were well out at sea.

The sailors did not enjoy this constant sermonizing, and

sneeringly asked, "When shall we come to ye Holie Land?" And when the ministers sought to buy provisions, they replied, "Ye are so full of the spirit, ye need nothing more."

But religion was not the only topic on which they conversed. In the joy of escape they became even humorous, and actually ventured upon a witticism in regard to the three ministers on board. A hooker was a small fishing boat still in use at the Orkneys, and some facetious passenger gave out that they were well provided for, having Cotton for their clothing, Stone for their building, and a Hooker for their fishing.

A majority of the company settled at Cambridge, then called New Town, but two years later jealousies and animosities sprang up between this place and Boston, and under the slender pretext that they were straitened for want of land, they asked of the General Court permission to remove to Hartford, Conn.

On May 31, 1636, fivescore persons, including Rev. Thomas Hooker and Rev. Samuel Stone, set forth on their perilous journey through pathless woods, with only a compass and a few obscure Indian trails to guide them.

In Hartford and adjoining towns they soon found homes, and for many years lived peacefully and prosperously. So close was the friendship between William Goodwin and the Rev. Mr. Stone that both before and after this journey their houses were built side by side. But after the death of Mr. Hooker, Mr. Goodwin and his pastor became alienated and even embittered against one another. Nearly all of the Massachusetts Colonists were church members and their children had been baptized into the same faith. Some of their sons had grown to manhood without making a public profession of religion, though leading exemplary lives. These persons found themselves deprived of the right to vote in town meeting, denied the ordinance of baptism for their children, and debarred from having any voice in the selection of a minister. This roused their indignation, and a great wave of dissatisfaction arose in the Hartford Church, spreading in ever widening ripples until the whole country was a sea of discontent. Some even went so far as to propose that all men whose lives were of good report should be allowed to partake of the communion. Councils were held, but nothing decisive was accomplished.

Elder Goodwin bitterly opposed the agitation of this question. It seemed to him like breaking down the gates into the fold, and a large minority of the church sympathized with him. Not so the pastor, Rev. Mr. Stone. He had always been less rigid in his views than many of his brethren, and had often disturbed good Mr. Hooker by his habit of smoking, his liberal ideas of orthodoxy, and other such matters. So now he gave his hearty assent to the Halfway Covenant, as it was termed, which had been approved by the council at Boston in 1657. This council decreed that non-church members who owned the covenant, and had nothing scandalous in their lives, should not be denied the rite of baptism for their children; but this did not give them the privilege of partaking of the Lord's Supper.

The intrusion of this article of belief among the inhabitants of South Hadley, about eighty years later, was the occasion of a violent religious quarrel, rending the church, and ending in the expulsion of the town's first minister, Rev. Grindal Rawson.

Feeling ran so high that Elder Goodwin determined to withdraw, with his followers, from the Hartford Church, and to return to what he called "Ye pious and Godly government of Massachusetts Bay."

Rev. John Russell, of Wethersfield, and most of his congregation, were in unison with Mr. Goodwin, and joined in his plan of removal to Norwottuck, the present town of Hadley. Of the pilgrimage thither, we know but little; we hear of an accomplished journey, but none of its details. Yet it must have been an arduous undertaking. It may be that by day the October sunshine filtered through the crimson and golden leaves, making a glory about their heads; but the nights were chill, and the bear, the wolf, and the catamount were always out watching for their prey in the far-reaching forests.

No sooner had they arrived at their destination than the woods rang with the sound of their axes, and the work of building went rapidly on.

The history of Hadley from this time onward has been so

minutely and accurately told by the late Sylvester Judd that no other hand is needed to bridge the gulf between the centuries.

One incident that he relates finds confirmation among the descendants of Lieut. Samuel Smith, Peter Tilton, Timothy Nash, Nathaniel Dickinson, and Elder John White. Many of their descendants are still living in South Hadley and Granby, and five of them have made affidavit in the presence of a Notary Public to the fact that the following story had been handed down in their families, from father to son, for over two hundred years.

Few events in the history of Hadley have excited such universal interest as the long concealment of the regicides by Rev. John Russell, assisted by Lieut. Samuel Smith and the Hon. Peter Tilton, and the unlooked-for aid of General Goffe in repelling an Indian attack. The story is too widely known to need more than a brief repetition.

General Whalley and his son-in-law, General Goffe, were two of the judges who had condemned Charles I of England to death. Upon the accession of his son to the throne, a price was set upon their heads, and they were obliged to flee to America. Here, being closely pursued, they were compelled to hide in cave, ravine or forest, finally finding a refuge in a well-contrived chamber in the minister's house at Hadley.

Some of the carpenters of that day had evidently learned, during the persecutions in England, the art of concealment, for this room gave access to the cellar, probably by means of a sliding panel, such as was found in demolishing an old house in another part of the town, and which dated back to the same period.

During King Philip's war, the towns which lay upon the outskirts of civilization were in constant and extreme danger from roving bands of Indians. Hadley was peculiarly defenceless, not only as a frontier town, but because the Connecticut River afforded such a swift and silent path of approach for Indian canoes. Each day seemed a terror, each night a menace, and the "Holy text of pike and gun" was in all minds.

The story of General Goffe's appearance was often related to a resident of South Hadley by her grandmother, just as it had been told to the latter by her grandfather, Nathaniel Dick-

THE ORIGIN OF THE TOWN

inson, who was living at the time the incident occurred. Although but a boy, the fact that his father was slain by the Indians at about the same time may have impressed the events of the year upon his memory.

The minister at Hadley, recognizing the great danger to be apprehended from Indian invasion, had appointed a day of fasting and prayer, and on this occasion every member of Mr. Russell's household, excepting the two regicides, attended divine service at the meeting-house. This left the two voluntary captives at liberty to roam about the house at pleasure and look from the windows. General Goffe, noting the approach of the Indians, hastily descended to the street. Two courses lay open before him; he would risk discovery if he showed himself in the town, and the English government was still searching for him, but, on the other hand, if the settlers were overpowered, pillage, fire, and massacre were sure to follow.

The Hadley men had no leader and were beginning to waver before the onslaught of their savage foes, when Goffe, with a roar like that of a wild beast, placed himself in the front ranks. Perhaps the old-time vigor came back for a moment; at all events, he rallied the men and charged the Indians with such power and skill that they were soon in full retreat. During the pursuit, Goffe quietly slipped aside and, returning to the house of Mr. Russell, became again a self-immured prisoner.

There was much questioning after the battle as to the identity of their unexpected ally. The paleness engendered by years of confinement, and perhaps the long and snowy beard (for smooth faces were then coming into vogue), evidently suggested to some imaginative mind the idea that the strange visitor was of supernatural origin. It was not until after William ascended the throne of England, and the search for the regicides ceased, that it was considered safe to make known the real facts in the case.

Some modern iconoclasts have tried to wrest this incident from the pages of history, but with little success, and generations yet unborn will repeat to their children, and children's children, the story of Goffe, the Angel who Saved the Town.

The early settlement of South Hadley may be attributed to the energy, courage, and perseverance of six persons—Peter, William and Luke Montague, Chileab Smith, Jr., John Preston, and Ebenezer Marsh.

These men were linked together, not merely by the ties of kindred, but by a common hope and ambition, and the history of their enterprise should be preserved in picture, song, and story, as long as the town endures.

Seventeen hundred came and went without finding, it was said, a single pauper in the whole Connecticut Valley. But a vague spirit of unrest had begun to creep into the quiet town of Hadley. It gathered strength as the years went on, till we find it recorded that the young people complained of being straitened for the want of room. Now, surrounded as they were with the vast areas of unmapped country, and in a village where many a family owned hundreds of acres of untilled land, their discontent must have referred to the crowded state of their households—too many families in one dwelling being the rule.

Thus, John Preston, Sr., married one of four sisters, each of whom brought her husband home to live under the paternal roof. And the children of William Montague, whose relatives were among the richest people of the town, lived in the same house with their uncles, aunts, and cousin, to say nothing of their father, mother, and grandparents.

In order to remedy this difficulty, and possibly to gratify their spirit of adventure, certain men in the community resolved to colonize south of Mount Holyoke.

The proposal aroused a fine commotion in the town. People shook their heads and declared that those sandy slopes and wooded intervales were incapable of cultivation, generally ending with the cheerful forecast that their families would certainly starve. The old folks, with tears in their eyes, begged them to give up their mad plan. But nothing daunted their courage, for already the very air seemed to be electric with the coming possibilities of the new town.

THE ANGEL OF HADLEY, 1675

THE ORIGIN OF THE TOWN

Tradition tells us that at last a town meeting was called, from which was wrung a reluctant consent to the exodus. But, be this as it may, we know that in the spring of 1720, a day of fasting and prayer was appointed from the pulpit, in order to implore the Divine Blessing upon this hazardous undertaking.

Others, outside the list of names previously mentioned, had at first joined in the enterprise, but without a just estimate of the danger, privation, and incessant labor that the task involved.

First of all, roads must be located, and within their boundaries trees must be felled and stumps uprooted, in order to open even the roughest kind of a cart-track. After the site of a house had been decided upon, ground must be cleared in order to give space for working and for the tent which would be their only shelter until the roof was covered with shingles, which latter must be made by hand. Their tools were clumsy and often dull, yet no scamping of their work was tolerated.

If the half-dozen men, who remained true to their purpose, needed a Nestor, they certainly found one in the person of Chileab Smith, Sr., since three of their number were his grandsons, a fourth was his son, the fifth his granddaughter's husband, and the sixth a brother of his son's wife.

The great event of 1720 in Hadley was the laying out of home lots south of Mt. Holyoke. For several years this matter had been under discussion without reaching any definite result.

The winter of 1717 had been one of unexampled severity. Noah Webster has stated that at this time there were snowdrifts from sixteen to eighteen feet deep, so that in order to leave their houses some persons were compelled to put on snow shoes and climb out of the second story windows.

This fact may have deferred the enterprise, but three years later there still remained a resolute purpose to—as the old records express it—"make a village, or precinct, behind the mountain." In February of 1720 a town meeting was called and a committee appointed who should lay out one thousand acres of the best farming land to be found there.

Their report included nine divisions of land. The first of

these, possibly in continuance of its Indian name, was called Leaping Well. It contained four home lots, number one being chosen by Nathaniel Ingram, whose descendants retained possession of it for more than a century and a half.

The second division was called "North of Stony Brook." It consisted of nine home lots, and lay upon the west side of College street, beginning near the residence of I. N. Day and extending northerly nearly, or quite, to the schoolhouse grounds. The latter place was at this time part of a highway ten rods wide, which, beginning at the schoolhouse, extended westerly down the slope of the hill till at the foot of the ravine it turned, running northward to Hadley street. This road formed part of the main thoroughfare from Springfield to Hadley, since the cross street in front of J. S. Preston's house had not then been opened.

About thirty rods southwest of the post office was a quagmire, and the whole section was spoken of in the ancient records as "The Gutter, or Lubber's Hole."

Tradition gives us this account of the manner in which it gained its name, though two centuries have so changed the conformation of the ground that the story loses much of its significance. Three very fleshy men, so the old folks say, were once journeying from Springfield to Hadley. They traveled in company, partly for the sake of sociability, but chiefly as a means of mutual protection against wild animals. One of the number, who had been partaking too freely of old New England rum, wandered from the road and ended by falling into the quagmire. Owing to his great weight and half-intoxicated condition, it was almost impossible to extricate him. The definition of a lubber was "a heavy, clumsy fellow," and this incident fixed the name of Lubber's Hole upon a region that has always been noted for the industry and enterprise of its citizens.

Many of these early names were given in recognition of some supposed characteristic. Misery Swamp, near the Slipe, was tenanted by wolves, who made night hideous with their dismal howling. Bare Hill (now Prospect) was almost wholly destitute of vegetation, while Bear Mountain was the favorite haunt of Sir Bruin. Cold Hill is still swept by the chilly northwesters that led to its early name, and Buttery Brook, too, has a little story of its own.

A buttery at first denoted a place where butter was kept, but in process of time its signification broadened, and it came to be synonymous with pantry, a place where food was stored. In those days it was customary, when a deer was killed in springtime or during the summer, to separate the flesh from the bones, the former being, to quote from J. G. Holland, "stored in a spring whose water, summer and winter alike, was almost at freezing point." This particular location in South Hadley Falls was recorded in 1720 as "Markham's Buttery," so named, probably, in honor of William Markham of Hadley, a son-in-law of Governor John Webster. He may have been an unusually successful hunter and one who shared generously the products of his skill, for thirty years after he had gone upon his last journey the Proprietor's Book still speaks of Markham's Buttery.

The third division of land was called "North of Lubber's Hole." It contained eighteen home lots, one of which (a part of the Eastman homestead, now owned by J. A. Skinner) was set aside for, as the records says, "The first well larnt, orthodox minister as shall settle south of Mt. Holyoke." This division began upon the west side of Woodbridge street, near the foot of Mrs. Hollingsworth's garden, and extended northward to the house owned by Hinsdale Smith.

These lots were, as the committee reported, curiously shaped, "something triangular at the rear of them, and each one of them longest upon the southerly side."

The White family chose their lots near the site now owned by A. S. Kinney, and by purchase eventually obtained the whole of this division.

"The fourth division, west of Stony Brook," comprised twenty-eight home lots upon the east side of College, Woodbridge and Amherst streets, beginning near the Perkins Mill and reaching almost to Bittersweet Lane. It provided also for a highway, eight rods wide, to be located a little below the present Morgan street. The land which formed the original Seminary Campus was chosen by William Murray and Peter Montague, Jr.

The fifth division, "north of Peachawomiche Road," began at nearly the same point where the fourth ended, and extended northerly to Bachelor's Brook. The land of Samuel Porter, who had drawn home lot number sixty-four, included both sides of Amherst street, that highway not being laid out until a dozen years later, when it was so narrow it was known only as Hubbard's Path, which followed the old Indian trail from the Notch to Cold Hill.

The sixth division consisted of twenty-seven lots upon the western side of Cold Hill, eight of these being chosen by as many individual Smiths.

In the seventh division, "east of Cold Hill," were fourteen lots, from which three more Smith families and six Dickinsons chose their homes.

The eighth division lay "east of Bare Hill, in the bow of Stony Brook." Here the leading owners were the Kelloggs, who retained a part of this land until 1909.

The ninth and last division was "south of Bare Hill," near the Preston homestead.

The distribution of these one thousand acres of land was effected in a somewhat singular manner. There were at this time one hundred and seventeen proprietors holding taxable property within the limits of Hadley, and it was voted that the size of each person's home lot should be in proportion to his ratable estate. In consequence of this provision, and of the fact that the lots were laid out from a quarter to a half mile in depth, it came about that while the rich men had a frontage on the street of from three hundred to seven hundred feet, the unfortunate owner of lot number seventy-five found himself possessed of a long strip of land only six feet, two and one-fourth inches in width.

The method of determining the order in which each proprietor should make choice of his land was by "the lot." A

IN THE BOW OF STONY BROOK

THE ORIGIN OF THE TOWN

town meeting was called and the presiding officer placed in a hat or box slips of paper numbered from one to one hundred and eighteen. Each proprietor as his name was called took out one of these slips, which denoted not the number of his home lot, but that of his turn for choosing his land. The fortunate person who drew number one had his first choice of the whole territory then laid out. He who drew the last number must take whatever piece of land was left.

After the distribution of the home lots had been completed, it was soon found that very few of the proprietors were ready to face the difficulties and dangers attendant upon the beginning of a new settlement. Only the six, whose names have already been given, adhered firmly to their purpose. The latter, it was said, had entered into a compact to work in rotation at clearing the land and building one another's houses.

The following account of the manner in which this enterprise was conducted was derived partly from tradition and partly from ancient records, but is probably correct in nearly every detail.

The pioneers of South Hadley, with the exception of Luke Montague, who, not being of age, was not yet entitled to draw a home lot, were all married men whose ages ranged from twenty-eight to thirty-seven years. Since Peter Montague would have the assistance of his younger brother, it would naturally be expected that his should be the first house to be framed, especially as he had shrewdly selected his land in a central location, and just opposite the point of junction where the two roads leading from Hadley came together, but before this house could be built great trees must be felled, great beams hewed, and planks be sawed, to say nothing of joists, shingles and hand-made nails.

It was soon learned that the best timber for this purpose was to be found upon Chileab Smith's home lot, which he had, perhaps, chosen with a view to this very end. His land was embraced in the farm formerly occupied by the late Mr. Albert Goldthwait, and the first field ever cleared in South Hadley lay a little southeast of the house of Deacon Calvin Preston.

For nearly two centuries this piece of ground was known distinctively as "The Old Field."

The old Proprietor's Book speaks of the mill pond (south of Mrs. Dunklee's land), on which at this time a saw mill was said to have been standing, and a rough cart track between this place and Chileab Smith's home lot could be quickly opened.

No sooner was the unseasoned timber for the new house prepared for weathering than other work lay ready at hand. Ebenezer Marsh had acquired possession of a piece of land northwest from the home of Sheriff Brockway. This must be cleared and prepared for the first apple orchard ever set out in South Hadley. Within a distance of eight miles were nurseries from which young trees could be transplanted, and in old account books from 1732 to 1740 we find frequent entries like the following: "Bo't of Eb. Marsh, 2 Barils of Syder."

While this work was progressing, it is said that these first settlers went back to Hadley every Saturday afternoon, returning to their work Monday morning, bringing with them loaves of rye and Indian bread, nut cakes, gingerbread, and like dainties. As for more substantial food, fish, deer and wild turkeys were never far to seek.

It is doubtful whether the house of Peter Montague was completed during this first summer. Months were required for seasoning the green timber so that it would neither shrink nor warp; then, too, the chimney must be taken into consideration, ground must be excavated to the depth of several feet, that its foundation might be below the reach of frost.

Early in 1721 we find our pioneers buying more land south of Mt. Holyoke, this last winter (spent in Hadley) having in nowise discouraged them. During the summer of 1721, more land was cleared, material for John Preston's house was prepared and fruit trees planted, Peter Montague setting out young apple trees and placing a pear tree at the very corner of his house. The latter is thought to have survived one hundred and fifteen years.

As summer waned, a new danger threatened, since a fresh Indian war was imminent. For more than a year it had been

PRESENT VIEW FROM "BARE HILL".

THE ORIGIN OF THE TOWN 13

the law that every man should keep arms and ammunition within his house, and the weight of their heavy matchlocks, which must always be kept within reach while they worked, added much to the labor of building.

In the early days there had been a law that every town upon the Connecticut River should keep in readiness "ninety coats basted with cotton wool and made defensive against Indian arrows," and when, as was customary, the minister preached to and prayed with the soldiers before their setting out, his text was usually an inspiration, as, "Thou shalt not be afraid for the arrow that flieth by day." But, now, in spite of the law strictly prohibiting the sale of firearms to the Indians, they had learned their use, owned them, and had lost their superstitious fear of the stick that sent thunder and lightning.

During the last two decades many white men had been slain near the banks of the Connecticut, some when working in the fields and others in their own homes. At this time the Indians, instigated by their French allies, had already taken captive whole families of the English and carried them to Canada.

Hadley, early in 1722, in spite of the threatening aspect of affairs, made a second grant of land south of Mt. Holyoke. This grant was five times the size of the previous one, and the success of the new settlement seemed now to be assured.

In this distribution of land William Montague appears to have cared but little for his own original home lot, which stood on Woodbridge street, desiring a more remote location. When the day appointed for the choosing of land arrived, he, followed possibly by Peter Domo, who located near him, desired to go farther afield. It is said that William Montague, after reaching Woodbridge street, declared himself ready to walk eastward, following an old Indian trail, until sunset. Nightfall found him at the McGrath Spring on Batchelor street. Although the land eventually decided upon lay farther to the south and near Granby Center, yet he kept his promise of settling east of the first nine divisions.

The importance of having new roads, whereby intending

settlers could reach their meadows and pasture lands, soon became apparent. The first highway laid out in the town, aside from the usual thoroughfare between Springfield and Hadley, was on Moshier street, which extended northerly to the house of J. W. Waite, then easterly to South street, in Granby—the surveyors choosing, as the old record said, "The hardest and evenest land."

We also read that on April 20, 1722, "We laid out a highway running easterly from ye Cold Hill to ye end of our Bounds, which run as ye Old Path runs. Excepting some perticular places where we run streighter or other places where ye ground was better going. This is called by some ye Peachawomache Road, which is eight rods wide." On the following day a highway was laid out from the Krug Homestead to Smith's Ferry, but this was not cleared of trees until many years later. The locations of these old roads have in most cases been somewhat changed.

Perhaps no better proof can be found of the kind feeling and sense of justice which prevailed in those days than their method of locating new roads. Many of our allotments of land were laid out in tiers so that some persons were unable to reach their own grounds without crossing those of their neighbors. In such cases the latter was forbidden by law to plow up the land traversed by the former. A committee was appointed who apprised the land for the road and the man who wanted the right of way paid for it and held it. The expense of felling the trees and digging up the stumps in these long highways would have been a heavy burden for the town to assume, and later on it was accordingly voted that those settlers who needed fuel in order to replenish their winter fires should have liberty to clear the timber from the roads. As the boundaries of the highway were not very clearly defined, it was sometimes a great temptation to encroach upon the land of some other proprietor. A man who was once reproved for cutting a fine tree beyond the bounds replied that "The highway is always widest where the best timber grows."

The work of constructing these roads was soon interrupted

THE ORIGIN OF THE TOWN

by the fourth Indian war, which was terminated only by the Long Peace of 1726. During this time the depredations of the red men were so great that the government, in order to stimulate watchfulness, offered a bounty of one hundred pounds for every Indian scalp. Under these circumstances, life south of Mt. Holyoke would be deemed very unsafe.

John Preston and his associates had not forgotten how the red men, a few years before, had climbed to the summit of Mt. Tom in order to mark the position of the scattered houses in the village beneath, and had then descended to massacre more than a score of its unsuspecting inhabitants. A portion of the great Indian trail from Connecticut to Canada lay directly through South Hadley; it extended from the ford near the bridge in the Connecticut River to Turkey Pass, or The Notch, as it is now called. Why should not Mt. Holyoke prove to be an equally good vantage ground for the savage foe? Prudence certainly dictated that the new settlement should be abandoned for a time.

Ancient records indicate that this course was the one pursued, and again forest and copse echoed the evening song of the wood-thrush.

There were still, however, brief journeys to the embryo town. In 1725, John Preston, desiring to be near his kinsman, purchased the land adjoining Chileab Smith's home lot on the west. This place, known as the Preston Farm, has remained in the possession of his descendants ever since.

Here, as soon as the war was over, he erected the second frame dwelling house ever built in South Hadley. Its massive and well-seasoned timbers were fastened strongly together with large wooden pegs. His original home lot had been on College street, and included what has been known as the Old Howard Place.

Several decades after the erection of this second dwelling house there came a winter of unusual length and severity. The snow lay so deep upon the levels that on the 20th of March this building was drawn across to College street over the tops of the fences, and after being set a short distance west of the highway became the southern ell of the Howard house. This dwelling was consumed by fire some years since or South Hadley's second house might have survived for centuries to come.

Early in 1727 a change of sentiment in regard to the South Precinct became manifest. Many new settlers determined to occupy the land previously allotted them. A party which included five families of Smiths, three of Kelloggs, three of Taylors, and others, commenced the work of building their houses.

Luke Montague, a stalwart bachelor of twenty-seven, had now returned to South Hadley. He brought with him the famous Courting Stick, which was so useful on cold winter nights when there being but one fire in the house, the whole family must be present at the wooing. This Courting Stick was a hollow tube about five feet in length, through which two lovers could whisper to one another without their conversation being audible to those about them.

Peter Montague's first house appears to have been occupied at this time by Daniel Nash, Jr., who subsequently purchased the premises. He was apparently not quite satisfied with the location of the house, which, it is said, after taking down the stone chimney, he moved to the present site of the Art Building. Here he erected a huge chimney formed of hand-made bricks. Attached to the house was a gunsmith's shop, wherein also he shod horses and oxen.

As for Ebenezer Marsh, aged people many years ago claimed that the old kitchen still at the rear of Fred Loomer's dwelling contained the big chimney and ponderous beams of "Eb's" first domicile.

The number of settlers south of the mountain began to increase so rapidly that within five years nearly forty families were living there.

The work of building these early houses was of necessity a slow and laborious one. They spent little time in digging cellars, but turned their attention at once to preparing material for chimneys, the bricks for which must all be made by hand. For this purpose sand must be thoroughly mixed with the clay in order to prevent it from cracking, and as they had none of our modern machinery this could be accomplished only by the trampling of heavy feet. If the chimney were to be a large one the sand and clay were placed together upon the ground, and for two days the patient oxen were driven back and forth, back and forth, till the two ingredients were well mingled. Molding it into form and drying it in the sun before putting it into their primitive kilns must also be done by hand. The number of bricks that went into the making of these chimneys would be almost incredible in our day. A grandson of one of our pioneers, building a house here in 1791, used 10,000 hand-made bricks in constructing a single chimney.

In the beginning all worked together, in turn, upon one another's houses, their joint labor being a necessity when heavy lifting was to be done. Confederacy was also a measure of safety at night when the tenants of the forests must be guarded against. Not only did the wolves issue from their lairs, but Sir Bruin, less fierce yet a clever marauder, might be sleeping in the very door yard. Then, too, the presence of venomous reptiles entailed constant vigilance. Rattlesnakes came down from the mountain in search of water and were often found at the very threshold. One woman, returning from a fierce encounter in which she had routed his snakeship, said, excitedly, but without a thought of irreverence, "I have killed the Devil." So numerous and venomous were these reptiles that more than a century later it was a common saying in Amherst College that no student was worthy of his diploma unless he had killed a rattlesnake. A member of the Class of 1830 said at a commencement dinner that at the time of his graduation there were not students enough in the college to keep the campus free from snakes.

Old Mr. Root, who lived in the next town, was always ready to tell of his adventure with wolves. He had been down to the meadow to see if the grass was ready to cut, and, it being a time of peace with the Indians, had left his heavy matchlock at home. On his way back he heard a strange noise, and, looking up, saw a pack of wolves coming toward him. He had not even a stick with which to defend himself, and reflecting that God alone could save him, he stood still in the path, closed his eyes, and prayed that for the sake of his wife and little ones the Lord would preserve him. He could hear the shuffling of the wolves' feet as he breathed his petition and expected every moment to feel their fangs in his throat. Presently the sound appeared to grow fainter and recede. Opening his eyes he saw the last one disappearing and knew that he was saved.

Bears were not at this time considered dangerous to the human race unless angered or very hungry. Instances are told of little children in this vicinity passing them unharmed. The author's great-grandfather used to relate the story of a narrow escape which he once had. He was going courting, and riding on horseback through the forests, saw before him a large black bear sitting upright beside the woodland path. He looked so dignified that the young man, in his light-heartedness, ventured on a joke. As he passed by he lifted his hat and bowed low. "Your servant, sir," he said. But the bear evidently considered this a challenge to mortal combat, for, with a fierce growl, he instantly started in pursuit. Mile after mile the horse's feet, winged by fear, rushed madly on, but close behind them, like a relentless fate, came the padding sound of the infuriated brute. At last the panting horse, exhausted by the race for life, began to falter and the end seemed near, when, lo, beside the path stood a house and yard encircled by a fence. The gate was, fortunately, open, and horse and rider entered. The bear stopped to gaze suspiciously at the fence, then with a disappointed growl turned and went back into the forest.

During the early settlement of the town there prevailed among its inhabitants an almost universal spirit of kinship and a generous regard for one another's interests. To every newcomer there was straightway given what was called a Chopping Bee. On the appointed morning men might be seen coming from every direction, carrying axes, saws and other implements of labor. When, at sunset, the grateful proprietor surveyed the transformation that had been effected, he could hardly believe the testimony of his own eyes. This great change had been brought about by what was then called the drive; this

HUSKING FOR A NEIGHBOR

meant that the woods had been leveled in the following manner: A row of trees was selected, the first one of which was felled and removed; the others were then partly cut, all of them upon the same side toward the front, the smaller trees being chopped into until the middle of the trunk had been reached, while the larger ones were penetrated still more deeply. The last tree in the row was felled in such a manner that it would drop upon the preceding one, and when the crashing sound that followed had ceased it would be found that all the trees had fallen in the same manner that a long row of ninepins can be thrown down by a single blow administered at one end of the line.

Most of these early houses were small, one-story affairs, and if any attempt was made at having a cellar the latter could only be reached by means of a short ladder let down through a trap door in the kitchen floor.

In 1728 Peter Montague, returning to South Hadley, purchased the land southwest of Bachelor Brook, where he built his second house, which was at that date the finest dwelling south of Mt. Holyoke. Four of its large rooms contained each a big, open fireplace; one of these, a chamber in the second story, being called the spinning room.

It had been one of the early laws that boys, girls and women should spin thirty weeks each year, and it was the duty of the selectmen to see that this edict was carried into effect. During the twenty-two weeks of cold weather very few of our inhabitants had any means of heating their spinning room. South Hadley did not intend that the crime of laziness should take root within her borders, and a special committee was appointed to look after idle persons. This duty later on developed upon the tithing men, whose office was not simply to preserve order in church, but to see that in every family the spinning and weaving of flax and wool provided sufficient clothing for the household. They were at that time called inspectors of the neighbors. Any families who neglected to comply with their demands were warned by the constable that they must leave the town.

Habits of enforced industry were continued until far into

the nineteenth century. Each of the young people had a certain amount of work allotted them, which was called their stint or stent, and no recreation was allowed until this task had been accomplished. Even the younger boys, upon their return from school, were required to knit a certain number of rounds upon their stockings before they could have a moment of play time.

There was often a friendly rivalry among young girls in the same neighborhood. Our minister's daughter, Julia Hayes, in the old parsonage now occupied by Mrs. Lester, Clarissa Dwight, who lived on the present site of the Art Building, and Sally White, whose father kept a tavern, each had the same amount of spinning allotted to them. This trio had agreed among themselves that whoever first finished her task should hang a towel from the window, and every morning found the girls at the very earliest peep of day sitting at their spinning wheels, each ambitious of being the first to hang out the signal that her stent was accomplished.

In such ways did our forefathers teach their children to respect the old saying that "Idleness travels very slowly and poverty soon overtakes her."

CHAPTER SECOND

EARLY LIFE IN SOUTH HADLEY

MANIFOLD were the devices whereby our early housewives were aided in their struggle with the privations incident to the settlement of a new town.

Then, as now, Monday was washing day. The larger home lots had been so carefully laid out that nearly every one contained a stream of water, where in summer the clothing of the family could be washed and then hung upon the bushes to dry.

But when winter came and the brooks were fettered with ice some substitute for the modern tub must be devised. Nature, however, had anticipated many of their needs. Ready at hand in our swamps stood a species of the black gum, called the peperidge tree, whose trunk when old was hollow or filled with a soft, spongy substance which could be easily removed. A section of the trunk was sawed off, two projections being left upon the upper side, which would later be made into handles, and a round disk of wood was fitted into the other end. The records show that a washing tub was considered the equivalent in value of a half bushel measure. Churns, keelers for washing dishes, mortars, and miniature barrels, which served as a receptacle for soft soap, were made in a similar manner. A softer kind of wood, with a less twisted grain, was used in the manufacture of the wooden plates, bowls, platters, and other dishes in common use. The children ate their bread and milk with spoons whittled out by their fathers, or cunningly shaped from gourds, raised for this purpose. Even the first communion service may have been in this, as in other towns, a wooden one.

Upon the advent of visitors, the dinner table was adorned with pewter plates and dishes, shining like so much silver. Only at neighborhood tea parties did the few bits of china appear. At these each guest was supposed to bring his or her own cup, saucer, teaspoon, and possibly an earthen plate. The tea was cooled in and drank from the saucer, and a spoon placed in the cup was a signal to the hostess that it needed replenishing. These festive occasions were bright spots amid the ceaseless drudgery of the settlers' life. The pound-cake that graced the center of the table was intended for ornament as well as consumption. "Gest to let her see that I knew what manners was, I passed it a second time, and she up and took another hull piece," was the complaint uttered by one of these ancient matrons.

About this time the small two-tined forks, with handles of horn, had come into use here, but they were still rare, as one of our richest men, whose family consisted of ten persons, owned but five knives and forks, and seven silver spoons. In these days the meat was cut into small pieces before placing it upon the table, and each child was given a bit of stout twig, from which the bark had been removed. Its two prongs having been well sharpened, served as a substitute for the new-fangled fork.

From the ancient records we gain many a glimpse of the manners and customs of that day. The aforesaid family possessed but one looking-glass, this being considered a patrician luxury. They had, however, four spinning wheels and a weaver's loom, these articles being classed among the necessities of life. Upon them had been manufactured the thirteen linen sheets, in common use, the latter being valued in the appraisal at one shilling each, while the pair of cotton sheets, kept for the most distinguished guests, were set down at thirty shillings.

This weaving and spinning must be done by daylight, for the inventory includes only two candlesticks, both of them being of iron. If any greater illumination was needed, a candlestick could be improvised from a turnip.

In the making of candles, we find another instance of the abounding hospitality that prevailed. Those dipped in melted tallow were considered good enough for ordinary use, but the company candles had their wicks first dipped in turpentine in order to make them burn with a brighter flame. It must be remembered that the ruddy glow which flooded the room from

Used by Permission of Silver, Burdett & Co., Publishers
"THE PLACE OF GENERAL RESORT".

the burning logs in the wide-mouthed fireplace did much toward lighting the big kitchen, which was the general place of resort during the long winter evenings, and in whose dusky depths young lovers clasped hands and murmured their fond vows, unheeded by their elders.

Our town had at that time a silent form of courtship, borrowed from the Indians. The bashful youth who would fain offer himself to the maiden of his choice plucked a sprig of southernwood, and at some opportune moment placed it in her hand. Quick to interpret its meaning, her answer might be given in three different ways. If she ruthlessly broke it in pieces and threw it away, this betokened a complete rejection of his suit. If she looked at it and then gently returned it, this was equivalent to saying, "I do not yet know my own mind, but you may continue to come here." If she kept it, raising it to her face in order to inhale its spicy fragrance, then indeed were the gates of Paradise flung wide before him.

Courtesy toward even unwelcome guests was always a marked characteristic of this place. He who had spent a night in any household expected, as a matter of course, an invitation to conduct the morning devotions, and sometimes prolonged them beyond the usual limits. Upon one of these occasions a little South Hadley boy, whose knees were weary from the long kneeling, remarked in a distinctly audible voice, "You've prayered long enough." This brought the orison to a speedy close, but the boy was afterwards interviewed by one of his parents and never repeated the misbehavior.

The "everyday" apple pies were made with a rye crust, and sweetened with maple sugar; but there must always be a company pie with wheaten crust, and well seasoned with spice, and white or brown sugar.

A child's first instruction in school was in regard to politeness. Before learning his A B C's he was taught to make his manners. This meant that he should watch the slow descent of the teacher's hand—his toes placed carefully upon the line—and at the psychological moment, should bend his body forward in an awkward bow. "Children should be seen and not heard," was the instant reproof if the little ones attempted to speak at the noon repast. There was no trouble at morning and night, for they were not allowed to come to table during breakfast or supper, but ate their bread and milk, or hasty pudding, sitting upon a joint stool. The reason of this exclusion from the two meals may have been that the one was too early and the other too late; for in summer the farmer's family breakfasted at five o'clock and supped at seven, while in winter the usual hour was six o'clock, both morning and night. Giving plenty of time for sleep to the occupants of the trundle bed was one of the old-time cardinal virtues.

The late Dr. J. G. Holland, poet and historian, who was formerly a resident of our town, and who often said that he loved South Hadley and was glad that he could count himself among her sons, when he heard someone quote, "The necessary hours of sleep are six for a man, seven for a woman, and eight for a fool," is said to have remarked dryly that the man who originated that saying had better sleep eight hours in order to verify his own statement.

The moral and spiritual welfare of children was watched over with no less degree of care than their physical development. The birch rod was considered a necessary adjunct of nearly every household, and usually lay ready at hand upon the mantelpiece. After correction had been duly administered, some parents required the sobbing culprit to stand in front of them and repeat these exasperating lines:

"Solomon says, his words are mild,
'Spare the rod and spoil the child.'
Oh, no, dear mother, don't do so,
But whip me well, and make me do."

Should a child exhibit signs of a dawning vanity in a new bonnet or dress, Dr. Watts supplied just the words they needed to learn:

"How should our garments, made to hide
Our sin and shame, provoke our pride,
For the poor sheep and silkworm wore
The very clothing long before."

Or, if little brothers and sisters quarreled, the punishment was supposed to receive added emphasis by having them repeat immediately after it:

"Let dogs delight to bark and bite,
 For God hath made them so;
Let bears and lions growl and fight,
 For 'tis their nature to.
But, children, you should never let
 Your angry passions rise;
Your little hands were never made
 To tear each others eyes."

As the years went on, the rhymes grew a little milder. Major David Smith, who, after the Revolutionary War, had been made a deacon in our church, having become a merchant, went, at stated intervals, to Boston in order to replenish his stock of goods. About a century ago he appears to have introduced wooden dolls with glass eyes and vermilion cheeks, which were to the children a perpetual joy, they being to a certain degree indestructible. Coincident with this was the publication of a new poem:

"Miss Jenny and Molly had each a new dolly,
 With rosy red cheeks and blue eyes,
Dressed in ribbons and gauze, and they quarreled because
 The dolls were not both of a size.
Oh, silly Miss Jenny to be such a ninny,
 To make so much trouble and noise;
For the very next day her mamma took away
 The doll with red cheeks and blue eyes."

One of the mothers in an adjoining town publicly declared that she should bring up her children without whipping them. This was a heresy that could not be countenanced, and the church committee were sent to call upon her in order to convince her of the error of her ways. They reminded her that Solomon, the wisest man that ever lived, said "Chasten thy son while there is hope, and let not thy soul spare for his crying," and repeated other passages of like import. "I am not patterning my life after Solomon's," she answered firmly, "but after the Lord

Jesus. *We* are living under the New Dispensation," and she gave them such apt quotations from the Testament that they were glad to beat a retreat. It is worthy of note that every one of her sons became either a minister or a deacon.

Children, as soon as they were too old to sit in lap, were taught to stand at table during the noontide meal. They were not allowed to sit until they had become so tall that it was inconvenient to convey their food from the plate to the mouth. Tables were much lower than at the present time, and sometimes a child borrowed grandma's cricket to stand upon.

It was expected at this time that every boy should read the Bible through at least once. This could be accomplished in a year's time by reading three chapters every day, and ten every Sunday. We find in our old account books how this or that boy was paid twenty-five cents for having read the Bible through.

About the middle of the forenoon, in haying time, the laborers always stopped for a snack, as it was termed, and while they ate, some boy, detailed for the purpose, brought his Bible and read aloud to them, thus combining at the same time bodily and spiritual refreshment.

"Five feather beds" is one of the items in the inventory previously referred to. From the refuse of their flax the settlers made a kind of coarse canvas called "tow cloth." This was sewed into ticks, two for each bed. One of them was filled with straw for summer use, and the other with feathers, since, during the winter, in the fireless rooms, they were needed for warmth as well as repose. These feathers were obtained from the wild turkeys, which were so plentiful. Nat Goodale used to say, "There was not an acre of land between Bittersweet Lane and Mt. Holyoke upon which he had not shot a wild turkey."

It was not until after the Revolution that even the richest inhabitants had a "tame" turkey for the Thanksgiving dinner. Before the advent of brooms the wings of these fowls were used not only for dusting the furniture, but in the hands of children as a means of keeping the floor clean. The stiff tail feathers were fastened together at the quills, forming an immense fan

THE NOONTIDE MEAL

which was used to keep at bay the buzzing flies that on Sundays in summer swarmed through the unscreened windows of the meeting house.

As more land was cleared, the beds were much improved by the substitution of what were known as "live geese feathers." This indicated that a piece of ground, situated near a running stream, had been enclosed in a goose pen. Three times each year were its inmates deprived of some part of their downy covering. At every other new moon during the spring and early summer each goose was caught in turn, an old stocking pulled over its head to prevent it from biting, and about five ounces of soft feathers taken, after which it was released. Whenever a suggestion was made to the old people in regard to the seeming cruelty of this operation, it was indignantly repelled with the assertion that at this season of the year the geese often pulled out their own feathers.

The employments now assigned respectively to boys and girls were then considered as interchangeable. Young boys were taught to spin and knit, wash dishes, and, if necessary, make beds; girls learned to rake hay, milk the cow, and weed the garden. It was the boast of one of our Cold Hill farmers that with the help of his four daughters he needed no hired man.

The geese were usually driven back and forth, to and from their pasture, by a girl, who always received a feather bed, bolster and two pillows as a part of her wedding dowry. Esther K., who lived in the "Over-the-Brook" district, had been goose girl for many years and felt that when she left the paternal roof she had earned more than one feather bed. But custom was inexorable. So she wove herself a tick, a little larger than the ordinary size, and stuffed it with feathers till her friends said it was so hard it would prove uncomfortable. She took no notice of this remark, but after arriving at her new home, calmly drew from her hair trunk a second tick, and having transferred nearly half of the feathers, pointed with pride to her two nice beds, and all the neighbors agreed that Mr. M. had found a very capable wife.

It was a common saying here that no girl was fit to be married until she had a pillow case full of stockings, the wool for which must be carded, spun, and knit by her own hands.

A wedding was the favorite merrymaking with both young and old. The elder people knew that the long afternoon would afford them ample time for talking politics, indulging in friendly gossip, or exchanging recipes for new dishes, which in the absence of cook books was deemed a matter of importance. Then, too, they were certain of having a substantial supper, veal, beef, and other attractive viands, with unlimited supplies of liquid refreshment.

For the young people there was the evening dance, prolonged, as a peculiar privilege, until ten o'clock. But they must trip the "light fantastic toe" to the music of a different violin from the one which led the Sunday service of song. To use the same instrument at both church and dance would have seemed in that day a most unsanctified proceeding, even though the minister himself closed the merrymaking with the Benediction.

Colonial laws strictly forbade the wooing of a maiden without having first obtained the consent of her parents; this sometimes caused an unscheduled change in the marriage ceremony. The author's grandfather used to tell how a daughter of the Widow H. was about to wed a young man of excellent repute, though not a member of the church. On the wedding day, hardly had the minister finished his first prayer when the mother of the bride interposed. Calling the young man by name, she demanded from him a promise that if he married her daughter he would immediately institute family worship and have morning and evening devotions every day. After some hesitation he consented. Then she asked him if he were prepared to acknowledge that, owing to the death of her husband, she, and she alone, had the right to give or withhold her daughter in marriage. To this, upon due reflection, he assented, upon which she triumphantly produced a paper which contained the legal relinquishment of the daughter's share in her father's estate, leaving it to the widow to give the bride only such portion as she might see fit. She requested him to sign the paper. This he refused to do, upon which Mrs. H. forbade the continuance of

READING THE BIBLE TO THE HAYMAKERS

the ceremony. The minister was perplexed; the guests nervous; but the mother remained calm and firm. At length the unhappy bridegroom yielded, and the minister used to say that he finished that ceremony with a celerity seldom witnessed.

About the year 1800 marriage notices were sent to the newspapers, and were always accompanied by a piece of the wedding cake. These notices were generally printed in a complimentary style. We find in an old newspaper:

"Mr. John Powers was married to the amiable and much accomplished Miss Jerusha Preston, daughter of Leftenant Preston of South Hadley."

The amount of the bride's fortune was frequently included in the marriage notices, for by law the wife's dowry became at once the property of her husband.

But there were other and less joyous gatherings than those which marked the wedding festivities. In their desire to avoid all resemblance to the English ceremonial, our ancestors at first held no religious services at funerals, and during the first few years of our town burials were very unlike those of to-day. Old people used to tell us their grandfathers claimed that they could hew from a log, planks so smooth that one would suppose they had been nicely planed. Out of these planks were probably constructed oblong boxes, which, when painted black, served as coffins. Later, the better class of carpenters in our town became known as cabinetmakers, and were expected to keep constantly on hand a supply of coffins, large at the head and tapering at the foot. We find in the old account books, about 1770, "To a coffin with a door to it, fifty shillings." "To a coffin with a door hung," etc. This doubtless referred to the panel in the lid, which, when, removed, left the face exposed to view.

One of the chief requisites for a burial was an abundant supply of cider and other spirituous liquors. These were dispensed both before and after the interment.

In accordance with their belief that the two sexes should be separated during divine service at the meeting house, men and women were not permitted to sit together at funerals. If the deceased person were a woman then the women sat in the same room with the coffin, and told one another in whispers of the different omens that had forewarned of death. For more than a century the friendly whippoorwills of Mt. Holyoke were in the habit of coming down to the settlement in search of food, and sometimes alighted upon the ridgepole, that being their favorite perch. But if the plaintive note of this bird was heard over a house wherein a sick person lay, the case was considered hopeless. A long bit of wick in an unsnuffed candle was called a winding sheet, and was said to betoken that one would soon be needed in that neighborhood.

For more than a hundred years a certain kind of wood tick, which made a curious little drumming sound with its head, added to the superstitious fears of our fathers. It was called the death watch, and though it was often in the walls the sick who heard it felt sure that death was near. But if the sound ceased, everyone made haste to repeat these encouraging words:

"The omen is broken, the danger is over,
The insect will die, and the sick will recover."

Women were at this time said to have been excluded from funeral processions; they remained at the house, setting tables and preparing food of which all were to partake on the return from the grave.

As the years rolled on, it became the custom for the minister to make a prayer at the house, and for the members of the bereaved family to read aloud appropriate texts of Scripture.

About 1800 there had been still greater changes in the method of conducting services for the dead. Now, at every funeral, the minister preached a sermon, usually a laudatory one, and closing with personal remarks addressed to different members of the bereaved family. If the deceased had been a large landholder he was spoken of as a man of substance.

In a sermon preached upon the death of one of our richest men, the widow was adjured "not to repine at her loss, but rather to wonder at the divine mercy that had spared her." We learn from an old diary that Deacon Smith's funeral sermon "touched upon his character and the loss sustained by the town and the church by the death of so great, so wise, and so pious a man, in that most useful age of his life."

After the Revolution women were no longer excluded from the funeral procession, and were even allowed to be present during the committal to the grave. If the deceased person were a woman, then they walked two and two directly behind the bier, the men following in like manner. If the deceased were a man, then this order was reversed, men having the precedence. The horsemen rode behind the mourners two abreast, while the rear was filled with chaises and other vehicles. So great was the respect shown toward the dead that during the conveyance from the house to the burying ground the street was kept clear of both persons and horses so that no one would either meet or pass the procession upon its way.

There were at that time no professional undertakers, but once in five years a committee was appointed by our town, one in each school district, whose duty it was to "regulate the processions at funerals." This committee was usually composed of the leading men, courtly in their manners, but of firm, well-disciplined wills. Among them we find in our town records such names as these: Col. Ruggles Woodbridge, Major Eliphaz Moody, Lieut. Titus Goodman, Dr. Stebbins, Lieut. Joseph White, etc.

Six bearers, using what was termed a shoulder bier, carried the coffin from the home of the deceased to the graveyard, a distance of several miles. Later their number was reduced to four, but sometimes relays of men preceded them, and, at stated intervals, relieved the bearers by taking their places. This shoulder bier was still in use here in 1837. It was usually concealed beneath a black cloth, called a pall. The latter was owned by the town. We find in the records of January 13, 1745: "Voted that Daniel Moody make a grave cloth."

At this period all persons were expected to lay aside their daily occupations in order to be present at funerals, attendance there being considered hardly less obligatory than at church services.

It used to be said that the ordeal which awaited the mourners upon the ensuing Sabbath was even harder to bear than the funeral exercises. It was customary for the minister to read from the pulpit such notices as the following: "Mr. and Mrs. ——— desire the prayers of this church and congregation that the recent death of their son may be sanctified to them for their spiritual good. Their children join in the same request." Then the whole family arose and stood in their pew while the pastor prayed for them.

Friends of the sick also sent in requests for prayers, and within a century notices like the following were read in the South Hadley meeting house: "Mr. ———, who this week sets out for York State, asks the prayers of the congregation for his safe return."

The story of South Hadley's first burial place, as it has been handed down from generation to generation, forms one of the most pathetic incidents in the history of the town. In 1727 the insistent courage and energy of John Preston had enabled him to build the second frame dwelling house ever erected south of Mt. Holyoke. One of the first public necessities of a new settlement was the "God's Acre," consecrated to the repose of the dead. It was usually placed near the meeting house in order that the worshipers might be constantly reminded of their own mortality. We had at this time no church building nearer than Hadley, and public opinion demanded that the burying ground should be so central that the mourners could walk from the house to the grave. We find local ministers as late as 1841 telling their congregations that the only proper method of procedure at funerals was for the bereaved family and friends to walk from the home to the place of interment.

Early in 1728 John Preston, who owned a tract of land on the west side of College street, nearly opposite the Mary Lyon Chapel, offered to give three acres to be used as a resting place for the dead. It had been known as Sandy Hill, and, lying at the junction of two highways, it seemed a convenient place of burial. In February of this year he was called to Hadley, probably owing to the illness of his parents. During his absence there occurred the death of an infant, and a message was

THE GAYLORD LIBRARY

sent to him begging him to return to South Hadley long enough to decide upon a place of interment. Being near the Connecticut he borrowed a canoe and came doyn the river to South Harbor (Smith's Ferry). After landing he threaded the narrow footpath up to Sandy Hill, and located what was afterwards known as the Old Graveyard. Upon his return a cold rain set in, and the pitiless sleet fell ceaselessly upon the open boat. This exposure was followed by a severe illness.

A town meeting had been appointed in Hadley for the purpose of ratifying his gift, and on March fourth the records tell us that it was voted: "Jno. Nash and Lieut. Jno. Smith be Improved to View the place, and Lay it out in such form and quantitee as they shall think Best, not to exceed three Acres in quantitee." It was on this very day that the donor breathed his last.

Stalwart men brought John Preston home, for it would have been looked upon as an unparalleled disrespect if oxen or horses had been permitted to aid in the conveyance. He was interred upon the exact spot where now stands the Gaylord Library, a fitting memorial for the two generous men, one of whom gave the land and the other the building. His headstone, which has been moved farther west, bears the following inscription:

JOHN PRESTON

DYE^D ON MARCH $\overset{e}{Y}$ 4 1727^8

AGED 41 YEAR AND THE

$\overset{e}{Y}$ FIRST HERE BURIED

He was buried with his feet toward the east in order that he might rise facing the dawn, where he believed that Christ would appear on the morning of the Resurrection. This practice was continued in the Old Cemetery until after 1800.

There was a curious superstition in regard to the treatment of honey bees, when, as sometimes happened, a death occurred in the family of their owner. It was a common belief that if the news of this event were not conveyed to these little insects, they might be angered and return to the wooded sides of Mt. Holyoke.

The messenger usually selected, if one may judge from the old-time paintings of her, was a young girl clad in the habiliments of mourning, and carrying a piece of black cloth to place upon the hive.

Mr. A., one of the farmers in this vicinity, has left us his experience. Previous to his father's last illness the bees had all been carried into an unused chamber, in order to protect them from the wintry storms and snow. He said that just before his father's death they became restless and uneasy, and strange sounds were heard within the hive. This lasted for several days, but after the funeral the bees having been told what had happened again became quiet.

A New England poet thus describes the customary method of imparting this information:

"Before them, under the garden wall,
    Forward and back,
Went drearily singing the chore-girl small,
    Draping each hive with a shred of black.
And the song she was singing ever since
    In my ear sounds on:
'Stay at home, pretty bees, fly not hence!
    Mistress Mary is dead and gone!'"

CHAPTER THIRD

EARLY LIFE IN SOUTH HADLEY (CONCLUDED)

NEIGHBORHOOD gatherings were far more frequent in olden times than at the present day, for whenever there was extra work to be done the young people promptly suggested having a Bee.

We find from the records that on an average each family used from ten to fifteen barrels of cider a year. This, however, was not intended wholly for use as a beverage. During the autumn fresh, sweet cider was boiled down into a syrup, and great kegs of cider apple sauce, more delicious than most preserves, were stored in the cellar for the winter's use. Its preparation entailed the paring, quartering and coring of many bushels of apples, and gave occasion for holding a paring bee.

Upon the appointed evening the young men, with their jack-knives sharpened to a fine edge, repaired to the home of the hostess, whither the girls had already preceded them. The latter were provided with long wooden trenchers, intended for the reception of the cores and parings, and the hearts of the maidens fluttered with uncertainty as to which of the comely swains would ask to share her trencher, and so work beside her through the flying hours.

As they neared the end of their labors, each youth in turn selected a smooth, round apple and pared it carefully so that he might not break the skin. Taking this paring in his hand he whirled it above his head, then threw it upon the table. The judges decided which letter of the alphabet it most resembled, this being supposed to indicate the initial of the girl's name whom he was—in the parlance of that day—to see home. If the letter could be construed into an "S" or a "P," it was sure to be translated into Sally Piper, for that fun-loving damsel was a great favorite among her young companions, albeit she was on Sundays the despair of the tithing man, whose voice could sometimes be heard halfway across the meeting house, "Attention! Sally Piper, attention!"

After the apples were finished came games and refreshments. Wooden keelers were heaped high with nut cakes,—more familiarly known now as raised doughnuts,—pewter platters were piled with squares of golden gingerbread, sweetened with maple syrup, since molasses must be brought from far. There were cheese and cider everywhere, but when the hour of nine arrived, cordial good-nights were exchanged, and the crowd of merry-makers went home.

These social methods of bearing one another's burdens were a marked characteristic of both South Hadley and Granby. There were spinning bees, knitting bees, quiltings, chopping bees, mowing bees and husking parties; to say nothing of the raisings, which were always convivial affairs.

At the raising of Dr. Dwight's new house (now the College Infirmary), he purchased a new washtub to be used as a punch bowl. The day was a rainy one and a shelter was erected in which to take refuge when the storm was too violent, and the impromptu punch bowl proved so alluring that even the deacon went staggering home. But this was before the days of the temperance reformation.

The raising of a meeting house was an even more thirsty affair. Volunteers came from other towns to assist, and the cider barrel that had received several decanters of wine, was considered suitable for such occasions.

Deacon David Nash went from here as a delegate to a neighboring town which was about to build a church. The committee, of which he was one, staked out the site, while the townspeople held a meeting and voted to "procure a sufficient quantity of rum for raising the frame of the meeting house."

Spinning bees appear to have been the ones that ranked highest in the estimation of our great-grandmothers. These were of two kinds. The first was an informal affair; the girls in the neighborhood, between services on Sunday, agreed upon the day when and the house where they would meet. At the appointed time and place all appeared, bringing their small wheels and bunches of flax. The afternoon was spent in friendly gossip, with a bit of half-suppressed rivalry as to which of them would first finish her stent. Then home to supper, singing blithely as they went.

The other kind of spinning bees were somewhat like a surprise party. If any woman were ill or unable to provide clothing for her family, or if the minister's wife had a young babe to care for, then the elder women joined with the younger, and ox carts conveyed the large wheels to the desired place. Some carried flax or wool, others gave their time and work, but each one brought some article of food for the sumptuous repast that closed the afternoon, and at which the preserves were put up pound for pound, and the hung beef was beyond the imagination of any modern epicure.

Prettiest of all were the children's knitting bees. Every child carried his or her stocking to the party. At a given signal each one put in a mark, and they knit with a swiftness and evenness that could find no parallel among the youth of to-day.

The men and women of past generations, in Granby and South Hadley, strong both physically and morally, proved that the old-fashioned bees had not been held in vain. Their comparative and mutual isolation from the outside world may have accounted in some measure for the social activity of these two towns. Hemmed in on the north by the Holyoke Range, and on the west by the Connecticut, they were bounded on the south partly by the river and partly by a line through, or near, that dreaded lair, Misery Swamp. Upon the east lay a strip of woodland, broken only by a single cart track, so rough that about 1760 the town was indicted for "not keeping in repair the road to Cold Spring."

In the early years, when Granby and South Hadley were one, this seclusion seemed to make of it a miniature republic. There was no postal service, no stage route to give communication with the outer world.

Towns in this vicinity received and sent mail but twice a month, for the post-carriers had been allowed nine days in which to travel forty miles with their letters and papers.

Each house here was a small apothecary shop, for in case of illness in the family no doctor could be obtained except by crossing Mt. Holyoke, or, making a wide detour around its base. And if a physician came, he charged for every visit eight times his usual fee. Ministers were at that era expected to bleed their parishioners if necessary, and to be able to administer calomel and other medicines. Parson Woodbridge probably had some medical knowledge, for his eldest son began practice as a physician here in 1765.

In this community of interests, they were able to build their own houses; manufacture their own clothing; provide their own lighting; and raise crops which, with the aid of their hunting and fishing, furnished sufficient food for their families.

The men were all farmers, even to the minister, but most of them had some other occupation. One was a carpenter, another a blacksmith, the third a tanner, while the shoemaker, the pumpmaker, and a score of others could meet any emergency.

Exchange of labor, or as they termed it, "swapping work," and barter, left but few money transactions to be recorded. Their old account books read thus: the carpenter credits John Lane* with a twenty-two pound salmon, five shillings and adds, "John Lane, Dr. to mending your flore, seven shillings." The cobbler debits Joseph Hillyer. "To making and mending shews, 3£ dew to me." "In ye yere 1732 to help mak smoak house, 3 shil. 6d." "Credit one fox skin 8 shil. 6d."

The first pumpmaker in our town was Ephraim Nash, a man who might justly have been proud of his lineage since he was a grandson of that eminent divine, Rev. Samuel Stone. He was one of the earliest settlers, coming in 1727, but apparently found small opportunity for exercising his craft.

---

*John Lane was a famous athlete, a man of remarkable strength; it is said that he once asked a neighbor for the loan of a large iron kettle. She replied that he was welcome to the use of it, but it was so heavy she feared he could not carry it a long distance. Upon this he swung the kettle up, and placed it upon his head. He then carried it into the woods in order to use it in making maple sugar. He once walked from here to Westminster, Vermont, in a single day, a distance of over sixty miles. He was janitor of our first meeting house, sweeping the building with husk brooms, or birch twigs, and on Sunday mornings he went through the streets blowing a conch shell to remind people that it was time to assemble at the meeting house.

THE PUMP

People remembered the long well-sweeps and old oaken buckets, and distrusted the new invention. But after a time wooden pumps came into use, big, clumsy affairs, with a handle three or four feet long. The spout was a flat piece of wood, with projections upon two sides to prevent the overflow of water, which despite this precaution would spatter to a distance of several feet if the handle were moved quickly or with a jerk.

The following account of their introduction was given to the author by an aged man, and though there is no definite proof that the incident occurred within our boundaries, it may not be uninteresting as showing the difficulties that Ephraim Nash was obliged to encounter:

One of the progressive farmers of the town announced that upon a certain day, at nine o'clock in the morning, he would bring up water from his well without the aid of his iron-bound bucket. This promise was treated with derisive merriment, yet at the appointed time a crowd had assembled. They saw only a tall figure, shrouded in white, standing on the edge of the well, and beside it the farmer, who explained that something was wrong. He requested them to retire for half an hour to some place out of view and then return. The crowd departed with mocking laughter and jeering remarks. At the expiration of the time they came again, and saw to their surprise that the owner had divested his new pump of its covering. Lifting the handle he sent a stream of water into the waiting tub. When they had, as the old man said, "sensed it," it seemed to them like witchcraft, and they were quick to ask the owner's pardon for their previous gibes.

During the last few decades, all, or nearly all, of these old wooden pumps have disappeared from our town.

Wells played an important part in the household economy, for they assuaged thirst, promoted cleanliness, were the only firewardens, and during the August weather were the most convenient places for the preservation of fresh meat and yeast. These articles were each put into a pail and suspended above the surface of the water by a cord which was attached to a small bar near the top of the curb. This rendered it at times a rather insecure refrigerator, for if the cord were old, or carelessly tied, it was liable to drop, letting the pail and its contents fall to the bottom of the well. Lowering a lighted candle, the big, three-pronged well hook,—one of which must be kept in every neighborhood,—was now produced, and the subsequent fishing was apt to be a long process.

Some inventive, or imitative, genius persuaded a few of our leading families to try a new experiment which, it was claimed, would obviate this trouble. An oblong pit was dug in the ground, in a shady place, its sides being stoned like those of a well. In winter this pit was filled with blocks of ice, carefully packed in hay, and thick planks were laid across the top. Over these was placed a roof, not more than seven feet in height at the apex, and slanting sharply to the ground. In one of the gables was a door, and a short ladder always lay beside it ready for use as the season advanced. By the middle, or at most by the last of July, the contents of the pit were all melted.

A son of one of our early settlers, whose father had removed to Granby, determined to try building an icehouse above ground. This idea was scoffed at by our townsmen. "If ice could not be preserved under ground, it never would remain frozen near the surface," said they. Paying no heed to this adverse opinion, he proceeded to erect a stout reservoir, more than twelve feet square, and this he banked with earth till one might have expected to see an ancient mound-builder issuing therefrom.

Over the top of this he placed a one-roomed structure, which was known as the milkhouse or dairy. A trap door in the floor of the latter gave access to the chamber beneath. This icehouse was intended mainly for the preservation of food, since cold water for drinking purposes could be obtained at any hour from the time-honored bucket that hung in the well. A pipe had been so arranged that water could be easily pumped into the tank. As soon as the cold weather of winter had penetrated its thick walls to such a degree that it would freeze water, this huge cistern was flooded, to a depth of two or three inches, which by the next morning would be changed to ice. This process was repeated day by day until the tank was filled with a solid block of ice, twelve

THE OLD OAKEN BUCKET

feet square, some part of which remained congealed until the ensuing autumn.

The South Hadley yeomanry immediately patterned after this new device, but, as they believed, improved upon their model. In building their reservoirs, they inserted a door in the northern wall in order that they might fill it with blocks of ice from the nearest pond. These were obtained by cutting them out with axes or saws, but were so irregular in shape that after being packed great air spaces remained between them. This they remedied by closing up the door and pouring cold water from above till every crevice was filled. This formed a mass of ice that kept their own food and that of their neighbors fresh and sweet through the sultry August weather.

Improvements in arts and crafts were, at the first, almost wholly dependent upon the skill and ingenuity of the settlers, since their communication with the rest of the world was but limited. Letters and newspapers, which might have been such a solace, were in a great measure denied them. It was not until 1792 that a postoffice was established in Northampton, which received and sent out a mail once a week. We know that South Hadley and Granby were allowed to share in its benefits, for in Northampton's first list of unclaimed letters occurs the name of Joseph Eastman, Granby. During the next decade getting the mail proved to be an arduous undertaking, but on January 1, 1803, to the great joy of our inhabitants, a postoffice was established here, probably bringing the weekly mail on Fridays. The former strictness in regard to Sabbath observance was so far relaxed that on Sundays the postoffice was opened during the intermission between the morning and afternoon services, in order that those of the congregation who lived in remote neighborhoods could get their mail. It was argued that as the laws compelling church attendance under penalty of fine and imprisonment had been repealed, this would prove an incentive for the worshipers to be present at divine service.

In 1816 Northampton had three mails a week, and in case of illness or emergency, individuals going from here could obtain their Saturday night's mail. The inconvenience of this arrangement is well illustrated by the following extract from an old letter:

Dear Sister: "South Hadley, Dec. 7, 1808.

We have been long anxious, very anxious about you. It is bad getting to Northampton; Bachelor's Brook overflows, and there is ice in the river—but we can go over the bridge at Hadley.

We sent Horace on Sunday after a letter, but he could not get over the river, on account of the wind being very high. In the evening we hired Barber to go, and he rode nearly twenty miles, bro't the letter, got here at eleven o'clock.''

Though the doings of the external world were but slightly known here before the Revolution, that was not the case in regard to local happenings. With the aid of social gatherings, the itinerant shoemaker, the school teacher who boarded round, and later on the tailoress and the dressmaker, who made semi-annual visits to each family, but little news remained untold.

The advent of the shoemaker and his bench was hailed with delight by both young and old, for it was a cardinal article of belief that every person should have each year a new pair of leather shoes: stout cowhide for the men; calfskin for the women and children. When the shoemaker came with his wooden lasts, lapstone and the implements of his trade, he established himself near the big fireplace, in order to use its light to work by in the evenings; and his favorite ditty was:

"There was a cobbler who lived in a coom,
    And all he wanted was elbow room, elbow room.''

He measured the feet of each member of the family, and if he had no last of their exact size, promptly shaped one out of wood. He always expected a pitcher of cider to be placed ready at hand. A certain family once forgot this requirement. Wishing to remind them of it, he tried to soften his request by putting it into rhyme, and calmly remarked:

"While here I set, and work and sweat
    By candle and by fire,.
My throat grows dry, I can't deny
    Some cider I require.''

Upon this the longed-for beverage was at once forthcoming. The shoes were usually paid for in skins, which required a year's time for tanning into leather; but there was so little money in circulation that even the hired girl's wages were paid by barter, as witness this extract from an old account book:

"January, 1770.

Elizabeth Lemon came Frydey night, Jan. 5, and tarried til Saterday noon, May 5, save two days.

She hed two pair of shoes	$1.98
2 second-hand quilts (agreed)	.98
4½ yards of shallon	2.00
Money	2.00
Shoes mended several times	.20
A Portion of Species Hiera Cure	.20
A check'd Linnen Apron (agreed)	.50
Six coppers to balance	.52
	$8.38"

A servant girl's wages at this era averaged from fifty to seventy-five cents per week, but she was never called a servant; she was known as the help, or as one of our later ministers dubbed her, "my wife's domestic coadjutor."

This scarcity of money gave rise to many inconveniences, and among them may be numbered the dearth of hymn books in the Sunday services of song. This compelled the "lining out" of the stanzas. Either a deacon or the precentor read the first line and the congregation then sang it, and each line was followed in the same manner to the end of the hymn.

The old tuning fork which set the pitch was found in the garret of the old Woodbridge House.

It was an old saying that a good singer could marry any woman that he pleased; or, as an English poet expressed it:

"A blockhead of melodious voice
In boarding schools can take his choice."

In providing good music for the sanctuary, South Hadley antedated many of the surrounding towns. In 1765 John Stickney brought to this vicinity new methods and tunes for singers.

Nathaniel White was at this time a lad of sixteen, while his brother Ezekiel was five years younger. Both boys became so deeply interested that the elder one afterwards taught a singing school for twenty-six seasons, and the younger supplied his brother's place, it is believed, during the latter's absence in the army. John Stickney, too, was so much pleased at his cordial reception here, that he eventually made this town his home, and the committee in charge of seating the people in church assigned him a place in a big, square pew with two widows, one of whom he is said to have married.

There had been another teacher of singing, Josiah Draper, the Fall Woods' schoolmaster, but his lack of patience disqualified him for this office. He was very nervous and if a pupil failed in keeping exact time it put him in a passion, and his penalties were severe. He was precentor in 1777, and judging from his diary, the number of tunes with which he had become acquainted was for those days surprisingly great.

These three men, officered doubtless by John Stickney, had brought about a great change in our Sunday services. There had been a determined effort on the part of the young people to do away with the "lining out" of the hymns and to have the singing conducted by a choir, who should occupy the gallery opposite the pulpit. This proposal had awakened a fierce storm of opposition on the part of the older members of the congregation, who declared they would not attend church under such circumstances. They protested against the extravagance of paying so much for new singing books, and were sure that it would be an entering wedge for the introduction of wooden and brass musical instruments into the meeting house, as indeed proved true. Their ancestors, they said, had come hither to avoid the set forms of prayer used in the Church of England, but now if they began to sing by rule they would soon pray by rule.

Everyone had been taught six tunes, three for the forenoon and three for the afternoon service, and anything more was simply superfluous.

Feeling ran so high in this and adjacent towns, that one

minister complained of a certain parishioner, who refused to return his salutation when they met, and entered in his diary,—"Several of my neighbors seemed very uneasy about the singing, some, I fear, kept from meeting upon this account. Lord help and direct! Compose their minds that are ruffled! Oh, chain up Satan! Forgive and direct me."

Tradition tells us that the first concession in South Hadley, was the omitting to line out the closing hymn on Sunday afternoon, permission to retire from the house having first been given to those who did not wish to listen to the choir. This arrangement did not satisfy either party. It seemed to detract from the sanctity of worship to see a part of the congregation rise and file out with flashing eyes and angry steps. The exciting events that culminated in the battle of Lexington, brought our town into greater contact with the outside world, and a broader vision of the future opened before them. In 1776 the whole of the afternoon service, as far as the music was concerned, was given up to the choir, and no longer could the sonorous voice of Josiah Draper ring out the words of his old-fashioned Psalm—

"My soul gave me a sudden twitch,
That made me nimbly slide,
Like unto the chariot in which
Amminadab did ride."

With the advent of Dr. G. W. Lucas as the singing master, a new and varied list of tunes was introduced. He was a very tall man, of gentlemanly bearing, and polished speech. The singing schools were held in our old Mount Tom Academy, and he was often annoyed by the older boys who lingered near the fire after the hour for opening had arrived. One evening he said to them, "If those who have imbibed a sufficient degree of caloric will approximate to their seats, we can begin." Awed by the mingled dignity and length of words, the shivering youths obeyed.

After the national and state quarrels had been settled, a musical war arose in South Hadley. The choir had been arranged according to their rank, the best singer being placed at the head of the line, and the poorest at the foot. This gave rise to much bitterness and jealousy. One of the leading sopranos, who was angry because the minister's daughter had been seated above her, said rudely: "Who are you, anyway? Your father is supported by the town." In one family the eldest daughter had won the highest place at the head of the choir, while her sister was number three. As they had but one book between them, and wished to look it over together, they asked number two to change places with the younger sister. This she promptly refused to do, but offered to exchange with the elder one. The trouble increased as others took sides in the affair, and the matter was finally referred to the minister for settlement. After mature deliberation, he decided that number two should sit at the head of the choir half of the time, but upon every alternate Sabbath should take her place as third, bringing the two sisters side by side at each service, and thus was harmony restored.

These bickerings were done away with in 1835, when Mr. Dexter Ingraham was made chorister. He arranged his singers in the order of their ages, and remembering the old adage, "Where McGregor sits, that is the head of the table," he taught them that where the best singer sat would be the real head of the choir. He was a man whose heart was fully given to music, and for twenty-five years imparted his enthusiasm to his fellow musicians. He was succeeded, at his own request, by Mr. William Smith, whose gentleness and tact kept the chorus of sixty voices united and peaceful for another quarter of a century. This chorus was led by an orchestra consisting of the large and the small bass viols, three violins, a bassoon, and a cornopeian, aided by the soft notes of a flute played by John Dwight, the donor of the art gallery.

Deacon Hastings, for so many years the efficient superintendent of our Sunday School, presided over the big bass-viol, and Mr. Norman Preston, so highly respected and loved both as school teacher and "committeeman," was one of the violinists. It was not he, however, who went to the minister for permission to exchange the lines in the hymn book—

"Oh, may my heart in tune be found
Like David's harp of solemn sound."
and sing in their stead,
"Oh, may my heart be tuned within
Like David's solemn violin."

Our grandfathers used to tell us that the irate parson returned with ready satire, "Fine as your version is, Brother, I think I can suggest a better. How would it do to sing—

"Oh, may my heart go diddle, diddle,
Like Uncle David's sacred fiddle."

Whether in South Hadley or not, the incident actually occurred.

There had been some opposition at first on the part of the ministers to admitting so much instrumental music. One of our pastors, who had no ear for the "Concord of Sweet Sounds," happened to come to church early one Sunday morning, while the orchestra were turning their instruments. As soon as the service was concluded, he hastened to the gallery stairs, in order to meet the players on their way out, and informed them in a severe tone that he wanted no more dance music in his church.

Another clergyman, not of our town, when the musicians sat down at the close of the anthem, opened his Bible at the twentieth chapter of Acts, and slowly began reading,—"And after the uproar was ceased———," there was a perceptible pause before he finished the verse.

The Psalms and Hymns of Isaac Watts had now come into use, and so great was their popularity here and elsewhere that at the middle of the nineteenth century the publishers sold annually over fifty thousand copies, which was for those times a wonderful record.

CHAPTER FOURTH

FROM DAME SCHOOL TO COLLEGE

OUR first minister, having been for years a successful teacher, it is not to be wondered at that even before the completion of the meeting house, a school building was in course of erection, upon the site now occupied by the dental office of Dr. Preston.

There must have been a school previous to this, and it is not impossible that our ancestors returned to the old English custom of having it kept in the minister's house, for the living room in our first parsonage was twenty-five feet long and twenty feet in width, and the fuel to heat it was supplied by the parish. It is a fact worthy of notice that the precinct did not vote to build a schoolhouse until about the time of Rev. Grindall Rawson's marriage, so that during his preceding years of loneliness he may have gladly welcomed the children of his parishioners. The schoolhouse when completed contained but one room. Across its southern side yawned an immense fireplace, nearly five feet deep and wide enough to take in logs eight or ten feet long.

In order to sustain the winter fire, each boy—girls were not allowed to attend the public schools at this era—was expected to furnish a cord of wood; and if any careless or neglectful parent failed to centribute his quota, his unhappy son was straightway "sent to Coventry." This phrase meant that his fellows would neither speak to nor play with him, and that he would be scoffed at and jeered till the desired wood was forthcoming.

The entire frontage of the schoolhouse was twenty-three feet, five of which were used in enclosing the rough chimney built of stones and hand-made bricks. Beneath the schoolroom was a cellar, a rare thing in South Hadley in those days,—but it had been excavated simply as a place of retreat in case of Indian attack. By means of an underground tunnel, it was connected with the cellar of the Woodbridge parsonage just across the street. Miss Nancy Burr, who taught in 1821, said that on rainy days the children often amused themselves by creeping in and out of the tunnel; but now the earth has fallen in, and no trace of it remains.

Around the sides of the room not occupied by the fireplace two series of boards were fastened to the wall, one above the other, a few inches apart. These served as desks to hold their scanty books and present a hard surface upon which they could use their quill pens in ciphering; for at that time slates and lead pencils were still unknown, and paper was so scarce and expensive that some of our ancestors used to "do their sums" with a sharp-pointed stick in the smooth sand outside—for our village center was at first known only as Sand Hill.

For such pupils as were rich enough to afford paper, a wild goose must be shot in order to provide pens, and it was not the quills surmounted with long, handsome feathers that were in request, but those that were short and stubby; and the art of making them into pens was taught in our schools. A clay inkstand in use here in 1740 has four apertures besides the inkwell, evidently intended to hold the quills which were thus at hand in case of breakage.

Their ink was prepared by boiling the bark from an oak tree or a hard maple for several days, adding a little sugar to the decoction in order to give the writing a glossy appearance.

This unfading ink has preserved for us the records, diaries and account books of our early settlers, which after one hundred and eighty years are still legible.

Another process by which ink was manufactured was as follows: Green peelings of walnuts were soaked in rain water for a fortnight; "Stir it pretty often," said the rule. To a quart of this solution, carefully strained, was added four ounces of oak galls, two ounces of gum arabic, and in order to prevent it from molding, a little salt. The receipt concludes thus: "Let these ingredients stand together in a large stone bottle; shake, roll, or stir it well once each day, and in a month's time you will have excellent ink."

In our primitive schoolroom, long benches made of plank

extended in front of the rude desks, and upon these forms were seated the pupils, facing the wall, and with their backs toward the master. He, within the hollow square thus formed, kept, or at least attempted to keep, good order. If he caught sight of a boy whispering, playing, or grossly inattentive to his books, the ruler was thrown with unerring precision, and the detected culprit was then ordered to bring the ferrule back. Upon returning it he was sternly directed to hold out his hand, and the number and severity of the blows was in proportion to the gravity of the offense.

The boys were expected to learn reading, writing, and the rudiments of arithmetic. As to spelling, the orthography of our ancient records would indicate that this branch of learning received but scant attention. Thus the name of Timothy Hillyer—in whose honor one of the peaks of Mt. Holyoke was christened Hilliard's Knob—was spelled in the old deeds in seven different ways. Even the teachers grew careless; a chair became a "cheer" upon which to "set" down; till at last a town official in hiring a new schoolmaster adjured him to be "Pertickler about the pronounce-ation of his words."

A would-be instructor of youth advertising in our county paper, placed among his list of qualifications, "I teaches gografy, and all them outlandish things." In order to understand the full significance of this remark, it would be necessary to read one of the old geographies brought to South Hadley by Ephraim Nash, and others, a few extracts from which are subjoined.

"There grows in some part of Russia, a strange sort of melon called Boranetz (i. e., the Little Lamb). In figure it resembles a lamb, and such is its vegetable heat that it consumes and eats up all the grass, or rather herbs, within its reach. As the fruit doth ripen, the stalk decays, and is covered with a substance exactly the same with wool. A part of the skin of this remarkable plant is to be seen in the King of Denmark's public repository of rarities at Copenhagen. Many of the Muscovites use the skin of this rare vegetable instead of furs for lining of their vests."

"Take a native Spaniard, strip him of his good qualities

THE RUDIMENTS OF ARITHMETIC

(which may be quickly done), that person then remaining will be a complete Portuguese."

"In Germany, near St. Omers, is a large lake in which are divers floating islands, most of them inhabited, and movable by ropes tied to strong poles, fixed fast in the ground."

"There is a certain European island the northernmost part whereof doth frequently alter its longitude and latitude."

In summer time the older boys worked on the farm, while the girls and younger children were expected to attend a dame school, taught by a woman, or by a superannuated schoolmaster, unable, on account of age or infirmity, to manage boys.

The town, with unusual liberality, allowed some of the public money to be expended in payment of these teachers. Here the children were taught to knit, sew, and to read short words. The older girls learned to read the Bible, recite the catechism, and possibly to embroider samplers. Some of them were instructed in the art of writing. But the latter class were sadly in the minority.

A part of the dame schools were intended only for children, and were often taught by illiterate women, skilled, perhaps, in the art of amusing the young. We read that Tom's aunt, on a certain occasion, "Deposed verbatim, that the sade Tomme had been under her tuishuon laste summer, and had always behaved as a good skolur ote to du; and she never had ketched him in a ly, or fib, in her lyfe."

The following description of a dame school is derived, in part, from an old story edited by a schoolmaster, many years ago:

Imagine a little story-and-a-half house, its rear roof sloping almost to the ground, and over whose unpaneled door hangs a signboard. Here were daily gathered the boys and girls of the neighborhood; little tots that needed to be carried over the rough places in the road, up to children nine or ten years of age.

The dame sat in a high-backed chair, her throne of state, since she believed herself a model of social preëminence, for did she not rank, next to the minister's wife, as the first lady in the village? Towering above her head rose the crown of her tall mob cap, hiding thus the gray hair which proclaimed her threescore years. A snowy kerchief was pinned closely about her neck, and a white apron, trimmed upon three sides with a deep ruffle, concealed a part of her linen gown. At her side hung the indispensable work-pocket, containing strings with which to tie the hands of naughty children behind them, soft bandages for youthful hurts, and divers other articles that might be needed. Beside her stood a little carved table, upon which lay a nicely-trimmed birch rod. Every Monday morning the floor was spread with clean sand, and a fresh rod provided; for it was expected that the good dame would wear out at least one a week while keeping her little flock in order. The bare shoulders and feet of her pupils afforded an open field for chastisement, but oftentimes a threat of punishment was sufficient. If she caught a girl chewing the corners of her primer, she took up the rod with an "I'll teach you to munch your book as a rabbit does clover." But the tears and promises of the culprit generally availed, and the sentence was commuted to a sharp rebuke.

Even the very little children were taught to knit stockings, and up to seventy years ago, it was considered that the proper penalty for dropping stitches was to have the ears snapped with a thimble, or "finger hat," once for each stitch. But the dame was not always finding fault. There were times when her smile was so sweet that "Every little child's heart grew happy at seeing it."

There was a great cupboard in one corner, where the books and work were kept. Into the bottom of this the infant class crept, when the dame was not looking that way, and here they "whispered and twittered like a nest of young wrens."

Though it was then looked upon as far beneath the dignity of a schoolmistress to reason with her pupils in regard to bad conduct, yet the kindergartens of to-day will do well if they train up such strong and sterling men and women as came forth from that old oaken door, wreathed round with morning-glories, and crowned with the modest sign:

DAME SCHOOL.

CHILDREN TAUGHT TO READ.

Previous to 1760 education seems to have made but slight progress in our town. Schoolmasters were hard to find, and we hear of their being "entreated" to come. Men who were college graduates, and had made teaching a profession, were in great demand, and were often employed up to extreme old age. One of these early schoolmasters was the town's first pauper. Samuel Mighill was the son of a minister. Graduating from Harvard at the age of nineteen, he came to Hadley during the following year, and was installed as master of the Hopkins Grammar School. Here he fell in love with a young woman, five years older than himself, whom he subsequently married. He removed to Connecticut, where he taught school for twenty-two years. At the expiration of this time, his heart turned once more to Massachusetts, and, deserting his second wife, he returned to Hadley, from whence he moved to Amherst, and eventually to South Hadley, coming here, probably, about the time when the precinct first voted to hire a schoolmaster. Some years later he made a public complaint that he "a Master of Arts, although still able to teach a small school, of late, people had refused to employ him in that business." He was now seventy-four years old, and his disposition, never perhaps of the best, may not have improved with age.

The selectmen sent the constable, Deacon David Nash, to warn him that he must "depart and leave this district of South Hadley," lest he become a public burden. This was an insult not to be tolerated, and in November, 1759, Master Mighill sent to the court at Northampton a humble and pious letter, asking their advice in honeyed phrases, and praying that their worships and the honorable court "would consider his helpless and needy circumstances, and make such order for his relief and support as to law and justice belong."

Now, the court had complete jurisdiction in such cases; the law empowered magistrates to dispose of paupers, "into such towns as they shall judge to be most fit for the maintenance and employment of such persons and families, for the ease of this country."

Master Mighill's crafty appeal was not lost upon the court. The judge promptly decreed that this district should provide relief and support for him as long as he chose to remain a resident of the town. He continued to live here, at public expense, until his death, which occurred ten years later.

A few months after Mighill's successful appeal, South Hadley was once more summoned before the court, this time upon the unaccountable charge of having failed to keep a grammar school the preceding year.

The law of the commonwealth required that every town which contained a hundred families should have a school that would fit for college. But in a district like South Hadley, which at that time included 24,000 acres of land, and whose opposite boundaries were from six to ten miles apart, it would manifestly be impossible to collect all the pupils at one place, especially as our present smooth roads were then but bridle paths, or rough cart-tracks. The school had therefore been kept in rotation, two months at South Hadley Center, two at Falls Woods, and two at the inn of Deacon John Smith, which stood on the site afterwards occupied by the residence of the late Mr. Frank Taylor, in West Parish, now a part of Granby.

The selectmen of 1760 had been very fortunate in their choice of an instructor for that year. Josiah Pierce had taught for twelve years in the Hopkins school at Hadley; he could read both Latin and Greek, and even preach a sermon if occasion required. He was as good a farmer as teacher, and appears to have been the means of introducing the use of potatoes as an article of food among our forefathers, whose old account books show that in 1762 the price here was three dollars a bushel, and the largest amount taken by any one customer was two pecks. In the evenings, Master Pierce, who was said to have been a good "arithmeticker," had a class in ciphering. This may have been necessary from the fact that some of the older boys were required to work at home during a part of the day; but another reason existed: the old arithmetics were but a brief collection

TEACHING ARITHMETIC

of rules, often with only one example given under each, so that the instructor was obliged to compose his own sums, or problems, the copying and explanation of which required time, especially the Golden Rule, as the rule of three in proportion was then termed.

In order that no infraction of law should go unpunished, Massachusetts had established a system of government well calculated to develop a generation of spies. When a crime was committed, he who reported it to the court received from one-third to one-half of the fine. In the present case against South Hadley the informer was the famous, or rather infamous, Joseph Ashley, whose name was to the populace as the red flag of the matador.

At the opening of the court in February, 1761, the town's attorney, Hon. Charles Phelps, of Hadley, stated the facts in the case, with such a pleasing humility that the judge summarily ordered the indictment to be quashed. So the discomfited Joseph went home minus even his ferriage, to the great joy of his fellow citizens. He, however, continued in his role of informer with varying success, until he was driven from the place, at the breaking out of the Revolutionary war.

Josiah Draper was the next teacher to leave us a record of his personal experiences, not in an interleaved almanac, like that of Master Pierce, but on the stout sermon paper in use among ministers of that day. His character was one of strange contradictions; at one moment generous to a fault; at another, close and calculating. He was an ardent patriot, ready to do or suffer anything for his country; yet upon the younger generation, his punishments were so severe that he put even the Middle Ages to the blush. He was a constant attendant at church; as chorister, he set the tunes with his ancient pitch-pipe; and as precentor, he lined out the hymns as they were sung.

Yet this same leader among men, after long years of service, was finally deprived of his office, because his habits of intemperance were past all enduring. One instance of his severity when under the influence of liquor was long remembered among his pupils. It was a bitterly cold day; so much of the heat went up the wide chimney that those who sat at the rear of the schoolroom said that their numbed fingers could hardly hold their books. They asked permission to go to the fire. "Yes," answered Master Draper, grimly, "and I will make you warm enough to last all winter." He placed them in a row across the front of the fireplace, and piled on logs till the flames roared up the chimney. He allowed no one to step back, but kept them in that scorching heat till both faces and hands were blistered. The narrator of this incident added significantly, "No one asked to go to the fire again that winter."

A true account of the brutalities that passed unnoticed in this old schoolhouse would seem hardly credible to the reader of to-day. It was an era of whipping, and every time a new master was hired, he was expected to enter the schoolroom on the day of opening with a large bundle of hazel rods under his arm (the latter shrub being considered a more efficacious means of discipline than birch), and carrying in his hand a hardwood ferrule. In the eighteenth century flogging was looked upon as the natural penalty of crime; and in the Revolutionary Army, desertion, stealing, and like misdemeanors, were almost invariably punished in this manner.

Within the first week of the term there generally ensued a battle royal between the new pedagogue and the ringleader of the boys. If the former failed of being conqueror, his stay would be but brief. One of our old masters thus addressed his school: "Boys, there is one thing I *cannot* have, and I *will not* have; it is NOISE!" and he thumped the desk lustily with his fist. He was a man of great muscular strength, but lacking in that moral force which is so essential to success.

On the third day, while the boys were walking around the room, talking aloud, and jumping from the windows, two town officials came in and dismissed the new master. Not so was Mr. W., who lived in town, working during the summer and teaching winters. If he caught one of his pupils whispering he was wont to remark, sardonically, that he knew of but one remedy, and that was red paint applied to the inside of the hand; and the ruler was then brought into requisition.

One of the later teachers, Mr. C., invented a cruel punishment of his own. Placing a lead pencil between two fingers, he held them firmly together while he twisted the pencil round and round. This soon brought the most stubborn to their knees. The result, however, was that the boys rose en masse, and bringing in wood blocked him from the schoolroom, which he never entered again.

But the masters were not all like this: there were men of dignity and worth, whose names were deeply graven in those little halls of fame that always find a lodgment in every human heart.

Josiah Draper, in spite of his severity, continued to teach school for many years, the town, as was customary, giving him a piece of land. This was situated in Falls Woods, and here, in the summer time, he raised corn, and subsequently built himself a house. But in winter, while teaching, he still preferred "boarding 'round, a week in each family," as he says in his diary. This meant that he would be the honored guest in a succession of visits; would sleep amid the linen-crested billows of the best feather bed, and would partake of the choicest viands the house could afford. If any family, through poverty or ill will, did not wish to receive him, their names would be placed at the end of the list, and would not be reached until it was time for the term to close.

Should there chance to be in any neighborhood a house that was noted for its poor cookery and meager fare, where the brass warming-pan never removed the chill that lurked beneath the canopied splendor of the four-poster, then the kindly neighbors vied with one another in sending invitations to the unfortunate teacher, so that without too much discomfort the week would come to an end.

And South Hadley *was* kind. Even poor old Samuel Mighill, in his letter to the court, spoke of the "charity, humanity, and benevolence," of its citizens.

Boarding 'round was not always an unmixed joy, especially in summer, when the schools were taught by young women. It is not agreeable to be continuously in the lime-light, as was one of the South Hadley girls, who wrote thus of her introduction to a new boarding place: "Opening the door, I beheld the whole family ranged against the wall in the exact order of their height, and looking like a pair of stairs. The mother stepped forward and said, 'Children, this is the Marm, and I want you to watch her, and do jest as she does, and talk jest as she talks, so as to grow up pooty ladies.' There was no place in which I could remove the dust of my day's work except the woodshed. Here, upon a wooden bench, stood a tin dipper and a dish of soft soap, also a coarse towel, upon which all the family had dried their faces and hands. 'Mabbe you'd like to wash,' suggested Mrs. H. At supper, platters of meat, potatoes, and bread, garnished the center of the table. As soon as the blessing had been asked, the children speared these articles with wonderful dexterity, and consumed their food with such rapidity that they were nearly half through before I was ready to begin my repast. It was all so new and strange that, though I went early to bed, I could not sleep. Presently through the thinly-boarded walls of my chamber I heard the voice of one of my pupils, praying. He said: 'O God, please to keep all houses from burning down to-night; and, O God, please to specially keep our house from burning down to-night, cause the Marm is here.' Then, soothed and comforted, I fell into such a sound sleep that I did not waken until cockcrow in the morning." There were some teachers who needed not the usual injunction to "Make yerself to hum." Miss Mary N. one day called to her desk a boy with whose widowed mother she was then boarding. He received what she called "a good ferruling," he meanwhile having no idea for what crime he was being punished. "There!" she said, when she had finished, "now we'll see whether you will make up faces at your mother the next time she tells you you are to have hasty pudding and milk for breakfast."

Holding down a nail in the floor, balancing books on the extended arm, and other old-fashioned methods of punishment, remained in force during the winter schools until nearly the middle of the nineteenth century. But after 1820, both boys and girls were admitted to the public schools at all seasons, and a much milder form of discipline prevailed in the summer time. Then if a boy whispered he was sent to sit with some good girl, whose example would be beneficial.

Miss T., who taught in Moody Corner, had a variation of this method which seems to have been all her own. If a boy and girl were caught playing in school time, the right arm of the one was bound firmly to the left arm of the other; the pair were then directed to knock at the door and show themselves to the residents of three neighboring houses, the teacher, doubtless, watching them from the window to see that her orders were carried out.

The Dunce Block was intended for the indolent and stupid, rather than for the mischievous pupil. A section of log, about two feet long, was made smooth at both ends and placed upright upon the floor. Upon this the delinquent was obliged to stand, wearing upon his or her head a tall, pointed cap of white paper, with the word DUNCE printed in large capitals across the front.

Some of our old teachers prayed with their pupils before whipping them. But even these orisons were less dreaded than the old-time punishment of "sitting in a whig chair." This was never used except in connection with the oldest and most turbulent boys; for, as the offender was compelled to assume a sitting position with nothing to sustain his weight, the crouching attitude was soon productive of severe cramps, impossible to be borne.

In looking backward, it must be remembered that the status of the teacher in those times was far different from that of the present. Then each school was a miniature kingdom, and the master, who chose to play the despot, found few to dispute his sway.

Occasionally some teacher tried to dispense with rod and ferrule. The experience of one such master was given in the newspapers of that day. He attempted to lead his pupils to the right by reasoning with them. This failing, he tried to drive them through a sense of shame; then he thought by praising to flatter them into well-doing, till he had "coaxed away his own authority."

Now there chanced to be in the school a youth whose too-indulgent mother had forewarned the master that her son was not to be corrected. This boy had begun to "throw down books, and huff out 'wills' and 'won'ts' with much emphasis." In despair, the master gave him one blow, upon which the boy kicked him and ran crying to his mother, who told him his teacher was a cruel blockhead. She immediately summoned her husband and bade him go and turn the master out of the school. He had but little liking for the task; his wife, however, who wore the purple in that household, insisted. A meeting was held, and the neighbors came in to express their approbation of the instructor; but the mother continued to "huff and ding at those who espoused the cause of the master, calling their children beggars, liars, and ill-bred scullions." Quarrels ensued, and the article closed with a sneer at the man who was "Under the control of what some call Ribocracy."

Methods of instruction, as well as those of discipline, changed with the passing years. The arithmetic of 1760 arrogated to itself a supreme place in the schoolroom, claiming to be the basis of all arts, and therefore it ought to be understood "before other branches were meddled with." The most minute details were given in regard to its different subjects. The first unit of weight, it informed us, was "A corn of wheat, gathered out of the middle of the ear, and well dried." Thirty-two of these were supposed to equal the weight of a penny. Later the number was reduced to twenty-four, and as the expression had changed to "grains of wheat," the table began, "Twenty-four grains make one penny-weight." Problems in arithmetic were also expected to do their part toward the moral as well as mental improvement of the pupils, as: "A gentleman told his son if he would be a good boy and attend closely to his school, he should have one-half of the chickens, one-third of the turkeys, and one-fifth of the goslings that should be hatched that year. The number of turkeys was three times the number of goslings, and the number of the goslings was one-half the number of chickens hatched by five hens, setting on twelve eggs each. When they had grown, the boy carried his part to market and received fifty cents each for his turkeys, twenty cents for his chickens, and two shillings for his geese. Can you tell me how much he gained by being a good boy, besides the approbation of his parents and the improvement he had made at school?"

Copy books, too, were supposed to inculcate lessons of wisdom. The oldest writing book to be found in South Hadley was brought here probably by one of the first settlers as a relic of his schooldays. The copy set on May 24, 1708, was: "Enter no serious Friendship with the mutilogonous man, for he cannot keep thy counsel."

After the rhyming fever developed itself in this region, such copies as this were used:

"Your delight and your care
Will make you write fair."

or

"If you would live in peace and rest,
You must hear, and see, and say the best."

For nearly a century our schools were both opened and closed with reading the Scriptures and prayer, and it was looked upon as a most disgraceful punishment when a pupil was required to stand beside the master and face the school during the concluding exercises.

J. W. Tuck, afterwards the Congregational minister at Ludlow, may have been the last to continue this practice, for about 1840 the recitation of Bible verses was substituted in place of the closing devotions.

Mr. Tuck had been the pupil of the famous Miss N., of whom mention has previously been made, and of whom it used to be said that she whipped wisdom into her pupils, using the rod in moderation if she thought that would do, but unsparingly if she considered it necessary. But the gentle firmness of Mr. Tuck won both the respect and good-will of all about him, and it was only upon rare occasions that he found it necessary to call in the service of Doctor Birch. He taught in the small schoolhouse, now used as a dwelling, on the east side of Amherst Street, a little south of Bittersweet Lane. This building, erected about 1816, furnished a good illustration of the second period of schoolhouse architecture.

Around three sides of the room, a long bench was fastened to the wall, with an elevated platform beneath it; this was known as the Backseat, and was intended for the older pupils. In front of it were three tiers of desks and seats, each of the latter being a step lower than the one behind it, so that the aisles were like a little pair of stairs. Upon the east side stood the fireplace and a door opening into the entry. But before the advent of Mr. Tuck the room had been modernized; the desks placed in rows upon a level floor and all facing the same way, and the fireplace exchanged for a large box stove.

The children and youth from Moody Corner and Pearl City, joined to those of "District Number Four," formed a school of from sixty to seventy pupils of all ages, from the ABCdarians to the stalwart boy already almost out of his teens. It was obviously impossible for one teacher to hear such a multiplicity of recitations, and Mr. Tuck appointed two of the older girls as monitors, Clara Montague and Irene Moody, who assisted him by teaching the younger classes. Then the old, old story, so new and wonderful to every passing generation, repeated itself, and two days before his installation at Ludlow, Mr. Tuck and Irene Moody were married. There was one brief year of happiness, then she sailed out over the Unknown Sea, on the returnless voyage that awaits us all.

Mr. Tuck, like other old masters, inculcated a deep respect for the ministry. Massachusetts had passed a law, some years before, making it obligatory for the ministers to visit the schools. Mr. Condit did this, and whenever he passed the schoolhouse during the recess or noon intermission, he beheld what in our day would be an unaccustomed sight. No sooner did his one-horse shay appear at the head of the street than all the games ceased. The boys were usually playing leap frog, jumping from a springboard, or having a series of Marathon races round the schoolhouse (the yard being then fully treble its present size), and the girls and little children were honeycombing the opposite bank, in unconscious imitation of the mound-builders.

Both parties immediately ranged themselves in lines on either side of the street, with the cry, "The minister is coming!" When Mr. Condit reached them he leaned out of the chaise, bowing to right and left with a cheerful, "Good day, boys!" "Good day, girls!" The latter courtesied, while the boys scraped their feet backward, with an awkward obeisance; then the ceremony was over, and the old horse jogged on.

We had another schoolmaster whose fame still survives. Daniel Paine was known far and near for his skill in managing unruly boys, and wherever there was a rebellion in school, other towns were sure to send for Master Paine. Not that his punishments were frequent, or unusually severe; but he had what Andrew Jackson called "The shoot in his eye." After he ceased teaching and was made a member of the School Committee, he was always spoken of as Squire Paine. On examination days his closing remarks to the pupils were certain to end with this inspiring forecast: "Perhaps I see before me some future President of the United States. Remember, boys, that this office is within the reach of the poor as well as the rich."

When the jurisdiction of schools was taken from the ministers and selectmen and given to a special committee, appointed in each town for that purpose, some of the new members felt that Solomon in all his wisdom was not equipped like one of them. One of the wiseacres in this vicinity finished his examination day speech in this manner: "Children, you are now slowly climbing up the Hill of Knowledge. But take courage; keep on; and do not forget that *when you reach the summit, I shall be there to welcome you.*" These same semi-annual examinations held a most important place in the calendar. On the preceding day each girl brought a wash-dipper and a large piece of cloth. Some kind neighbor volunteered a dish of soft soap. A part of the boys were detailed to bring hot water, and with a sand bank near by, the scrubbing and scouring began. Meantime, the rest of the boys had gone in search of evergreen, which was festooned about the walls and windows; the rusty old stove being concealed beneath a mountain of feathery asparagus. There was sure to be a crowd of visitors on the fateful day, and many teachers were sorely tempted to give out in advance the list of questions that they intended to ask their dullest scholars. This practice, however, did not always turn out according to their expectations. The old folks used to tell of a schoolmaster who had one pupil so stupid that he positively could not learn anything. So on the day before the examination he told this boy that he should ask him, in the geography class, "What is the shape of the earth?" and directed him to answer, "It is round like a ball or orange." Now, at this time, the habit of using tobacco was almost universal, and it was considered courteous for the master to offer his snuff box to visitors. The one that he usually carried was square, but he had a new one for Sundays that was round, and this he promised to bring the following day and hand to the committee if the boy forgot his lesson. This, as might have been expected, he did, and to the question could only return a "I dunno." "Think a moment," said the teacher, encouragingly, as he took out the new snuff box. "I know," cried the boy eagerly. "It is round, sir, on Sundays, and square the rest of the week."

Many were the revelations of the schoolroom. Mr. E., the oldest man in town, tells of a boy in his class who was learning the alphabet. He gave correctly the names of Q, R and S, but could not tell what T stood for. "What did your mother drink at breakfast time this morning?" asked the teacher, and the pupil answered truthfully, "Rum and molasses, sir."

Mr. Carter could seldom refrain from a smile when telling of his efforts to teach a stupid and overgrown boy, who lived a long distance from school. "C-er-a-er-k-er-e-er," he drawled one day at recitation. "Well, what does c-a-k-e spell?" asked Mr. C. The boy shook his head despairingly. "Think what you have in your dinner pail, and try it once more," urged the master. The boy began, "C-er-a-er-k-er-e-er. Didn't brung the same things to-day that I did yistiddy; brung slapjacks to-day."

About a century ago there began to be a marked revival of interest in the art of spelling. The teachers vied with one another in producing long fourteen-syllabled words, which trained the memory, but were of little practical use. One of their favorites was Ho-no-ri-fi-ca-bi-li-tu-di-ni-ta-te-bus-que, and was spelled in this way: "H-o Ho, there's your ho, n-o no, there's your no, hono, there's your hono, r-i ri, there's your ri, honori, there's your honori, and so on to the end. The banner pupils could reverse the process and spell it backward in the same way.

Spelling schools have been often described, but few writers have alluded to the joy and glory of the encounter, when one district challenged another to "match up sides." Each school appointed its best speller as leader, and they severally chose a picked crew from among the brightest pupils of their respective districts.

On the evening in question, each boy and girl among the challengers brought a tallow candle and a potato or turnip to be hollowed out and used as a candlestick, so that the visitors, upon their arrival, found the room ablaze with light. The judge, who had been mutually agreed upon, stood up and gave out the words, at first easy ones, but finally coming to Phthisic, Feoffment, Hautboy, etc. The contestants were arranged in two lines facing one another, and if a pupil failed on a word (only one trial being allowed), his or her opposite spelled it, and if correctly, the leader on the latter side called over one of the opposing faction to augment his own strength. Sometimes the leader alone was left, and consequently obliged to spell every alternate word; but this often resulted in stemming the tide of victory and bringing defeat to his opponents, since he could call back the best spellers from both sides. After this, if time permitted, came a bout of spelling down. Each pupil, who missed a word, was immediately seated, till none were left.

Teaching was not a lucrative profession. Our district records show that a dollar a week in summer and a dollar and a half in winter, boarding 'round, was looked upon as fair pay.

Some of these old records are interesting reading. Pearl City District voted that every member who failed to set out a tree in the schoolyard that summer should be fined fifty cents;

and if he did not assist Harry Smith in leveling the ground his fine should be double.

Falls Woods voted that any pupil who used profane language in the schoolhouse yard should be punished; for at this time the moral and religious education of the young was deemed a matter of paramount importance. Teachers of children were required to show certificates that they were persons of sober life and conversation; and the law directed that in early stages of life they should instill a sense of piety and virtue, and teach decent behavior.

When a master came to us from another town, he must bring with him a certificate from his minister and the selectmen, stating that he sustained a good moral character. If the Rev. Joel Hayes, during the last forty years of his pastorate here, with the consent of the selectmen, had allowed an instructor to teach in our public schools without such a certificate, he and they would have been subject to a fine, one-half of which went to the informer, and the rest to the poor of South Hadley.

Master Hiram Bagg was one of our teachers who held firmly to Solomon's dictum in regard to the training of youth, that "the rod and reproof give wisdom," and he maintained such good order in his schools that his services were constantly in demand. He usually began the term with these words: "If scholars try to be good they always find me the kindest and pleasantest man you ever saw, BUT—," and the unfinished sentence carried more weight than a dozen threats would have done.

Soon after came the transition from master to mistress in our winter schools. This change was not easily effected. Miss T. taught for several summers in the Center District with such marked success that the Committee felt justified in offering her a position in the winter school. This was an innovation indeed; a woman to teach big boys! Her friends all begged her to refuse, but she had confidence in herself and accepted the appointment. The result of the experiment, however, was such a mortifying failure that she immediately learned dressmaking, and as long as she lived never again taught school.

It was rumored that the Prudential Committee in District Number Four had hired the daughter of a minister in a neighboring town to teach their winter school. There arose a great cry against it, for the policy had always been to employ home talent, and the public money, they asserted, should be kept in the town.

The young woman came; strong, purposeful and with abundant tact; before the close of the term the whole district were ready to kneel at her shrine, and the dynasty of men as teachers in Number Four was at an end.

With the advent of women in our winter schools the style of punishment was changed. Such brutalities as "sitting in a whig chair," "holding down a nail," etc., were dropped and milder penalties substituted. One Granby teacher earned the perpetual hatred of her pupils by introducing the use of leather spectacles which, covering the eyes, entailed temporary blindness and gave the offender ample time in which to reflect upon his ill doing.

Very young children were now admitted to public schools, and the little three-year-old girls were distinguished as Totty Smith, Totty Clark, etc. They were placed at the foot of the primer class and taught the alphabet. The first question to be asked them was, "Who made you?" and they were taught to answer, reverently, "God;" but they sometimes developed an unexpected theology of their own. One little tot, in reply to a teacher's question if she did not think God was very good and kind to give her her little feet to run about with, answered, stoutly, "No. Dod *wanted* to div me my little feet. He didn't want to see me stumpin' round the house and backin' down stairs."

At the head of this class stood the children who could read c-a-t, cat, d-o-g, dog; and sometimes a boy who was in words of four letters. One of the latter, without a thought of irony, persisted in reading goat g-o, go, a-t, at, go-at, and the only specimen in the vicinity always justified that pronunciation of its name.

This class learned many improving rhymes, such as:

"Sixty seconds make a minute,
  Sixty minutes make an hour;
I wish I were a little linnet,
  Sitting in her leafy bower,
Then I should not have to sing it—
  Sixty seconds make a minute.

"Twenty-four hours make a day,
  And seven days will make a week;
I'd rather jump upon the hay,
  Or play at charming hide and seek,
Than count the hours that make a day,
  Or tell the days that make a week.

"Four weeks will make a month,
  And twelve whole months will make a year;
Now, I must say it o'er and o'er,
  Or else it never will be clear;
So once again I will begin it—
  Sixty seconds make a minute."

The teachers composed simple rhymes for their pupils to learn. The following by a country schoolmistress was considered her masterpiece, and was given here at the close of school on examination days.

"Parents and friends, we're very glad
  That you have come to-day
To listen to the simple things
  We children have to say.

"We learn to read, we learn to spell,
  We learn to write and cipher, too,
And hope to act our part as well
  In life as our dear parents do.

"Some of us will be ministers,
And some will lawyers be,
Doctors, merchants, farmers, too,
Upon these seats you see.

"But this is future, none can tell it,
We may be men of might and dollars,
But all we ask for now's the credit
Of being very decent scholars.

"Parents and friends, our task is done,
My speech is now quite through,
With your permission, honored sir (bowing to the committee),
I leave the floor to you."

The lead pencils that first came into use were almost indelible. It was customary in some of our schools for the teacher to make a large "X" upon the forehead of every pupil who misbehaved. This served a double purpose; it was a present disgrace, and, its significance being understood, it made known to the parents at home the guilt of the offender.

One schoolmistress provided herself with small wooden pegs, and whenever she caught a pupil in the act of whispering, one of these was placed in such a manner as to distend the mouth, rendering speech impossible. But this method of discipline was of short duration, for the children soon grew expert in the art of moving and replacing the peg with the tongue, and by holding the mouth open when the teacher was looking that way they were able, while hidden behind the big slate and bigger atlas, to greatly abate the rigor of this punishment.

It was not until the time of the Civil War that the teachers learned the full meaning of the old lines:

"O'er wayward childhood wouldst thou hold firm rule,
And sun thee in the light of happy faces?
Love, Hope and *Patience*, these must be thy graces,
And in thine *own heart* let them first keep school."

CHAPTER FIFTH

FROM DAME SCHOOL TO COLLEGE (CONCLUDED)

SO MUCH has been written in regard to Mary Lyon's School for Girls, people are in danger of forgetting that a famous boys' school was also located in South Hadley.

Soon after the Rebellion of 1786, Col. Ruggles Woodbridge, who was now the wealthiest man in town, began the building of his beautiful home, now owned by Mrs. Hollingsworth. The ornamental carving within was all hand work, and a well-known antiquarian once said that it was amongst the finest in the State. The large house, with its curiously paneled doors, was at first but a lonely home. Col. Woodbridge had been one of a family of eight children, and, including visitors and servants, his father's household had never been a small one. He had never married, since most of his life had been spent in an era of continual excitement on account of impending conflict or actual warfare. Even in the later insurrection it was he who gathered a small party of men at the old Woodbridge Parsonage, ready for battle, until finding from his scouts that he would be outnumbered by Shay's men, and lives would be sacrificed in the fight, he became convinced that prudence forbade his making a sally. But if the present quiet of his dwelling grew irksome, his active mind soon devised a remedy. He had always been a friend to the education of youth, his own college course having been of great assistance to him in life.

He was an original thinker in advance of his time, and his theses during his curriculum often puzzled the professors. He now decided to open the "Woodbridge School for Boys," and it met with such success that he was compelled to make one addition after another to his house, till people said that if it had a few more wings it would be able to fly. Hartford and New York City alone sent thirty students. The first teacher was Samuel Ely, but the Colonel was head master as far as discipline was concerned.

WOODBRIDGE SCHOOL

A single example will illustrate his methods. After some years of faithful service, Jerusha, the "hired girl," received an advantageous offer of marriage from a well-to-do farmer, who was also the precentor at church. Her kindness to the boys had been so great that Col. W. not only presented her with a set of furs, the muff of which was two feet long, but also offered to give her a wedding. On the day before the ceremony a bride's loaf of rich cake was carefully frosted and placed upon the upper shelf in the pantry. About midnight, a venturesome youth stole downstairs barefooted, captured the cake, and bore it in triumph to the third story. The boys then lowered it and themselves to the piazza roof, and climbing down to the ground, went into the orchard to eat it, leaving no telltale crumbs to betray their exploit. Next morning there was great excitement; the teachers said the boys who had done this should be expelled. "No," answered the Colonel, "that would disgrace them for life. I think I know of a better way."

After conducting the morning devotions, he asked every pupil to look him straight in the eye, and his keen vision singled out the culprits by their guilty blushes. "His eyes bored right through us like a gimlet," said one of them afterwards. The teachers agreed that these lads should at least be locked in their rooms during the wedding. Again Colonel Woodbridge said "No." He told the midnight marauders that every one of them must be present at the ceremony, but if any of them, when the cake was passed, ventured to take a piece, he would be expelled the next morning. Fifty years later these lads used to say that Colonel Woodbridge had been the making of them.

The pupils were obliged to dress in uniform, and on Sunday march two and two into church with military precision. Every Sabbath morning they had a Bible lesson at home, and every day at the close of school each boy recited a verse of Scripture.

Most of the pupils came from old and aristocratic families. They wore tall hats, which gave great offense to the town boys, and there were frequent collisions in which fists were freely used. These quarrels were discountenanced by the teachers, and after some of the South Hadley boys entered the school a semblance of peace was maintained.

A long list might be given of the governors and other leading men of Massachusetts, who were educated in this school, which ranked high in its intellectual as well as its moral influence.

The following advertisement appeared in an old Hampshire Gazette:

"BOARDING SCHOOL.

"Miss Wright's School will commence in this town the first Wednesday of May next, where the usual branches of education taught in her school and in other female academies will be duly attended to.

"Particular attention will be paid to the manners and morals of those who may be committed to her care.

"South Hadley, March 25, 1809."

The plan for this, as well as that of the boys' school, originated with Colonel Woodbridge, and for the preceding six years it had been a decided succuss.

Previous to 1800, girls appear to have been excluded from our public schools, except for a few weeks in the early summer. Any woman who could read in Cumming's Catechism, sign a deed if necessary, and was able to calculate how much eight pounds of butter would come to at seventeen cents per pound, was looked upon as having all the education that was needful, or in any way befitting her sphere. But in 1803 the progress toward modern methods received a new impulse from the installation of our first postoffice, and the establishment of Miss Abby Wright's School, one of the very earliest academies devoted exclusively to girls that was opened in Western Massachusetts. Miss Wright was for those times a lady of rare culture, and though she taught the most exquisite needlework, was still more careful to see that her pupils were well grounded in mathematics and other essential branches.

A few extracts from Miss Wright's journal and letters may give a brief glimpse of her school:

"South Hadley, July 22, 1803—My school is very agreeable, though the attention they require renders my task pretty laborious. The scholars are very ambitious and I am glad to encourage them. I tell them they may come as early as they please and I will attend to them. Sometimes they come in at six o'clock in the morning. I am of the opinion that ten shillings per week is not enough for such a school, but when I wrote to Col. Woodbridge I set my price at that and did not limit the number, though I did not expect there would be more than twenty scholars."

"South Hadley, Jan. 25, 1804—I have an excellent place to board, which is in the family of Dr. Stebbins. They live in a kind of genteel snugness, and Mrs. S. has not failed to show herself as friendly as a sister on every occasion in which I have needed the assistance of a friend."

"May 29, 1804—My school goes on cleverly, and I have no reason to regret staying here. I keep in Mr. Goodman's hall a very convenient room. Five or six young ladies from Granby who attend my school board at Dea. Joseph White's. The number who have applied for admission has exceeded my expectations. I admitted forty and applications were made until I positively refused to take another. The major part of them are from out of town, are from fourteen to twenty-one years old and upward, and are in general very studious and attentive to the rules of propriety.

"The school has acquired a greater degree of celebrity than I wish and I believe much greater than it deserves. On many accounts this is an excellent place for a female academy. It is pleasantly situated, very healthy, and there are few objects to divert the attention of the scholar."

"August 3, 1805—I am now boarding at Rev. Joel Hayes. I had the honor of riding out with him—on Col. Woodbridge's best horse—to visit at Rev. Mr. Gridley's. Mrs. Hayes, Dr. and Mrs. Stebbins, Mrs. Dwight, Mr. and Mrs. Joseph White, rode in carriages."

Two days later she writes:

"August 5, 1805—We called in Springfield to see a piece of needlework lately executed at a celebrated school in Boston.

It was an elegant piece, and yet I have some in my school which I should not blush to compare with it, if the expense of each might be admitted in the comparison. The piece I refer to was wrought by a Miss Lyman, in memory of both her parents. It consists of a large willow, a monument, and two urns, the figures of a lady and gentleman and a little boy. The expense of the limner in drawing and painting the faces was eight dollars, and six months spent in Boston in working it."

The following sensible advice was given to her pupils upon the opening day of the term:

"Perhaps in no period of a woman's life is her conduct more criticized and her actions more liable to censure than when attending a boarding school * * * Be diligent, then, in improving your time; content not yourselves with being merely pretty or agreeable, but endeavor to be useful. Remember that amusement is not the business of life, but use it as a relaxation from its cares that you may return to its duties with redoubled ardor, and remember that the more good you do the more happiness you will enjoy."

A short extract from her farewell address to the members of the graduating class will illustrate the spirit and character of her teaching:

"My Dear Girls: You are now arrived at an age when your characters are to be established for life. How necessary is it that you have some fixed principles by which to regulate your conduct, for she who is governed by the influence of the present moment, who acts without thinking and thinks without reflecting, is as sure to run into improprieties as the seaman who sails without a pilot or compass is to dash upon the rocks. * * * Let books be the constant companions of your lives, accustom yourselves every day to spend a little time in reading and let the Holy Scriptures make at least some part of your studies."

The termination of this school was a source of deep regret to the people of South Hadley, but all were glad that Miss Wright, as the wife of Captain Peter Allen, would remain a member of the town. The marriage proved to be a happy one, and in her hospitable home, which stood just in front of the present Pearson Hall, Mary Lyon was a frequent and always welcome visitor, especially while the Seminary Building was in process of erection. It was said that Mrs. Allen's age and experience enabled her to be of great use to Miss Lyon during this period.

Her commanding influence made her a power in the church, and she was the acknowledged leader in all benevolent enterprises. Her death occurred in 1842, in the sixty-ninth year of her age, and her funeral sermon was preached from the text: "Precious in the sight of the Lord is the death of His saints."

On a bleak hillside in Buckland, near the door of a small house, a young girl was standing. She looked toward the stone-walled pasture, where the sheep were leisurely browsing, for she knew that from them must come the thick, woolen dress for her daily winter wear—always a red dress, everyone said red was such a durable color. But she knew the wool must first be carded and spun, dyed and woven, and already she was learning to knit, spin and weave. In the field of flax near-by she saw the brown linen gown for summer's use, but swingle, and hetchel, wheel, and loom must each do their appointed task. As she mused, a voice from the doorway called, "Mary!" and she could easily guess the duty that awaited her. The long potatoes of that day formed an essential part of the midday meal, and since there was no stove in the house they must be roasted in the hot ashes of the big fireplace. People were at this time expected to eat the whole of the baked potato, including the outer covering, or skin. In order to do this, every trace of the ashes must be removed before bringing them to the table. The wings of the wild turkey furnished the substitute for our modern brushes, and it was a frequent request in the Lyon household that Mary should be the one to "wing the potatoes, because she makes them so clean." By these habits of patient industry, Mary Lyon was laying the foundations of a character which would eventually win her an honored place in the Hall of Fame.

In spite of poverty, her early home was a happy one. Most of the food and clothing for the seven children was supplied by the little farm, and there was always something which they could share with a neighbor more in need than themselves. Though they had but few conveniences, their lot was but the common lot of all, for even in the minister's dwelling there was no stove. Our necessities were their luxuries.

Before Mary had completed her sixth year a dark shadow had fallen upon the household, a shadow that was never wholly lifted from their lives. In December of 1802, her father became alarmingly ill. On the day before his death he was constantly repeating "Thou art my rock and my fortress, my high tower and my deliverer," and other kindred texts. It was the common belief that a peculiar sanctity was attached to the words of those who were approaching death, and children were often carried for miles in order to receive what was termed the Dying Blessing. On the following morning Mr. Lyon summoned the family to his bedside and spoke tender words of farewell. The baby in the arms of her elder sister added pathos to the scene by calling now and then, in a pitiful little voice, "Papa! Papa!" Bidding them cling more closely to each other and always love one another, he added: "My dear children, what shall I say to you? God bless you, my children." These were his last words.

The girlhood of Mary Lyon was an uneventful one. Her teachers found her an apt scholar, diligent, quick to learn and possessing a most retentive memory. She was fond of books and might often be found in a corner of the kitchen preparing her lesson for the next day's recitation.

Her leading characteristic at this time appears to have been her deep reverence for the sacred hours of the Sabbath. In pleasant weather it was the fashion for the members of the congregation, during the intermission between the morning and afternoon service, to stroll out into the old burying ground. Here they ate their simple lunch and talked in low, subdued tones. It sometimes happened that a group of young people met, and, freed from the restraining presence of their elders, indulged in light conversation, which seemed to her ill befitting the day. Upon such occasions she always left them, and the silent reproof of her example was perhaps more potent than words.

Affectionately yours, Mary Lyon.

From a miniature painting in 1832.

In the present age it is difficult to realize the strictness in regard to the observance of the Sabbath which prevailed a century ago. Then no beds could be made, nor rooms swept until after sunset, and in many families no cooking of food was allowed on the Lord's Day.* Miss Lyon never permitted either herself or her pupils to write letters on Sunday. About 1840 one of the students in Mount Holyoke Seminary, whose mother was ill, asked permission on that account to write her on the Sabbath. In South Hadley the mail closed in the morning at nine o'clock. Miss Lyon asked her pupil if she could not write a letter on Monday before the mail went out. The girl replied that it would be impossible, as she had a recitation in Logic at eight o'clock. "Then," said Miss Lyon, "I will excuse you from the recitation and you can write your letter at that time."

A pupil once asked her if she considered it a sin to write religious letters on the Sabbath. Her reply was: "If you are deeply interested in the conversion of an impenitent friend, I do not say that it would be wrong to write to her on Sunday, but think how much greater weight the letter would carry if written during recreation hours."

She was equally strict in regard to herself. Upon one occasion she waited in Buffalo for the stage which was to convey her to her sister's home, waited from Saturday morning until four o'clock in the afternoon. When it came she found that by taking it she could reach her sister's house early the next morning,

---

* A grandson of Jonathan Edwards left us the following description of a Massachusetts man: "However busy the season, even when his crops were exposed to destruction by rain, he dismissed all the laborers so early on Saturday afternoon as to enable them to reach their own homes before sunset—the time when he began the Sabbath. His cattle were all fed, his cows milked, the vegetables for the ensuing day prepared, and his family summoned together previous to this sacred period. Until nine o'clock he spent the evening with his household in reading and prayer, and at this moment they uniformly retired to their beds. No room in his house was swept, no bed was made, nor was any act, except such as were acts of necessity and mercy in the strict sense, done until sunset on the succeeding day, when in his opinion the Sabbath terminated."

but felt that it would be a profanation of holy time to travel on Saturday night, and accordingly remained in Buffalo until the following Monday.

In the busy days of her early womanhood, Mary Lyon found little time for youthful love and romance. After she became a teacher, however, an incident occurred which showed her entire devotion to the cause of education. A young man, whose birthplace was but three or four miles from our South Hadley church, studied for the ministry and entered the missionary fields in what was then looked upon as the Far West. He spent two years in teaching the whites and Indians and then came East in order to find a wife who could assist him in his work. He confided his wishes to a friend, who suggested that Mary Lyon was well suited to this position. The young minister called upon Miss Lyon, and as a missionary's wooing was often a speedy one, after two or three interviews he asked her to marry him. She thanked him for the compliment he had paid her, but gently told him that her mind was so filled with plans for the elevation and improvement of schools for young women that she had room for but little else. She added, however: "I will do better for you than to marry you; I will introduce you to one of my friends, who is just suited to be your associate in this work, and who will, I feel sure, make your home a far happier one than I could ever hope to do." The young man followed her advice, and the wife proved a willing and able helper.

This was not the only occasion upon which Mary Lyon was compelled to explain to a disappointed suitor the high purpose of her life. Even after the Seminary Building was well on its way toward completion, a widower with six young daughters came to South Hadley because someone had told him that Miss Lyon was just the wife for him. The matter was whispered from one to another, and Mr. Joel Hayes, who was a son of our former minister, and who lived in our third parsonage, now owned by Mrs. Lester, volunteered to give a tea party in order that the two might be introduced to one another. Invitations were sent to Captain Peter Allen, Rev. Mr. Condit, Dr. Elihu

THIRD PARSONAGE

Dwight, Mr. E. T. Smith, Deacon Moses Montague, Mr. Cyrus White, and others. These invitations included their wives also, and Miss Lyon, who was at that time a guest at Captain Allen's. It was thought that this arrangement would enable the widower to accompany Miss Lyon home, when he could ask permission to "pay his addresses to her."

One of the company, who was a somewhat clumsy joker, told Miss Lyon in a low voice that he never expected to see her preside over Mount Holyoke Female Seminary. "And why not?" she asked quickly. "Because," he replied, "I think you will take a smaller school, with but a single pupil." Miss Lyon instantly divined the situation, and not wishing the matter to go farther, found a quiet moment in which she could hint to Mrs. Abby Wright Allen her desire to return home before the breaking up of the party.

At this time etiquette demanded that at the tea table husband and wife should sit next one another. This gave Mrs. Allen an opportunity to arrange with the Captain for their early departure. A little later the three excused themselves and went home, leaving the widower to his own reflections.

When Mary Lyon found that the dream of her life was nearing its fulfillment, a question arose in regard to the location of the new seminary. Rev. Roswell Hawks, who had resigned his pastorate in order to aid in the work, was an intimate friend of Rev. Artemas Boies, who was at this time our minister. The latter wrote to Mr. Hawks: "Do not let Miss Lyon decide upon a situation until she has seen South Hadley. This is an ideal place for such a school."

It was in response to this invitation that she first visited our town, with the view of finding a suitable place for locating the seminary. She finally decided to establish the school here, asking only that the townspeople should provide a site and help on the building to the utmost of their ability. Eight thousand dollars was promptly subscribed in work and money, but when the time for payment arrived many gave double the amount which they had promised.

Mr. Hawks and Miss Lyon solicited contributions for the seminary, both for the building itself and its needed furnishings, and for this purpose made frequent tours. Their friends in this vicinity sometimes loaned them their best horse and chaise, and sometimes, alas! a superannuated horse and decrepit vehicle.

The word "hospitality" has now lost much of its former significance. Then it meant that they would be welcomed everywhere, and breakfast, dinner, supper and lodging could be had for the asking. A single instance will illustrate their methods. "One bitter cold night in December, 1835, a gentleman and lady drove to the door of Mrs. F.'s early home and asked for a night's lodging. She gave them a cordial welcome, but told the gentleman he would have to care for his horse, as her husband had gone to meeting. She soon found her guests to be Rev. Roswell Hawks and Mary Lyon. They were on a pilgrimage through the towns of Western Massachusetts, soliciting funds and other donations for the new female seminary to be founded at South Hadley.

"A pleasant evening was passed, Mary Lyon taking out her knitting work and wisely plying her needles as she engaged in conversation. All were up at an early hour next morning, as was the custom of farmers, and the guests were anxious to make an early start. As the sleigh was brought out it was found to be sadly in need of repairs; the harness, too, needed mending, and after considerable delay in patching things, they started on their journey, rejoicing over a gift of fifty dollars from their host. In front of them in the sleigh was a tub filled with articles donated by friends."

Later, Mr. and Mrs. F. visited the seminary, and as they sat down to dinner Mary Lyon quietly remarked that this was their bread and milk day—plenty of sweet milk, good bread, stewed sweet apples and pie made up the menu for the day's dinner.

In 1835, a difference of opinion arose among Miss Lyon's co-workers in regard to the location of the new school. Some who lived in the eastern part of the state wished it to be near

Boston, others were equally insistent that it should be in the Connecticut Valley. Miss Lyon well knew that the Ipswich Seminary had for years occupied the field north of Boston, and this very summer Wheaton Female Seminary was opened about twenty-five miles south of that city. She, herself, taught in both institutions, and in the latter school is said to have taken a class through Adam's arithmetic in three weeks' time. Under such circumstances she adhered firmly to her purpose of locating at South Hadley, and the others all yielded to her decision.

It was now necessary to fix upon a site for the building. Her first plan was to place it upon the summit of Prospect Hill, which commands a fine view of the surrounding country. A beautiful landscape was, in her eyes, a continual education, but when she thought of the toil involved in the steep ascent—far steeper then than now—it seemed wiser to choose a more accessible spot, and another site was offered, which embraced the present summer residence of J. A. Skinner and gave a picturesque view of mountain and valley. This situation would have been entirely satisfactory but for its distance from church. She expected that her pupils would attend both morning and afternoon service, in storm as well as in sunshine, and it seemed better to place the building at a less distance from the meeting house, as at this time umbrellas were both rare and costly.

Opposite the Old Burying Ground was a sandy pasture, a part of which was covered with huckleberry bushes and the remainder was used as a boys' playground. Mr. David Choate, one of her friendly advisers, standing one day upon the present site of the Mary Lyon Chapel, said quietly: "This is the right place, I believe." At his side stood an old pear tree, which had probably shadowed the walls of South Hadley's first dwelling house. The owner of this tree had allowed the village boys to gather its fruit at their pleasure. Mr. J. once told the author that in 1836, when he was a boy, one summer morning he had climbed into the old pear tree, when a man named John Preston approached with an axe, saying that he had been directed to cut down the tree and dig up the stump, as this spot was needed for the new seminary. Hastily filling his pockets with fruit, he returned home with laggard steps, while across the street the little children asked with tearful voice, "Where shall we go huckleberrying?"

The laying of the cornerstone was a memorable affair in South Hadley, and great preparations were made for its celebration. Mr. Todd was engaged to deliver an address in the village church, and Mr. Dexter Ingraham, the leader of the choir, invited the young people to assist upon this occasion. He trained a chorus of nearly one hundred voices which, led by a good orchestra, furnished inspiring music.

After the services at the church were ended, the congregation formed in procession and marched, two and two, to the northwestern extremity of the Seminary Building. Here the cornerstone was laid with appropriate exercises, and upon this occasion it is said that Miss Lyon stooped down and wrote, "The Lord hath remembered our low estate."*

*Recollections of Mary Lyon, by Fidelia Fiske, page 93.

The following account of Miss Lyon's first years in South Hadley is from the pen of Mrs. Cynthia Wright Herrick, and was written soon after the fire of 1896:

"My remembrance of Mary Lyon, and the influence she exerted upon individuals with whom she came in contact, dates back to my fifth year of childhood. Our family had moved to South Hadley in order to obtain better facilities for schooling. When our home was first established there, her seminary building was nearing the third story. Her experiment was discussed around our hearth by neighbors and friends nearly every evening. The pros and cons as often against as for her. An open declaration of war with England would hardly have created more controversy. Even her well wishers predicted failure; her enemies felt that it would curse the town, and one good South Hadley deacon predicted there would not be a girl in the place worth marrying, with their higher education. It is well that none of them read with a prophetic eye.

"During this period I had no idea what kind of a creature this Mary Lyon was. I fully believed she was some kind of a

PROSPECT HILL

monster, but of what species I was ignorant. One day I ventured to ask one of my big brothers what kind of a lion a Mary lion was. He looked at me a moment with a twinkle in his eyes, and replied that it was a kind that fed on girls entirely and had no use for boys whatever; that there was to be a large, brick cage built, and there they would live with the Lyon till she disposed of them. He then informed me that I might be snapped up between times if I ran away, or stayed out late at night. I was also told that he had heard father say he should send me there when I was older. I assure you, I had my opinion of Mary Lyon after that, and the darkness never found me away from home.

"The first time I saw her she was sitting beside my invalid mother, her eyes sparkling, talking volubly of the need of quilts, pillows; anything that pertained to household furnishings. She pushed her chair nearer as she talked, and at last my mother consented to aid her, after Miss Lyon had taken her hand in her own and gently held it. No young lady who has ever felt the pressure of that hand will deny the magnetic influence that it exerted. I was standing behind the kitchen door looking through the crack to see a Mary lion, and she was just a blue-eyed, red-cheeked woman.

"About that time my father came in one morning and stated the fact that the seminary had completely disappeared off the face of the earth during the night. The three stories collapsed, and the plan of educating women was supposed to have incurred the Divine displeasure.

"When Miss Lyon saw the ruins of her long-cherished hopes, she exclaimed, 'How glad I am that no one is hurt.' It was discovered later that the foundation was permeated with quicksand, which caused the ruin.

"Miss Lyon soon rebuilt the seminary, having raised twenty-seven thousand dollars, which she collected in sums ranging from six cents, in three instances, to one thousand dollars in but two, and there were eighteen hundred subscribers.

"The cornerstone of Mt. Holyoke Seminary was laid October 3, 1836, and the school was opened with four teachers and eighty scholars on November 8, 1837. During the first year the number of scholars increased to one hundred and sixteen. At the time of Mary Lyon's death, in 1849, there were fourteen teachers and two hundred and twenty-nine pupils.

"Miss Lyon had a correct yet nimble and elastic judgment which could adapt itself to any situation. Her aim was singularly unselfish, and for this high purpose she put aside all merely personal matters. Declining marriage, a sacrifice much greater for her than for one less affectionate and domestic, she gave her life in as pure and lofty a devotion as ever characterized a Saint Theresa.

"I entered the seminary the year Miss Lyon died. She met me with a smile, called me her new daughter, and informed me that my trunk had been mislaid and I could have the pleasure of sharing a room with one of the teachers until my absent trunk was found.

"Miss Lyon had few duties in the school room. She taught only Butler's Analogy and Chemistry.

"The first week of the new scholars was to most of us a homesick season, but when Miss Lyon came into the seminary hall, with her Bible under her arm, and her face shining as if she had been in communion with Deity, she would speak words worth cherishing. It was then that she impressed upon us the power of littles—little habits, little sins, transient thoughts, cherished indulgences, and their importance in the formation of character. She always placed the sufferings of Christ and His self-denials in such a clear and vivid light that the common trials of a school girl's life were not for a moment to be thought of. At these times she seemed beautiful to me.

"One of my fellow students was taken very ill with malignant erysipelas, which proved fatal. Miss Lyon scarcely left her bedside and herself contracted the disease. The young lady's coffin was placed in front of the platform in the seminary hall, and Miss Lyon, with tears rolling down her cheeks, talked of the dear sister. Her last words to us were these, "Young ladies, if I could fold my hands and lay down in our dear sister's place, with God's voice saying, 'Your work is done, come up

MT. HOLYOKE SEMINARY, THE ORIGINAL BUILDING

higher,' I should be so glad to go." She only lived three days afterwards. It was predicted that the seminary would prove a failure after her death, but she had planted and pruned too wisely for the tree to die after all its early care, and now we are proud and a little boastful of Holyoke as the finest and most progressive school in the world."

One of Mary Lyon's greatest objects in founding the seminary was to bring education within reach of the poor. The trustees sympathized with this desire, and said that since the expense of the building had been defrayed by gifts of money, and voluntary labor, no charge should be made for room rent and the price of board, including tuition, should be placed at the small sum of one dollar and a half a week.

Under these circumstances no person of less executive ability than Miss Lyon could have carried the school through its first year to a successful finish.

As no help was hired, except one man for heavy lifting and the carrying of wood, the labor of the household devolved upon the young ladies, as Miss Lyon always called them. Each of these was assigned her part in what was termed their domestic work, which occupied on an average about an hour a day.

They were formed into circles, according to the different duties assigned them. The dinner circle prepared the food for the mid-day meal, after which the blue crockery circle washed and wiped the willow ware then in use. The work was all classified and carried on with unerring precision. If a pupil was absent, either by reason of illness or from some other cause, her place was promptly filled by a member of the miscellaneous circle, who could turn their hands to anything.

Nor were the pupils dissatisfied with this division of labor. They sang blithely at their work, or chatted merrily, and it would be hard to find even among the college girls of to-day a happier set of faces than those that brightened the old domestic hall in the days long gone by.

Five years after the school opened Miss Lyon wrote to a friend, "Everything is systematized, and Miss Moore and Miss Whitman urge forward the wheels so beautifully that all seems more than ever like clock-work." In her modesty, Mary Lyon did not realize that she was herself the mainspring of it all. Her firm will, sometimes half veiled under a playful manner, carried everything before it.

Mr. Hawks once differed from her in regard to some proposed plan, and being the president of the trustees, said with some dignity, "Miss Lyon, please to remember that I am the head of this institution." "Well," she returned, quickly, "if you are the head I am the neck that turns the head," and she had her way.

The pupils always complied with her wishes, and usually with cheerful readiness. Once she gave them an unexpected holiday, in order that they might visit Mount Holyoke. She had, as she supposed, guarded her plans with care, but hardly had her pupils reached the summit when she was told that a messenger on horseback had been seen riding post-haste through the notch to Amherst, and she knew that the college boys would soon be flocking toward the mountain. Sending for Mr. Hawks, she asked him to procure teams and go at once to Mount Holyoke with a summons for the immediate return of the party. He would gladly have been excused from this duty, but did as she desired. In spite of their disappointment, all yielded to her request. One of them, however, remarked in an audible voice as they descended the mountain, "It seems that we escaped from the Lyon's den only to fall into a Hawks' nest."

Few of their outings were better enjoyed than going berrying. On a pleasant Wednesday, when the swamp huckleberries were ripe, some of the good-natured farmers of this vicinity drove to the front of the seminary building with their big hay wagons and waited while the girls climbed joyfully in. Accompanied by Miss Lyon, or one of the older teachers, they rode across the plains with song and laughter, till they reached "the slipe." Tin pails and willow backets were then much in request, for all knew that the fruit of their afternoon's labor would add to the present menu, besides being in part preserved for winter's use, when dried huckleberry pies were not to be despised. And if, on the way home, each contributed an amusing story, Miss

THE DOMESTIC HALL

Lyon's was sure to be the best and wittiest one of all, though at its end, like the old edition of Aesop's Fables, there was generally a moral ready to be attached.

During the early years of the seminary, the furniture was simple and the food plain. This was a necessity since sixty dollars a year from each pupil must defray the cost of provision and the salaries of the teachers.

Tea and coffee never appeared upon the tables except on Sunday morning, at which time crust coffee was added to the usual menu. This was prepared by toasting dry pieces of bread very brown, and then pouring boiling water over them. This, though somewhat colorless, made, with the addition of milk and sugar, a pleasant beverage. But the girls never seemed to miss the luxuries of to-day, and their robust health made an isolated sickroom almost needless.

In case of a slight indisposition, tea and toast would be sent at meal times to the room of the pupil, but a small sum was charged as the price of this extra privilege. One girl, who had inherited an indolent disposition, but had brought with her an abundant supply of pocket money, fell into the habit of taking her breakfast in bed nearly every morning. This coming to the knowledge of Miss Lyon, she herself took the tray to the pupil's room one morning, saying that she had missed her from the dining hall, and inquiring solicitously in regard to her pupil's health. Before leaving she took up the tray and said, "My young ladies are all of them so busy that in future I will myself bring up your tea and toast whenever you need them." The invalid was by this time completely recovered, with no danger of a relapse.

While Mary Lyon allowed her pupils to bring rocking-chairs with them if they so desired, she discouraged their use as far as possible. She said it made people lazy to sit in them. She might well have echoed the plaint of an old man at South Hadley Falls, "Nothing's good enough since the Revolutionary War," said he, "it's nothing but change, change. Folks used to think when they was sick, or old, that they was well off with arms to their cheers. But now it's nothing but teeter up and teeter down in these 'ere rocking cheers.''

She often warned her pupils against boastfulness, and the assumption of social preëminence, relating to them an incident that occurred during the first years of the seminary. One of the students came to Miss Lyon with the request that she might at her own expense have eggs every day with her breakfast. She stated that her father was a rich man and she missed the home luxuries, and added that her constitution was too delicate to thrive upon warm griddle cakes with butter and molasses,— which was then the usual morning meal. After some discussion the desired permission was given. A few weeks later, happening to be in the town which was the birthplace of the young lady in question, and having an hour at her own disposal, she called upon the parents and found them living in a small, three-roomed, one-story house, with little furniture, and neither carpet nor rug, save two or three mats braided from strips of old cloth. She learned that the daughter had been out at service two years, earning the money to carry her through a year at the seminary, and to provide the showy gowns in which she delighted to appear. The mother invited her to stay for dinner, saying frankly that roasted potatoes and bread was all that she could offer her. Miss Lyon declined, as she had brought a lunch from home, and her concluding remark in repeating this incident was, ''Young ladies, you can each draw your own moral.''

One of the most striking features of the new institution was the unity of purpose and the sincere friendship that existed between the school and the town's people. If Saturday night brought a drifting snowstorm, so that by Sunday morning the seminary yard would look like a prison enclosure, the pupils well knew that volunteers, headed by Byron Smith and John Dwight, would appear, each carrying a shovel, and a broad path would soon be cleared from their very threshold to the door of the church.

Sometimes in summer, the pupils, while taking the long walks, which formed a part of each day's duty, paused to cast a longing glance at the trees laden with cherries, peaches or pears,

SEMINARY AND COLLEGE BUILDING DESTROYED BY FIRE, SEPTEMBER, '96

that were at this time abundant in South Hadley. If this were noticed by the owner, they were sure of a cordial invitation to come into the orchard and help themselves to the luscious fruit, nor were they ever allowed to return to the seminary empty handed.

If a teacher, wearied by the week's routine, went calling in the village on Wednesday afternoon, she was certain of an invitation to stay to tea, which meant that a most bountiful repast was in store for her, and often a little package of caraway cookies would be slipped into her hand at parting. It was the custom among the leading families of the town to invite all Miss Lyon's teachers to a substantial meal at least once in every year, and these outings did much to strengthen the friendly relations between them.

The hospitality, however, was not all on one side. On a Sabbath morning the pastor would give out notice from the pulpit that all members of the congregation who were more than fourteen years of age were invited to the seminary on Tuesday evening. At the time appointed the guests were received at the front door with words of welcome and were ushered into the stately and solemn north parlor. After a season of social converse, the company adjourned to the seminary hall and were entertained with music and calisthenics. Refreshments were served, sometimes consisting of raised biscuits and butter, cherry preserves, loaf-cake and tea.

At half past nine the minister read a chapter from the Bible, one or more hymns were sung, and after the closing prayer the people of the town went home.

Sometimes the youngest classes in the Sabbath School were invited to spend Wednesday afternoon at the seminary, and the pupils entertained them so beautifully that the children, when they went home, felt as if they had been on a trip to fairy land.

On the last Sabbath before the graduation exercises, notice was given at church of the public examinations on Tuesday and Wednesday, at which all the parish from twelve years of age upward were invited to be present. Between the recitations were interludes filled with music and compositions. The latter were always interesting. There was one on "The Moral Effect of Bad Bread," whose author became a famous Boston teacher. Another was entitled, "Minus a Garret," and depicted, in a witty manner, the trials of a family who moved into a house with a roof which gave no attic room for the storing of trunks, etc.

One of the seniors, three years after the founding of the seminary, wrote a farewell poem to her classmates, a few lines of which will be quoted below:

> Down, down to the tomb of the buried years,
> That are shrined in song, that are veiled in tears,
> Down, down with a soft and a stealthy tread,
> Behold how the hastening months have sped.
> And there cometh a hand on the wall to trace,
> 'They are numbered and finished, thy dearest days,
> But far o'er the earth though your steps may roam,
> * * * *
> Not a lovelier spot shall memory claim,
> And your bosoms shall thrill at Holyoke's name.'
> * * * *
> We are parting now, for a godlike race.
> Let the arm untwine from its last embrace,
> Be our course right on as the eagles fly,
> Right on to a glorious destiny.
> Give the farewell kiss, and the trembling hand,
> For we part but to meet in a holier land."

Not only spiritually and intellectually was Mary Lyon's life an inspiration to those about her, but in the home circle her tender, sympathetic nature drew all hearts toward her. Once she saw a pupil standing lonely and sad beside the window, and said to her, "I think you want to see your mother." The girl answered, "I have no mother." Upon hearing this Miss Lyon put her arms around her and said, tenderly, "I will be a mother to you. Come to me any time you would go to her, if she were here."

In describing her we might well misquote Emerson; one can teach simply by doing, and to Mary Lyon it was given to do that which would have been impossible to any other woman of her time.

"As chief commander, few her peers; none better knew to choose her aids. Here lies the secret of a grand and useful life."

The weeks that followed the death of Mary Lyon were a season of deep anxiety to the friends of the institution. None of the teachers desired to assume the position of principal. Finally, Miss Whitman, who had been associated with Miss Lyon for years, consented to take charge of the school for a time, but resigned before her marriage, which occurred in 1851. The position of acting principal was then given to Miss Mary W. Chapin, and the ensuing two years were perhaps the most critical period in the history of the seminary. Some of the pupils who had never known Miss Lyon desired to abate the former strictness of the rules, and believed that the new regime could be brought to accept their views. Two of them tried to incite an open revolt against certain wise and prudent regulations. The ringleaders were, strange to say, daughters of a clergyman of considerable note. It was now that the full value of an able and discreet counsellor became evident. Rev. Roswell Hawks, and family, resided within the building, and his services had been of inestimable worth to Mary Lyon from the first inception of her plans. The record states that "Mr. Hawks was enlisted in the cause as permanent agent as early as 1834. From town to town and from house to house in western Massachusetts he presented its claims with such clearness, good sense, and patient persistence, as to win people who had never before thought of doing anything for female education. Always devoted to the interests of the institution, he was president of its board of trustees for many years."

He was a great favorite among the pupils, who always spoke of him as "Pa Hawks," and invariably treated him with affectionate respect. He now called a meeting of the trustees, who promptly and unanimously voted that Miss Chapin should have their unqualified support. Several of the pupils were expelled, and others suspended, but Mr. Hawks managed matters with so much firmness, tact, and gentleness, that the incipient rebellion was crushed, and Miss Chapin continued to preside over the seminary for fourteen years, both honored and beloved by teachers and students.

After the foregoing episode it was the custom, in case any new pupil showed a continuous spirit of insubordination, to suggest to her that she "Stay out a year and mature." Such absences rarely failed of their object.

Early in 1888 application was made to the legislature for a change in the name of the institution. As "Mount Holyoke Seminary and College" it would share with other such schools the power of conferring degrees. On March 12, the day of the great blizzard, this request was granted, but it took forty-eight hours for the good news to force its way through the snowdrifts in order to reach South Hadley.

The standard of scholarship for the entrance examinations was, during the next few years, raised to such an extent that on January 31, 1893, the legislature voted to drop the word "Seminary," leaving the school a college.

Concerning this change, Miss Elizabeth Prentiss, a teacher from 1866 to 1904, thus writes:

"A new Mount Holyoke has gradually arisen on the foundations of the old. Fears that innovations may mar or diminish the precious legacy which the present holds in trust, have given place to that wise liberalism which, while preserving the best of the past, does not fear to take possession of the present and develop the larger and fuller life demanded by larger opportunities and responsibilities."

The following tribute to Miss Lyon is taken from a poem written by the late Mr. Andrew Judd, of South Hadley:

> The mountain halos here are cast,
> The nearer hills play loose and fast,
> Now, clad afresh, the trees appear
> Marking the spring-time of the year;
> Warmed with its breath the embryo leaves
> Spin the deft web the summer weaves.

MARY LYON'S GRAVE

Yon Campus holds a lowly mound,
Humble the shaft that marks the ground
Whereon its stands; whose grassy spears
Spring at the beck of watering tears
From those who felt the charm and grace
That mirrored her immortal face.
When hath there been sublimer thought,
In crucial test, more fitly wrought,
In unison with heart and brain,
Uttered in sweeter human strain
Than wakened by this pioneer,
This avant-courier, whose career
Thrilled with its throbbing pulse of steel
The world's best thought for highest weal?
She blazed a path untrod before;

* * * *

Out from the Book of books she wove
Her woof of life, to web of love;
How grateful now the thought appears
That on the circling round of years
Comes centering to our good old town
So much that adds to its renown.

CHAPTER SIX

THE EVOLUTION OF A CHURCH

PROGRESS in civilization was, in the opinion of our forefathers, measured by the improvement in church architecture. The rough, box-like structures, which the early colonists dignified by the name of "meeting-houses," were often but little more than log cabins covered within by a coat of coarse mortar.

South Hadley Center has had five successive church buildings, only the first and last of which still remain. One, now used as a dwelling, stands just west of Judson Hall, the other being the present Congregational Church.

One hundred and eighty years ago on Sunday mornings, in summer, the young people of the South Precinct might have been seen threading the woodland path that skirted the base of Mount Holyoke, on their way to the mother church in Old Hadley. They were barefooted (for in those days shoes were far too costly to be worn during the sixteen-mile tramp to and from church). When the bridge at Fort River was reached the whole procession halted, and, sitting upon the bank, laved their dusty feet in the cool water; then putting on their shoes and stockings they proceeded decorously to the quaint, old building on Meeting House Hill, prepared to listen to the prolonged discourses of the Rev. Isaac Chauncey.

The settlers of Moody Corner were so thrifty that they wore their ordinary working clothes to and from Fort River, exchanging upon its wooded sides the old suit for the Sunday best, and replacing them on their return.

If one considers the unremitting toil of the early colonists when, as the old people used to say, knitting stockings and chopping wood were their only recreations, it will not seem strange that ere long the task of walking to and from church proved irksome, and in November, 1727, we find them petitioning the General Court, at Boston, that they might be made into a separate precinct, which would entitle them to the privilege of having a meeting house and minister of their own. This the court was willing to grant, provided that at the expiration of two years they should have forty families and during the following year should settle a "learned and orthodox minister."

The first thing to be done was to agree upon a site for the new meeting house. The spot chosen being, as was the custom of that day, a slight elevation commanding a partial view of the surrounding country, which in case of war might, perhaps, warn of Indian approach. Their shrewd avoidance of forest fires was shown by placing the building near the center of a sandy field covered with low huckleberry bushes. This field included the present common of South Hadley Center.

The new meeting house was a plain, unpretentious, one-roomed structure, forty feet long and thirty feet wide.

In 1733 they had already made choice of a minister. Grindall Rawson had been a restless, impetuous youth, to whom the religious restraints of that age were almost unbearable. The Puritan Sabbath was a long day for the boy, and it is said that one Sunday afternoon, as a special privilege, he was allowed to sit in the orchard for an hour while he committed to memory a chapter from the Bible; at the expiration of that time the Book lay upon the ground unopened and the lad was found wholly absorbed in a mimic battle between insects, which he had caught and forced to fight.

Before he had entered upon his teens, the wise and tender care of his father was withdrawn by the stern hand of Death, and he found a temporary home in the house of Judge Sewall, and a congenial playmate in the person of the judge's grandson, Sam Hirst.

The laws of the commonwealth had long ago decreed that whenever a minister was settled a house should be provided for him, and the young and already overburdened community were now asked to build a parsonage. The erection of a meeting house had already taxed their energies to the utmost. Trees eighty feet high had been felled in order to "hugh" out the massive beams which are still a wonder to those who see them.

Such buildings were usually framed upon the ground and the raising of their heavy timbers was by no means an easy task. It sometimes required the services of sixty picked men for a week or more before the framework would stand in its proper position. This work was voluntary and unpaid for, and those men who lived at a distance of four or five miles found it difficult to be present at the early hour set for commencing labor. Their horses could not pace rapidly the narrow, winding cart tracks, and pacing was at that time considered the natural gait of a horse; trotting not coming into favor till several decades later.

The location of the minister's dwelling had already been provided for in the land grant of 1720. It was to stand upon the west side of the present Woodbridge street, and the old parsonage still exists as the rear ell of the house now occupied by the Misses Eastman. Its hand-made nails with their rough, irregular tops, and its carefully-prepared clapboards testify to the skill and patient industry that were required for its construction.

On March 30, 1733, a committee had been appointed "to order and proportion each man's labor, as near as may be convenient, about Mr. Rawson's house." This date is of interest as being that of the first town meeting of which South Hadley has preserved a record.

The living room of the new parsonage was of ample proportions. Extending half-way across the western end was a wide fireplace and an old-fashioned brick oven for the Saturday baking. In the northwest corner of the room was a deep well with its old, oaken bucket.

As the summer waned, the people became impatient of their long walk to the Hadley church, and in spite of the unfinished state of their meeting house, it was voted that the ordination of Rev. Grindall Rawson should take place on October 3, 1733.

The preparatory fast day, which always preceded the settlement of a new minister, was observed, and a committee was then appointed to take charge of the dinner and to send for the neighboring "Ministers and Messengers."

In the main, an ordination dinner was in those times a joy-

THE FIRST PARSONAGE

ous and, in many cases, even a hilarious occasion. After the solemn consecration of the candidate, by the laying on of hands and the other attendant religious ceremonies, had been duly performed, then clergy, as well as laity, gave themselves up to the enjoyment of social festivities. To "provide suitably" meant at that time to have the punch well brewed, the flip iron heated and the toddy stick prepared for frequent use.

There may or may not have been spiced wine at this South Hadley feast, but of a certainty there was an abundance of both cider and rum. No one but a deacon or a man of equal piety and probity was permitted to sell spirituous liquors, and his duty allowed him to deal it out simply to "cheer and not inebriate." Another qualification was also demanded of the vendor, as is evidenced by the licenses issued by our town officials. He must be, they state, not only a man of sound judgment, who could tell at a glance how much spirit a customer could bear, but he must also be a connoisseur whose cultured taste could select the delicate jorum "fit to be offered to ministers."

Doubtless the tables groaned beneath the weight of edibles that filled the pewter platters on that memorable third of October. There would be, first of all, according to the custom, a rich plum pudding; for dessert preceded the course of meats a century and a half ago. Then one looks for wild turkey, from the side of Mt. Holyoke, baked in a big Dutch oven before the fireplace and redolent of sage and other savory herbs. It was probably flanked by roasts of beef and pork, a leg of lamb and a venison pasty.

There were no potatoes to grace the festal board, turnips being used as a substitute, but it may be that they were enabled to offer their favorite apple and gooseberry tarts, for history tells us that the first settlers in Connecticut had with wise forethought brought apple seeds with them from England. Our ancestors had profited by their example, and they, in turn, had taken apple seeds from Connecticut, and already there was one flourishing orchard in South Hadley.

Some of our old inhabitants possessed spinits, a kind of circular gridiron with a rotary motion. Upon this useful utensil delicious salmon, fresh from the river, were wont to be broiled over the bed of coals.

Of the after-dinner speeches no record remains, but doubtless amusing stories were rehearsed; stories that have ever since gone echoing down the halls of time.

But soon the chill winds of November, the early snows of December and the tempestuous storms of January must have made a rather dreary outlook for the new preacher. The town had voted the preceding March to ceil and plaster the meeting house and to provide joists for the gallery, but this had not been done. The pulpit was simply a plain, wooden desk, behind which the preacher stood on these wintry days muffled in his great coat and with his hands incased in gloves or mittens to keep them from freezing.

There was no artificial heat in the meeting house, the iron boxes, known by the name of stoves, being then unheard and unthought of. The little footstoves made of perforated tin, inclosing an iron pan which contained a handful of coals buried in ashes, were just coming into use in the larger towns, but were probably unknown in South Hadley.

Sometimes the roar of the wind rushing through the gap between Mt. Tom and Mt. Holyoke must have almost drowned the voice of the speaker, whose welcome "tenthly" gave notice that the sermon was nearing its close.

In 1734 came the crucial test of the church harmony—the seating of the meeting house. The committee were directed to seat the congregation according to ratable estate, having due regard to age and ability. To adjust matters on this delicate scale often sowed seeds of dissension and bitterness that bore fruit for years afterward, but the present committee appear to have used rare tact, good judgment and care, for there was no public dissatisfaction recorded, as was the case upon similar occasions later on.

The first few years of the Rawson ministry were quiet and uneventful, but in 1737 trouble arose in the church. It may be that some family eccentricities now became apparent. It was said of his cousin, the other Rev. Grindall Rawson, that hear-

THE EVOLUTION OF A CHURCH

ing he had been made a subject of ridicule by certain members of his congregation he preached from the text "I Was the Song of the Drunkard," and the sermon was such a stinging one that at its close hardly a person was left in the house.

The first complaint against Mr. Rawson, brought by the South Hadley church, would seem a very trivial pretext upon which to hold a council of ministers. He was accused of having traded horses with someone outside the town. Perhaps his native shrewdness enabled him to get the best of the bargain and complaint was made of conduct "unbecoming a minister."

At all events, a council, of which Rev. Johnathan Edwards, of Northampton, was a member, was called. After hearing the evidence on both sides, the council voted that Grindall Rawson was "Learned, orthodox and moral," and as these were the three essentials required by law the incident was considered closed. It proved, however, to be the entering wedge whereby later dissensions crept into the church.

It should, perhaps, be added by way of explanation that although at that period the towns in this region yielded an outward show of reverence to their ministers, yet they often interfered in personal matters to a degree that would be deemed intolerable at the present day.

Thus, in the unpublished diary of a minister, who was settled in an adjoining town and who had some financial trouble with a parishioner to whom he had loaned money, we read such entries as the following:

May 28, went to Walter Fairfield's and bought his cattle. Gave him up a note that I had against him and I am to give him more, if Johnathan Bardwell and John Cowls say that I must."

This the two men did say a few days later. Afterward meeting one of his congregation, who had absented himself from church in order to go hunting, the pastor said to him, severely, "Phelps, you have not been at meeting for three Sabbaths. If you continue in your present course remember that very soon you will be in hell and there will be no preaching there."

"B-b-but, p-p-p-parson," stuttered his parishioner, "it w-won't be for the l-lack of m-m-ministers."

It may be that this trouble with the church deepened Mr. Rawson's desire for sympathy and companionship, for in the succeeding May we find preparations for a wedding going on in the house of the Hadley minister, Rev. Isaac Chauncey, whose daughter, Dorothy, was the promised bride of our pastor. He had meekly followed the tradition of the fathers, for there was in this section a general expectation that the younger divines would marry the daughters of other ministers. There was so much clannishness among the members of this profession in the early days that it even led them to propose that none but ministers should be eligible as deputies to the General Court, but this law failed of enactment.

There being no divinity schools at that time, students were obliged to study theology in the homes of older ministers, where they learned to be orthodox, and perhaps fell in love with one of the pretty daughters of the household. If there were none, the elder man usually gave to the younger at the close of his novitiate a letter of introduction to some other minister who had marriageable daughters, and under the transparent pretext of reviewing his theology the wooing was accomplished.

Some of the elderly people of South Hadley still recall an amusing instance of this kind which happened to a reverend ancestor of their family.

The pastor and his wife had been invited out to supper, and when a young minister appeared with his letter of introduction the three daughters with their little brother were obliged to do the honors of the house. The youthful minister had a very prominent nose and at the table the youngest daughter, intending to ask him to pass the cheese, said, unconsciously, "Will you please pass me your nose?" then, noticing her mistake, she blushed and said hastily, "I mean the cheese." He gravely handed the dish with no remark and nothing in his face betrayed his having heard the first question. On the morning of his departure two weeks later, her mother having sent her into the garden on an errand, the young man presently followed her and said, in an earnest voice, "On the day of my arrival you asked me to pass you my nose; will you permit me to offer with it my hand and my heart?" And the wedding occurred shortly after.

A minister's wedding in Hampshire county was at this time considered an affair of importance. The first thing to be done was to hold a town meeting in order to vote money for defraying the expenses of the entertainment.

If the laws of etiquette which the county demanded upon such occasions were obeyed, then a delegation of his parishioners would accompany Mr. Rawson to Hockanum, where a party from Hadley would meet them and all proceed together to the home of the bride. The marriage ceremony was usually performed "in the edge of the evening." On the following morning the party from South Hadley, increased by a score or more of the friends of the bride, would return home. The fair Mistress Dorothy riding, according to custom, on a pillion behind one of the deacons, perhaps in this case Ebenezer Moody, as he was one of the bridegroom's most intimate friends. At Hockanum they were probably met by a large company from our town who escorted them back to the house of Mr. Rawson, where fun and feasting reigned until late in the evening. On the following day the festivities were usually renewed so that those of the congregation who could only leave home in turn might also share in the joyous occasion.

Hardly had the wedding bells ceased their melody when a new difficulty arose in the church. Eighty years had elapsed since the first settlers of Hadley emigrated from Connecticut in order to escape the Half-way Covenant, and now the abhorred doctrine had followed and overtaken them in their new home. Championed by Rev. Solomon Stoddard, of Northampton, it had already become a prevailing article of belief in Western Massachusetts, and a majority of the South Hadley church members were ready to accept it as a tenet of their faith.

Then, too, the old superstition that the souls of infants dying unbaptized would be lost wakened into new life during this century, and our ministers baptized the children of their parishioners upon the very day of their birth or within a few days after that event. Many non-church members desired this sacrament for their children, deeming it consistent with the teachings of Scripture.

But not so the Rev. Grindall Rawson. His determined will, firm even to stubborness, opposed itself to this innovation and a strong minority of the church upheld him. This party included many of his kindred and intimate friends. Among them was Chileab Smith, Third, the great-grandfather of Mary Lyon, a man of dominant will and unflinching purpose, as beseemed her ancestor. Her intense loyalty to whatever she believed to be right, her unswerving honesty and truthfulness, and her high courage that could not brook defeat, all seemed a heritage from her brave old forefather.

Aside from the personal interest of the narrative, the story of his life is well worth the telling simply for the light it sheds upon the customs and manners of the day. His journal tells us that at the age of seventeen he was "Pricked to the heart, indeed, by the words of a dying young man." The words were these: "Forever, forever, what not one drop of water? forever, forever." These words being often repeated by him alarmed me to the purpose. Before this I used to be frequently with vain company but now I forsook them." This finally resulted in his conversion and later on he united with the South Hadley church.

Meanwhile three brothers named Clark, two of whom were Baptists, had settled in the eastern part of South Hadley. James Smith, brother of Chileab, who lived near them, was soon converted to their faith and Chileab also adopted the same Baptist belief.

This doughty warrior was generally victorious, as witness the following entry in his journal.

"Simeon Harvey, of Deerfield, slandered me and at last got to that pass that he threatened to take club-law, and then bragged that I was afraid to come to Deerfield, 'For,' says he, there are men here that will riddle him till they can see through him as through a riddle.' " (A riddle was a kind of coarse sieve in use at that day.)

But Simeon Harvey thus retracted his unkind speeches:
"January 28, 1772. I, Samuel Harvey, rashly and in a passion from time to time charged the said Smith unjustly, for which I am heartily sorry and ask his forgiveness, and all other peoples who heard me. Witness my hand—Simeon Harvey. I also promise to set up this paper on the door of my house to stand one month.

"Jonathan Wells In behalf of
"Samuel Montague the church."

In 1732 Chileab had married Sarah, the daughter of Deacon Ebenezer Moody, and as a part of her dowry received a certain tract of land situated in South Hadley, about a mile north of the church. It included a small elevation which has since always been known as Chileab's Hill, and was once a favorite Mecca of the student girls in the earlier days of Mt. Holyoke Seminary. Here he built himself a house which still remains as part of the dwelling of H. C. Talbot.

After the departure of Rev. Grindall Rawson, Chileab Smith, Third, went before the association and testified that "the South Hadley church was dead in trespasses and sin, and though they would not refuse to receive a converted person, yet never the sooner for his being converted, so that if a person is never no better than is required to be a member of their church he must perish eternally."

Alienated from the South Hadley church by their treatment of Mr. Rawson and himself, he afterward removed to Ashfield, where only two settlers had preceded him. There he built a house and planted an orchard.

As the colony increased in numbers, he began to hold divine service at his own house on the Sabbath. After the breaking out of the French and Indian War, finding that white men had been massacred or taken prisoners but a few miles away, the whole settlement migrated to the other towns. Three years later they returned to their own homes, and a stockade was erected which enclosed Chileab Smith's house, and was built mostly at his own expense. It was composed of logs fifteen feet long, of sufficient size to be bullet proof. These were placed side by side, having three feet sunken in the ground and twelve feet above the surface. This fort was nearly one-hundred and fifty feet square and had but one door of entrance, which was barricaded every night. Upon the roof of the house was a watch tower capable of containing six armed men. To this fort at night came all the inhabitants of the village that they might sleep in safety.

When the Ashfield church learned of Chileab's Baptist proclivities they dropped his name from their list of members. Afterwards he refused to pay "rates" toward the support of the minister. Church and town were at that time so closely connected that in consequence of this non-payment of rates the authorities sold at auction for thirty-five shillings his dwelling house, orchard, family burying ground, and twenty acres of land; and others of a like persuasion met with a similar fate.

Now, Chileab was not a man to be daunted even though his neighbors, apparently forgetting the generous shelter and protection that he had formerly afforded them, came in a body to mob him. They dug up his young apple trees and carried them away, but this was too much for the proud spirit of Deacon Moody's daughter, and tradition says that Mrs. Chileab went out with a shovel in her hand which she used with such good effect that presently the mob dispersed, bearing, however, in triumph the young fruit trees, which were transplanted with such care that to this day the chance visitor in that vicinity may still have pointed out to him the famous "Baptist Apple Trees."

But this was not to be the end of the matter. Chileab Smith determined to recover his property. Back and forth, to and from Boston he went, through forests whose only aisle was a narrow bridle path, and wearisome journeys they were. All the Baptists in the state took up the matter and the uncertain General Court knew not what to do. Finally, at the suggestion of Governor Hutchinson, the matter was referred to Royalty.

King George, the Third, in council, decreed that the land should be restored to its original owners, and Chileab, with those of his thirteen children who then survived, were reinstated in their rights.

He was married several times, his last wedding occurring

when he was more than ninety years of age. Mary Lyon, we are told, was present upon this occasion, as was also his son and namesake, Chileab, who was destined to become a centenarian, living until the success of Mount Holyoke Seminary was an accomplished fact.

Returning to the history of the Rev. Mr. Rawson, we find him up to 1740 treated with an outward show of respect. Each year his salary was voted and a day set on which to carry him wood. The seaters had been directed to make room for Madam Rawson in the meeting house, and when she and her husband entered the whole congregation rose and stood in silence until the two were seated.

The precinct had been very liberal with him in the matter of settlement. Besides the Home Lot, he had been given woodland, meadow and pasture, while the General Court had granted him a tract of land in the eastern part of Granby; the whole aggregating over three hundred and seventy acres. The large maple tree, still standing in front of the old parsonage, a little to the southeast, and the twin maple which formerly stood a little north of it, probably dated back to the time of our first minister, and indicated his love of nature.

In 1740, the Half Way Covenant had so leavened the churches of Hampshire County (which at this time included also those of Hampden and Franklin) that the records state that not a single church, and only one minister, upheld Jonathan Edwards in his protest against this very liberal theology. Yet the clearer vision of to-day approves the simple creed for which Mr. Rawson fought. Let us, therefore, bear in mind that he was in the right to such a degree that Protestantism has returned to his views, deeming them both Scriptural and proper.

On February 25, 1740, at a meeting held in South Hadley, it was voted that "It is the desire of this precinct that the Rev. Mr. Rawson be dismissed from and lay down the work of the ministry among us." Mr. Rawson took no notice of this request. On January 12, of the succeeding year, they voted that they would give him neither wood nor salary. Mr. Rawson insisted that until the town should settle its past indebtedness to him he was still legally their pastor and should continue to preach.

A committee had been appointed to keep the keys of the meeting house, it was not to be opened or shut except "According to their prudence." A minister not far away had been locked out by his parishioners, for the manners of that day were rude. Upon this the parson shouldered his axe and broke down the door, then mounting the pulpit in triumph he preached a vigorous sermon. Perhaps the committee people suspected that the present incumbent might be tempted to do the same thing, as indeed he was quite likely to.

Finally, on October 30, 1741, their last shred of patience gave way. A committee of fifteen were ordered, in more explicit language, in case he again attempted to preach, "*To put him forth from the meeting house.*" To this threat, which had been so often repeated, he paid no attention.

The committee met, thirteen of them agreeing that now they would obey instructions, only two dissenting. Some of the elders proposed to delegate their sons to perform the task that had been assigned them.

One Sabbath morning later on, Mr. Rawson appeared in church. When he had ascended the pulpit stairs, one of the deacons rose and solemnly warned him against attempting to officiate. Mr. Rawson's reply was simply to begin reading one of the Imprecatory Psalms, or, as another version of the story has it, commencing a long prayer. A number of men now advanced, and, taking him from the pulpit, either carried or dragged him from the church. Tradition tells us that he continued the prayer or psalm until a handkerchief was placed across his mouth.

This was Mr. Rawson's last attempt to enter the pulpit. It was expected that he would cause the arrest of the young men who had forcibly removed him from the meeting house, and ten pounds were raised to be used in their defense. He refrained from taking the matter into court, but, none the less, refused to resign his pastorate.

The precinct had previously voted that they would pay him

THE EVOLUTION OF A CHURCH

up to November 20, 1740, "but not after that." As he would not accept this overture, they extended the time until May of 1741, when the council had advised a separation. Finding him still obdurate, some peace-loving members of the community gave him their personal bonds for the payment of one hundred pounds if he would resign his pastoral office, which he did, and in 1742 the precinct repaid them.

Many of Mr. Rawson's friends had become so much embittered against the church that they removed to other towns. The discarded minister did not find it easy to secure another settlement. When pastors were engaged for life there were but few empty pulpits; he must wait until a new church was formed and a new building erected in some thinly populated district.

Three years passed and still he remained here. Then the people of Hadlyme, Conn., hired him to preach there for three months. At the expiration of the time they engaged him for three months more on probation. In May, 1745, they invited him to become their minister, taking the Cambridge Platform as the basis of belief.

There had been dissension among the people of Hadlyme in regard to the new church, but now they all united upon Mr. Rawson, and under his guidance they enjoyed a long season of "satisfaction and rest." At his death, in 1777, the faithful congregation erected a tombstone at their own expense.

After the resignation of their minister, the South Precinct were not long in finding a successor. About two hundred years before this, Rev. John Woodbridge, a clergyman of Wiltshire, England, had named a son after himself and educated him for the ministry. This practice had been continued from generation to generation, until now South Hadley's second minister was the ninth Rev. John Woodbridge in unbroken succession. His ancestral pride may have been gratified by the fact that his father was a grandson of Thomas, the Earl of Dudley, while his mother was a granddaughter of John Eliot, the "Apostle to the Indians." He, himself, had married the daughter of a well-known minister, and of his social supremacy there can be no doubt. Unlike his predecessor, he was dignified in bearing, prudent in council, and full of gentleness and sympathy toward all who were in sorrow. During the greater part of his pastorate, Mr. Rawson had refused, or at least neglected, to attend the meetings of the Ministers' Association, but Mr. Woodbridge soon became one of its most valued members. He was considered to be a man of such sound judgment that people came from far and near to consult him. A young divine, living nearly a dozen miles from here, was falsely accused of having stolen a silver watch, and was summoned to appear at the next session of the court in order to answer to the charge. Several witnesses, or, as they were then called, evidences, said they would testify that Mr. F...... had entered the watchmaker's shop on the afternoon of the day when the watch was first missed. In his trouble and perplexity he came to Rev. Mr. Woodbridge for counsel. "Go home and take up your work," said the latter, "and pay no attention to the matter. When the day of the trial comes God can plead your cause." This suggestion was followed, and the real culprit, "a coffee-colored negro," lulled into a feeling of security, incautiously revealed the fact that he, himself, was in the shop on the evening of the day in question. When the case was called in court, the defendant was promptly acquitted and the negro arrested. Taken by surprise, the latter confessed his guilt and made restitution. The young preacher entered in his journal (for in those days it was the fashion for ministers to keep a diary), "I bless God that I followed Mr. Woodbridge's advice."

April 21, 1742, was fixed upon as the date of the new minister's ordination. In the joy attendant upon his settlement, it was determined to make the dinner "An occasion." The precinct had raised ten pounds to be used in defense of the young men who took Mr. Rawson from the pulpit. This money, they now voted, should be used for the dinner; "as far as it will go" was considerately added."

For more than twenty years almonds and raisins, China oranges, and spiced wine had adorned the tables of Boston's elite, and who can say but that some ambitious member of the committee may have ordered them now; for the Smiths as a

REV. JOHN WOODBRIDGE

THE EVOLUTION OF A CHURCH

class were wealthy, and singularly enough the five men appointed to "pursue and accomplish what has been agreed on" in the matter of Mr. Woodbridge's settlement each answered to that surname. They were Deacon John Smith, Corporal John Smith, Jonathan Smith, Lieutenant Chileab Smith (not the ancestor of Mary Lyon), and William Smith.

For the past two months the people had been working busily on the new parsonage. They had learned wisdom since locating their first one. It could not have been a pleasant experience for Rev. Grindall Rawson to walk a quarter of a mile through pelting rains and drifting snows, in a town where umbrellas had never been heard of, and then to stand for two hours in a cold, damp church, his wet garments clinging about him. If, however, owing to the severity of the storm and the intensity of the cold, only seven worshipers were present, then the minister had permission to take his small audience home with him, and in the big living room preach the sermon he had previously prepared.

In consideration of these facts, they now placed their parsonage within a few rods of the meeting house, upon the east side of the street. The main part of the house, with its four large rooms and pulpit window, was probably not finished until several years later. In front of the old Dunlap house (our second parsonage) was placed a row of young poplars, this being, at that time, considered as the distinctive mark of a minister's residence.

A day of fasting and prayer preceded the ordination of Mr. Woodbridge (the term "installation" not having yet come into vogue), and his settlement was followed by a special service, when the congregation met to thank God for having given them so good a minister.

The precinct had agreed to give Mr. Woodbridge fifty loads of wood, and a date was set for its delivery. Wood Day was indeed a great day in South Hadley. Busy hands were at work in the parsonage long before sun-up; there were eggs to be beaten and flour sifted, butter and milk to be placed ready at hand, and apples to be pared.

Then, too, the big oven beside the chimney must be prepared for use. This had been built with three courses of bricks lying side by side, this thickness of the wall being necessary in order to absorb and retain sufficient heat for the baking. There was an opening into the chimney for the escape of smoke, which was called the up-take or draft, and could be closed by means of a piece of wrought iron attached to a long rod. The oven was nearly filled with long, slender sticks of dry wood which had been cut for this purpose, and a fire was kindled beneath them. When this had become a bed of coals, both the up-take and iron door of the oven were closed in order that the bricks might become thoroughly heated. A little later the coals and ashes were removed; then Madam Woodbridge advanced with arm bared to the elbow, and putting her hand into the oven as far as she could reach, counted up to thirty. If the heat were too great for her to bear, then the oven must be cooled before using. Later on another method came into use here. Flour was sprinkled upon the floor of the oven, and the expert housewife could judge of the heat by the quickness with which it browned.

A flat shovel with a long handle, called a slice, was now well floured, and from this loaves of wheat and of rye bread were deftly slipped to the farther end of the oven. At this era there were no bread pans, and when these useful articles did appear, about 1800, they were simply round, flat disks of tin, without sides.

It was customary in such families as the Woodbridge's to scatter oak leaves upon the floor of the oven, and while the mother was busy it was considered a nice plan to get the children out of the way by sending them leafing, as it was called.

Next after the bread came pandowdies, Indian puddings and loaf cake, followed by apple, mince and pumpkin pies, the remaining space being filled with ginger snaps and cookies. While they baked in quiet seclusion, the kettle of hissing fat that hung from the crane tossed and turned the golden brown nutcakes. Kindly neighbors, too, were bringing in provisions,

BRICK OVEN

Used by permission of Silver, Burdett & Co., publishers.

while meantime the sturdy farmers outside were cutting the wood and piling it up neatly, ready for use.

The quality of the wood given to a minister was said to be a sure test of his popularity. That brought by his friends was certain to be straight and sound, while those less kindly disposed toward him would sometimes bring sticks that were crooked and full of knots.

After the wood had all been piled, the men adjourned to the house, and the rooms echoed with the clamor of merry tongues and loud-voiced laughter. When the feast was spread, the beef, pork and mutton roasted on the spit, being flanked by dishes of cider-apple sauce and Dutch cheese, with, alas! flip, toddy and eggnogg everywhere; what then were the coveted husking bees and apple parings of the young people in comparison with the joys of Wood Day?

There was another annual appointment somewhat less jovial than this; it was Rate Day. It had been agreed that a certain part of Mr. Woodbridge's salary—sometimes a third, sometimes a quarter—should be paid in wheat, Indian corn, rye and flax. There were no corn barns at that time, and the people were expected to carry their grain up to the low-raftered chamber over the kitchen, or into the generous-sized garret, above the main house. It was now that a man's real character was made manifest. The generous brought large measure, and of their best; the stingy and avaricious used their poorer quality for this purpose and gave scanty weight. Sometimes, however, they were detected. A minister of the county records in his diary: "I declined taking some corn that Capt. C. sent here this day. I think I acted upon a principle of justice. I desire that the Captain may be kept calm and composed."

In 1743, this being the usual time for again seating the meeting house, a committee was appointed to take charge of the matter.

The size of the congregation had increased as new settlers joined the community, and additional seats had been made in the gallery, some of these being built from the public funds, others at the expense of private individuals. At the meeting on

March 14 it was generously voted that "those persons which have built pews in the gallery have liberty to sit in them during the pleasure of the precinct."

Since the men who had been chosen to seat the meeting house could not have the arrogance to assign themselves the highest places, and did not wish to sit for three years in the lowest ones, a second committee was appointed whose duty it was to seat the seaters.

William Montague, who lived in what is now Granby Center, was pretty sure to be on one or the other of the two boards, and he was given a place in the highest rank on the men's side. His wife sat with Madam Woodbridge, in the Great Pew, next the pulpit. The Widow Kellogg, who six years later became his second wife, had her choice between the foreseat and the third. She was the daughter of Deacon John Smith, whose father had died after a lingering illness which was supposed to have been brought upon him by the potent spell of a malevolent witch. She was treated with distinction, for during her eight years of widowhood she was supposed to look after the sick in a general way. Trained nurses were not to be had, and a serious case of illness was a neighborhood affair. The younger women were expected to go as "watchers" at night, while the older ones carried in food for the family and sat by the bedside of the patient by day. If the sickness proved fatal, two persons were detailed "to sit up all night with the corpse," and this custom was kept up in South Hadley until the middle of the last century.

In the pew by the east door sat Deacon John Smith and his wife, also their next neighbors on Cold Hill, Mr. and Mrs. Luke Montague.

The Northampton Church, five years before, had positively forbidden any intermingling of the sexes in seating the meeting house, and Deacon Smith 2d and Luke Montague were now the only men who ventured to sit with their families on the woman's side of the house. But public opinion followed their lead, and twenty years later the separation of the sexes in our church was abandoned.

In 1743 there devolved upon another John Smith the most difficult and perplexing duty that fell to the lot of the deacon's office. It is thus stated in the town records: "Voted that Deacon John Smith 1st acquaint people where to sit in the meeting house." This affair of "seating the meeting house" in most towns gave rise to much bitter wrangling and many neighborhood quarrels.

It was performed by a committee whose instructions in South Hadley at this time were: "To have regard to age, estate and qualifications." That the old people should sit near the pulpit in order to hear well, all were agreed, but when it came by placing the men of wealth in the high seats and the poorer brethren away back by the door—that was quite another matter. Then, too, in regard to "Qualifications," who should say whether or not the Hillyers, with their great strength and skill in boating, were superior to Nat Goodale, who lured the wild turkeys from Mt. Holyoke down to the very home lots of the settlers with his wonderful bird calls? Then, too, military titles entailed fresh complications, for the families of the officers were even more tenacious of their rank than were the officers themselves.

They used to tell of one old woman who was continually repeating that her son had been in the army. "He was either a genny-rill or a corpo-rill, I can never remember which, but it was some kind of a 'rill,' " she reiterated.

There was some kind of a rill in a good many families. Thus: In seating the John Smiths, of whom we had five, Sergeant John's wife must have a higher place than the wife of Corporal John, and plain John Smith must go still lower. Deacon John Smith 1st sat, of course, in front of the pulpit.

Once in every three years a new allotment of seats was made, and it was his duty for three successive Sabbaths to read the list aloud at the close of the morning service. If on the fourth Sabbath the congregation did not take the seats that had been assigned them it was his duty to reprove them.

In case any malcontent still refused to sit in his appointed place, the custom of other towns was to have the erring brother fined by the court; but our shrewd and kindly deacons simply ordered the tithing men (of whom we had three) to conduct the offender to the Pouting Pew, and if, during the ensuing week the children in the streets called after him, "There goes Pouting Thomas," or John, or Richard, or Samuel, as the case might be, there were none to say them nay.

Our number of deacons in active service was limited to two, as the Sacrament of the Lord's Supper was administered in a different way from our present system. The communicants ranged themselves in a procession, and going up one aisle passed in front of the deacons' pew. One of the latter handed them the bread, the other the wine. They then returned to their seats by another aisle, leaving, at least once a year, a contribution of twelve and one-half cents each upon the deacon's table to defray the expenses of the communion service.

Deacon Silas Smith and Deacon Enoch White both died in 1813, and two years later we find that Deacon Selah Smith and Deacon Levi Judd had left the pew under the pulpit and sat, except on Sacramental occasions, with the congregation.

When the church was remodeled in 1825, the deacon's pew was removed and modern methods were then adopted at our communion services.

In 1760 the population had increased to such an extent that the necessity for a larger meeting house was believed to be imperative. The dwellers in the eastern part of the town— now Granby—naturally expected that the new building would be placed, as they said, near the center of travel, and they suggested that it should be located on Cold Hill, a few rods northeast of the DeWitt homestead. This proposal was rejected, and a bitter contest ensued, which finally ended in the erection of two houses of worship, and a division of the town.

In 1761 South Hadley began building a meeting house upon nearly the same site as that of the present church. A party of men from the eastern precinct carried off one night several of the huge posts intended for use in the framework, and hid them in the Pichawamiche Swamp. The story that some of the Granby women seated themselves upon these timbers and sang

THE EVOLUTION OF A CHURCH

songs of triumph is said to be untrue, but one thing is certain, they composed upon this occasion verses that were handed down for over a century. The rhyming mania, so often prevalent in this section, sometimes proved an excellent safety valve.

The old folks used to tell how a certain man accused the tax collector of having cheated him, and was preparing to take summary vengeance. One of the deacons sought to dissuade him in calm and persuasive tones. The aggrieved taxpayer replied in the vernacular of that day:

> "No man on this 'arth
> Can let down my wrath
> Like you."

Upon this the deacon advised his companion to write the collector a letter in rhyme. The man consented, but before the poem was finished his anger had subsided, and the matter was adjusted to the satisfaction of both parties.

This second church was probably a fair type of the architectural fashion of that day. The building was sixty feet in length and forty-five in width, and there were three doors of entrance, two of which were eventually closed up. The pews were for the most part seven feet long and six feet wide. Hard, uncushioned seats ran round three sides of these generous enclosures, and in the center was an open space where the children could sit on their little footstools and crickets, and in summertime beguile the long hours by eating dill and caraway, or, better still, fennel, which grew in wild luxuriance in one corner of Mr. Woodbridge's garden. The wooden seats of the elders were hinged, and could be dropped down while the congregation were standing, allowing the old people to rest themselves by leaning against the high-backed pews. This could be done quietly, but mischievous boys sometimes tried to shorten the exercises by rattling the seats.

From a journal of a much-tried pastor living in this region, we glean the following:

"October 10th. After the first prayer, in the pew in which the young men sat, the seats made a terrible rattling, beyond what I should have thought possible. After the blessing was pronounced C. Clark spoke and said that such rattling was contrary to all order and a violation of the Sabbath, and he thought I ought to reprove them. I replied to him: 'I am sensible that this is indeed a violation of the Sabbath, and contrary to the gospel rule and order, but you know what Solomon says will be the fate of him who reproves a scorner. I have reproved them, but they will not forbear. I have done.' I went out of the pulpit. Mr. Clark said that he thought that all who feared God (or words to that purpose) ought to bear testimony against such practices, and that if the faithful would stand by him he would prosecute or drive it to the end of the law. I told him I would bear testimony against it in all proper ways. I went out of the meeting house, saw Sergeant B., and said to him: 'Sergeant B., I wonder that you would let or allow your son to be among them.' He said: 'I don't know that he is one of them.' I replied, 'It is time for you to know whether he is one of them or not. I have heard that he has said that you never forbid his rattling the seats. I would have you take care that you be not guilty of the sin of Eli.' The seats rattled P. M."

The pulpit stood on the east side of the meeting house; in front of it an aisle six feet in width, leading to the principal entrance at the west door, afforded ample room for the catechizing of children during the Sunday service. This broad aisle was also supposed to add dignity to the office of minister, since all conversation must cease, even in the slightest whisper, at the moment Rev. Mr. Woodbridge appeared. After the belfry tower was added, about 1792, the town gave a new mark of their appreciation to Rev. Joel Hayes, who was then its pastor. It was the rule that the bell should begin to ring fifteen minutes before the commencement of divine service. But someone was appointed to watch the house of Mr. Hayes, and inform the bell ringer the moment the minister and his family started for the church. Notice of this event was communicated by an immediate change from the ringing to the tolling of the bell. This sound recalled the congregation, who in summertime often loitered about the common, but were expected to be in their

From "Old Time Meeting Houses".—C. A. Wight

SECOND MEETING HOUSE

proper places when the minister entered. After Mr. Hayes had ascended the pulpit stairs and disposed of his hat, he turned and bowed to the people, which was the customary signal that they were at liberty to seat themselves.

The steep and narrow stairway which led into the pulpit had a railing on the side and at the top a latticed gate whereby the minister could shut out all intruders. The corresponding floor space upon the other side of the pulpit was occupied by a pew intended for widows, and may have been built in after the Revolutionary War. There being no vestibule, the one staircase leading to the gallery was placed in the southwest corner. Next it on the east stood a most undesirable pew, partly under the stairs. Some inventive mind suggested that this be named the Pouting Pew, and be used as a place of exile for unruly and violent members of the congregation. The proposal was received with favor, and the plan of the church in 1815 still retained this unique title.

In 1791 Colonel Woodbridge presented the church with a bell, and later a tower was added to the meeting house upon its northern side. The old sounding board was utilized, it is said, by becoming a part of the second story of the belfry tower. A red satin curtain, also the gift of Colonel Woodbridge, was hung behind the pulpit, making a cheerful background for the minister. About 1826 the house was remodeled, and "slips" were substituted for the old-fashioned pews. The high pulpit was moved to the north side, and the west door was replaced by a window. Twelve years later, the increasing number of seminary girls led to the erection of more seats in the unoccupied floor space at the rear of the house.

The front of a venerable Baptist church in Providence, Rhode Island, bore for many years this inscription: "Built for the worship of God, and to hold commencements in." Mary Lyon did not read this motto above the entrance to the South Hadley meeting house. She desired to have the graduating exercises of her first senior class take place in the seminary hall. This seemed to her the most fitting plan. The trustees did not agree with her, and she finally yielded to their wishes. The first "Anniversary Day" was celebrated in the church, which was crowded to its utmost capacity. The wisdom of this arrangement was soon evident. Many of the donors to this new enterprise witnessed its success with a feeling of gratified pride. For seven years all members of the seminary were given free sittings in our church, but their numbers increased to such an extent that in 1844 the parish was compelled to erect a new edifice. The seminary trustees contributed three thousand dollars towards the cost of the building, and until it was destroyed by fire in 1875, the school enjoyed the free use of every third pew all over the church, and were not asked to pay any part of the minister's salary or other expenses, unless they used extra sittings.

Miss Lyon showed her gratitude for this generosity by presenting the church with a large Bible, suitable for the pulpit. This was saved from two fires by the personal daring of men who entered the burning churches and rescued what is now a precious relic of the past. Many an able and vigorous sermon has been preached to us upon texts read aloud from this Bible, and in olden times the text of the sermon held a far more important place than at present. Some pastors even required their congregations to rise and stand while it was being read. The minister knew as he looked at his congregation that on Monday morning every pupil in our schools would be asked to repeat the text and as much of the sermon as he could remember, and woe to the child who had forgotten it, or misbehaved at church. The practice of repeating the text and the heads of the sermon was kept up in female seminaries till the middle of the nineteenth century. Old people always said that the value of the habit thus formed could hardly be overestimated.

Texts were at that time usually pertinent to the occasion. Thus, when on March 20, 1801, the Connecticut River, swollen by the greatest freshet ever known in its history, burst its bounds and carried away banks and bridges, sweeping out flocks and herds, and flooding some of our meadows to a depth of twenty feet, our minister preached from Amos 9:5: "And it shall rise up wholly like a flood." Upon the death of one of our pas-

From "Old Time Meeting Houses"—C. A. Wight
THIRD MEETING HOUSE

tors, the text of the funeral sermon was: "He maketh * * * his ministers a flame of fire." After the alarm at Lexington the text chosen was: "When the host goeth forth against thine enemies, then keep thee from every wicked thing." Later when a company of soldiers set out for the army, a sermon was preached from the words: "The Lord thy God walketh in the midst of thy camp, to deliver thee and to give up thine enemies before thee." The last clause of a text from Jeremiah was most comforting to the friends of these volunteers, "And they shall come again from the land of the enemy."

It was said of Rev. Joseph D. Condit, the town's fifth minister, that however severe upon evil-doers his sermon might be, his closing remarks always contained some gentle allusion to the boundless love and mercy of Christ, and his hearers went home with beautiful thoughts of God. He was a peace-loving man, and was greatly beloved in the community. Mr. Condit was in the habit of visiting each school once in two months, and his presence was welcomed in every neighborhood. His wife often accompanied him on his pastoral calls, and many and urgent were the requests that they would stay to tea. His usual reply was a pleasant "Thank you. But please remember that all we want for supper is your good bread and milk, and some of your gingerbread."

Upon one of these occasions it began to rain during the afternoon, and as he was at the time suffering from a severe cold, his wife was a little anxious. Just as they were leaving the home of their hostess a messenger appeared with the request that he come to the bedside of a sick man who desired to speak with him. "It would be a great risk," said Mrs. Condit, firmly, "and you cannot go." "The man needs me," he replied, "and whatever I ought to do I can do," and he accordingly went.

In 1847 he became very ill and one Sunday morning repeated slowly his favorite hymn, "Welcome, sweet day of rest." A few moments later he said, "Before this day closes I shall have entered into an eternal Sabbath." After the morning service had commenced he told those about him that he would like to bid each one of his people good-bye. This message was carried to the church, and one by one the worshipers went silently over to the parsonage, where he took each by the hand, speaking gentle words of farewell, and with tears in their eyes they returned to their places in the sanctuary. Before sunset he had, as the Hawaiians say, entered upon that narrow pathway which knows no backward turning. At his request there was placed upon his breast in the casket a paper containing only these three words—Grace, Grace, Grace. His daily rule of conduct was thus given in his own words: "Put off the world; put on Christ; live for God and an Eternal Heaven."

CHAPTER SEVEN

THE INDIANS

HALF a century ago the old people used to say that a certain elevation of land in the northern part of Granby, called Mt. Norwottuck, was formerly the winter headquarters of the Indian tribe who ranged our forests. The truth of this statement is confirmed by an incident which was related by the late Moses White, of Southwick.

One day in the month of February, many years ago, he was chopping wood on the south side of the Holyoke Range when his companion said: "I can show you cowslips in blossom," an assertion which Moses White doubted. The next day, after having eaten their dinner, his companion led him up the side of Mt. Norwottuck to the place where a warm spring was flowing from beneath a rock. For several feet around this spring the grass was as green as in the middle of May, and close to it the cowslips were in full bloom, while beyond this patch of green the ground was deeply covered by snow.

This may, at first thought, appear improbable, but a similar spring, it is said, still exists on Chicopee Plains, on the land belonging to Henry Baker, of Granby, and is one of those that unite to form Cooley's Brook, the source of Chicopee's water supply.

In summer the favorite camping grounds of the Indians were the one near the Slipe Meadow, in Granby, and the other a little above Smith's Ferry, between the two points of junction where Stony Brook and Bachelor's River, as it was then called, flow into the Connecticut.

But the advent of civilization has banished these ancient lords of the manor and the cutting away of the forests has so dwarfed the old-time river that it is now known only as Bachelor's Brook, and from like causes the spring upon the side of Mt. Norwottuck may also have disappeared. Most of the mounds, too, each of which was supposed to mark an Indian grave, have been leveled, although two of them remained on or near Woodbridge street as late as 1850. The principal burial ground of the red men was on Bridge street, a little north of the drinking fountain. Head smashers, stone axes, tomahawks, arrows and other implements of war are still uncovered by plow and harrow.

Many and varied are the legends that have been handed down by our forefathers; perhaps the earliest and least widely known is the following:

Although it was a time of peace, one of Hadley's young men had given great offense to the South Hadley Indians. It may be that he was too ardent and persevering a hunter south of the mountain upon lands that they looked upon as peculiarly their own, for in selling their domains they did not consider that they were giving up their right to dwell and hunt therein. But whatever may have been their cause of complaint the feeling against him became so bitter that a council was called in order to decide upon some fitting punishment. One shrewd Indian, well versed in the ways of white people, suggested that the capture of the young man's sweetheart would prove a most effective penalty for his crime. This plan met with approval and was carried out, the girl being concealed in their camp at South Hadley on the eastern bank of the Connecticut. So quietly had the abduction been managed that for weeks no trace of the captured maiden could be obtained.

At last her whereabouts was discovered; she was imprisoned in a wigwam at the rear of the Indian camp, and it is safe to conclude, since it was usual in all such cases, that two women slept side by side, across the doorway of the hut, making escape, as they supposed, impossible. One moonlight night the very best rowers in Hadley embarked at midnight and floated silently down the river. When they had nearly reached the encampment they beached their boat, and with a cunning which they had learned from the Indians themselves, stole softly through the woods until they had reached their goal, and breathed rather than whispered their instructions to the prisoner.

Long knives had been provided, the intention being to make

THE OX BOW

an opening in the back of the wigwam, an opening which would enable them to grasp the prostrate maiden by the shoulders and draw her gently forth. When this feat had been successfully accomplished the party retreated quickly and quietly to the boat. At this point a new difficulty awaited them. They had slipped silently down with the current, but oars must be used in the voyage up stream and the swish of the water would be sure to arouse the sleeping camp. The English had not yet learned the Indian art of rowing silently by turning the blade of the oar flat and taking their next stroke without lifting it from the water. Go they must, and go they did, but their forecast proved true, for an Indian canoe was speedily manned and sent in pursuit of them.

The young lover had chosen his crew wisely, and they held their distance well while with an even sweep the oars flashed and gleamed in the silver light. At the Oxbow they turned in order to make a circuit of the peninsula, the river not having then broken through its new channel, so that a neck of land connected it with the shore. Hardly had they rounded its western point when they saw that the Indians, instead of following in their wake, had landed, and were carrying the canoe upon their shoulders across this narrow strip of land. Launching it upon the other side, they were soon abreast of the white men and between them and Hadley. For the moment no hope remained. Then someone remembered that the chief, who lived upon the island north of them, was one whose authority was respected by every member of the tribe, and they resolved to ask his protection. The Indians divined their purpose, and they also steered for the island, the two parties landing at nearly the same time. The Indians wished to tomahawk the whites, but the old chief forbade them. Each told his story, both claiming the captive. After some meditation the chief announced that the case should be decided by a wrestling match between one from among the red men and one from the rescue party. Whoever first threw his opponent, his side won.

The Indians were jubilant, for one of their most famous athletes was with them, and he was immediately advanced as their champion. The young lover begged that he might be the one to contend with him. "It is your right," said his comrades, and the contest began. For some time victory seemed to hang in the balance, the one was supple and experienced, the other nerved to desperation by the peril of his sweetheart. At last, by an almost superhuman effort, the young white man threw his adversary.

The chief then directed the Indians to return to their camp, an order which was sullenly obeyed.

Then the exultant white men rowed merrily home, and if their song of triumph, as they passed down the broad street, wakened their sleeping neighbors, there were none to say them nay, for the whole town rejoiced at the return of the captive maiden.

There were other traditions with a more tragic ending. One of these was the story of the Indian girl whose lover had been slain by the white men, and who climbed to the summit of the cliff overhanging that mass of trap rock formerly called the Devil's Garden, stretching up her arms toward Heaven as if to invoke Divine vengeance upon her foes, she threw herself down the jagged incline, and among the early settlers the place was afterwards known as Heartbreak Hill.

Then, too, there is a legend that the last of his tribe stood on Titan's Pier and, surveying their once happy hunting ground, now tilled by the relentless hand of the white man, leaped, hopeless and disheartened, into the deep pool that waited beneath.

"South Hadley always hated the Indians," was the codicil to nearly every local legacy of fact which has been handed down to posterity concerning the aborigines, and indeed why should they not? The Norwottucks, it is true, were more quiet and peaceable than most of their race. But there were savage tribes farther afield whose unparalleled cruelties will never be forgotten. Take, for example, the case of Deacon Joseph Eastman, one of the early proprietors of our town and the friend and helper of our first minister.

Deacon Joseph was the ancestor of all the Eastmans and most of the Smiths in this region. Joseph, while still a youth,

ISLAND IN THE CONNECTICUT

entered the family of Rev. John Williams of Deerfield in order to prepare himself for the work of the ministry. Two soldiers who had been quartered there for the protection of the town slept in the second story of the dwelling.

One cold night in winter, when the ground was covered with ice and snow and the wind swept remorselessly past, they were awakened by the sound of heavy blows upon the front door and the voice of the minister calling up the stairway that the Indians were upon them. One of the soldiers, with a quickness of perception that easily accounted for his rapid promotion in military rank, threw his heavy cloak from the window and, barefooted as he was, jumped out upon it. Not so Joseph and the other soldier. Hardly had they time to grasp their shoes and stockings before the door crashed in and they found themselves in the hands of their savage foes. Bound hand and foot, they waited, shivering in the icy air, while the house was being pillaged. The baby, wakened by the noise, uttered a cry, but the little voice was instantly stilled forever.

So sudden and simultaneous had been the attack upon the whole neighborhood that the underground passages leading from house to house, which had been prepared for just such an emergency, proved wholly useless.

After the work of devastation was complete the captives were led from the house, which was then burned to the ground. Who can tell of that long journey to Canada?

By day Joseph marched side by side with his Indian master, over miles of ice and snow, and at night, weary, footsore, and half famished, laid himself down to a sleep broken by fitful dreams of the home he had left behind.

He was prevented from making any attempt to escape, not by the watchfulness of the savages, but by their dire threat, which he knew was certain of execution, that if any man fled in the night the remainder of the captives would be massacred the next day.

His one pleasant memory of the journey was of a kindly French woman, who invited them in and gave them a dinner. But great was the indignation of their Indian masters when she seated her white guests at table with herself and bade the red men eat their dinner sitting on mats before the fire.

After three years of captivity in Canada, Joseph Eastman was discovered and ransomed, mainly through the efforts of the clever young soldier who had escaped through the window. But the hardships and privations of that time had so dulled the fire and vigor of his youth that he no longer sought to enter the ministry, and returned to the farm of his grandfather, the Hon. Peter Tilton.

His son William was early in life appointed clerk of the church in South Hadley, and afterwards was for many years a deacon in Granby. Another son, Benjamin, generally known as Squire Eastman, lived at the Five Corners, in the house now owned by Henry Moody.

Although South Hadley suffered less at the hands of the Indians than did many of the neighboring towns, yet there was always this element of uncertainty in regard to the movements of the red men. No one could foretell what would be their next point of attack.

The treatment of the first white captive, the great-grandfather of the town's third minister, taken through South Hadley on his way to Canada, is thus described:

"Coming to South Hadley Falls, the party crossed the Connecticut River by fording and swimming and spent the ensuing night at the base of Mt. Holyoke. The captive was secured during the night by being placed upon his back with each arm and ankle strongly fastened to a sapling and with sticks so crossing his body as to be lain upon by an Indian on each side. He passed most of his nights bound in this manner, during his long march to Canada. His sufferings were excessive and almost without intermission, which in most cases would have brought the victim to the grave."

It was nearly seven years before he again stood at the foot of Mt. Holyoke, and this time as a free man.

The spirit of the red men toward the white was well illustrated by the answer of an old Indian woman who, in time of peace, had joined one of our local churches. A fellow member, having made some unkind remarks in regard to her, the minister gave him his choice between apologizing to Old Zuba or being suspended from communion. Rather sullenly he told the Indian woman that he was sorry and hoped she would forgive and forget. "Yes," she answered briskly, "I'll forgive and forget, but *I shall remember it as long as I live.*"

One of the strangest retributions of history dated back to the flight of the Indians from this and surrounding towns, which occurred on a certain Friday in August, 1676, after the downfall of Phillip.

Two hundred Indians, men, women and children, had gathered at South Hadley Falls, where during the afternoon they constructed rafts upon which they poled themselves across the Connecticut River, camping for the night upon the farther shore. Here they kindled many fires, partly for the purpose of cooking their suppers and partly, doubtless, as a protection against wild beasts. As there was at that time no human habitation between them and Mt. Holyoke, they apparently had no fear of discovery. But the vigilant eyes of Springfield's sentinels detected the columns of smoke, and the next day, finding that the trail of the Indians came from the Northeast, they so reported upon their return. Meanwhile the red men had proceeded westward and had passed Westfield, from whence a messenger was quickly despatched to Major Pynchon, at Springfield, telling him the Indians had skirted the town. While they considered the matter an unexpected ally arrived.

During the previous year every house in Brookfield had been burned by the Indians, and the inhabitants had been obliged to abandon the settlement, and in their once well-tilled fields the former were now raising a crop of corn.

To Major Talcott it seemed a pity that our land should afford sustenance for the savage foe, and taking with him both white men and Mohegans he went to Quabaug, as it was called, and cut down all the corn. Returning by way of Springfield he arrived on this very Saturday. Resting his men for a single night, he started in pursuit of the enemy. Not expecting such an army, the Westfield housekeepers had failed to fill their big ovens, and food was not to be had in large quantities. But Talcott and his men hurried forward on what was destined to be thenceforth known as "The Hungry March."

Sunday and Monday passed, but the Indians were not overtaken. Food was so scarce that the Major sent back all of his horses and the greater part of his men. He retained the provisions, of which little remained, and pressed on. Tuesday he came up with the Indians at the Housatonic River. Here he gave battle, killing forty-five and taking fifteen prisoners, with but the loss of one man, a Mohegan Indian.

In this battle the cruel and treacherous Sachem of Brookfield was slain; but the rest of the Indians, who escaped, crossed the state line between New York and Massachusetts and settled upon the farther side of the border.

The Governor of Connecticut was so much pleased with Major Talcott's exploit that he appointed a day of thanksgiving, which was kept all over the State.

These Indians remained undisturbed for nearly eighty years; the older members of the tribe handing down to their descendants the story of this terrible march from South Hadley to the Housatonic. The memory of this injury still unavenged, although slumbering, was not allowed to die.

Now, however, it was a time of peace and people had grown careless. Emboldened by the thought of their French allies, these Indian refugees believed that the time had come in which to avenge their ancestors. Sallying forth, burning, pillage and massacre, marked every step of their path; and thus did Hampshire County first learn that she must prepare for immediate war.

Within less than a decade Granby and South Hadley had sent forth their brave sons to do battle in the French and Indian wars that were devastating the land. Some of them had fallen by the wayside and some of them had languished in captivity. Yet such was the loyalty of our town that eighty names of soldiers were entered upon its service list. Nor were the other towns less patriotic. There were sharp crises in this war when mounted messengers rode in hot haste for reinforce-

From "Old Time Meeting Houses".—C. A. Wight
THE GRANBY CHURCH

ments. One of our adjoining towns sent in answer to this call every man between the ages of sixteen and sixty except the minister.

It seemed to us a dreadful thing when, during the Civil War, we learned that one in every ten among our able-bodied men had enlisted. Yet in the French and Indian War, in 1757, one-third of all the men in Massachusetts were in the field, and South Hadley had sent a still larger proportion of her sons.

Many strange things happened in Hampshire County during this war. The movements of the Indians were so silent and stealthy that the unsuspecting inhabitants often fell into ambush through mere carelessness. This was illustrated in the case of a little girl named Molly Smead, who lived a few miles to the north of us. She had been warned against going near the edge of the wood, but in the excitement of a game of tag ran to the very border of the forest. An Indian lurking near caught her up and, placing his hand over her mouth in order to stifle her cries for help, carried her back to the camp. From there she was sent to a village in Canada, whose chief showed her much compassion, shielding her as far as possible from cruel treatment.

The inhabitants of the village demanded that, as was the custom with other white captives, she should "run the gauntlet." The chief, believing that on account of her youth this would mean certain death, refused for a time to allow it, but the tumult increased to such a degree that he was obliged to yield, and appointed a day for this ordeal.

The decision was made known to Molly by an old Indian who could speak broken English. He had noticed that she was an attractive child and had a musical voice, and so added in a whisper: "Missey Molly, you sing and dance all the way and they not whip you so much."

At the appointed time all the men, women and children in the neighborhood were arranged facing one another, in two long lines, between which she must pass. They stood with right hand uplifted, each holding a pliant rod with which to strike her as she ran. Molly, following the instruction of her friendly adviser and singing in her sweetest voice, went dancing gaily down the line, while the Indians stood listening in motionless surprise. One old drunken woman gave her a stinging blow which made the flesh quiver beneath the one thin garment she was permitted to wear, but without hesitating for an instant she prolonged her song, until she had reached the end. Then arose a Babel of voices clamoring fiercely for her to run the gauntlet again, but this the chief refused.

Meantime the Connecticut troops had taken prisoner a young Indian girl, whom the Governor of that State offered in exchange for Molly Smead. To this the red men would not at first consent, but after a sufficiently large amount of redemption money had been added the transfer was effected, and Molly returned to her home in safety.

There were some humorous as well as tragical incidents in this war. In this same locality was a fort so large that in case of Indian alarm all the inhabitants of the village could find shelter for the night. Upon one such occasion the sentinel who went on duty at midnight was a young man of but little experience in Indian warfare.

Soon after twelve o'clock the moon arose, but obscured by clouds through which came a dull, uncertain light. Presently the young guard observed a figure beneath the spreading branches of a large oak tree which stood outside the fort. Thinking it some belated neighbor, he demanded, "Who goes there?" The figure moved slightly, but there was no reply. Raising his voice, he repeated his challenge a second time, with the same result as before. Aiming his gun carefully, he shouted, "Who goes there? Answer, or I fire." Again receiving no reply, he discharged his piece, which aroused the whole garrison, who at once commenced a furious fusillade against the dark object beneath the tree. Finding that they had produced no effect they rested on their arms, but watched until the first beams of morning light disclosed the innocent target of their marksmanship. A woman of the garrison had washed her dress and hung it from one of the lower branches of the oak to dry, where it had fluttered all night in the wind. It was, of course, ruined, being completely riddled with bullet holes, and the verdict of the sleepy and discomfited garrison was that it served her right for depriving them of a night's rest.

It will be remembered that from the beginning of King William's War, in 1688, to the Treaty of Paris, in 1763, more than half of the time was filled with scenes of war and bloodshed. The struggle between England and France for supremacy in America entailed incessant watchfulness on the part of the colonists. The Indians, inspired by their French allies, made fresh attacks upon some of the villages about us, compelling the inhabitants to forsake their homes and take refuge in the larger towns.

When the call came for more soldiers, South Hadley responded by giving the very flower of her young men to the army. Three of our pioneers sent their five sons to assist in the reduction of Canada, William, John, Peter and Josiah Montague and Phineas Smith.

Peter Montague was at the siege of Louisburg in 1745. No sooner had our troops landed than the French spiked the cannon in their outer fortifications and retired behind the inner defenses, which were supposed to be impregnable.

Now Peter's major was a gunsmith and declared the cannon could be repaired. Permission having been given, he selected twenty assistants, drilled out and reversed the cannon, and the siege was then commenced.

But it was necessary to drag their own artillery across a morass impassable for horses or oxen, so Peter and his comrades placed straps about their shoulders, and for fourteen nights dragged the cannon through mud and water reaching to the ankles, and in some cases even to the knees. They had no bed but Mother Earth and no tent to shelter them, only rude huts made of turf and brushwood. This hardship and exposure was too great for one so young as Peter, and the ultimate song of triumph fell upon ears that were deaf to its notes.

John Woodbridge, the eldest son of our minister, instead of studying theology as was expected, spent eight years in the defense of his country during the French and Indian wars. Entering the army as a private, he rose to the rank of lieutenant simply upon his own merit.

He was present at the siege of Quebec and took part in that memorable battle on the Plains of Abraham, in which both Wolfe and Montcalm were slain.

Doubtless he always remembered one incident of his perilous passage up the St. Lawrence on the evening preceding this assault. When the sentinel at the fort challenged them in French with the customary "Who goes there?" one of the oarsmen replied in the same language, "The provision boat. Don't speak so loud or the English will hear you," and, holding their breath with suppressed laughter, they glided past.

The death of Montcalm might not have seemed an undeserved retribution to Job Alvord, another of our young soldiers. He had been one of a beleaguered garrison surrounded by the army of Montcalm, which outnumbered them three to one. Messengers had been despatched to Fort Edward, fifteen miles away, for aid, a request which the commanding general refused, sending them in return a letter advising immediate surrender. This communication was intercepted by Montcalm, who forwarded it to the besieged garrison, offering terms of capitulation which for those times do not seem to have been severe.

On condition that they would not fight for a year and a half, they were promised safe escort to Fort Edward and permission to carry with them their arms and baggage. When they reached the woods a mile from the fort the Indians, contrary to all stipulations, fell upon them, killing some, wounding others and plundering all who came within their reach.

Job Alvord escaped with his life and probably considered that this act of treachery released him from his parole, for we hear of him shortly after as holding the position of lieutenant in the army.

The first marriage registered in our town was that of this

same Job Alvord and Rebekah Smith, both of South Hadley. There had, however, been other marriages previous to this which failed of registration, for Josiah, son of Peter Montague, had wedded his cousin Abigail, and was soon after sent on an expedition against the French at Crown Point, from which he did not return until three years later.

In one respect their manifold experiences by sea and land were fruitful of good to the men of our town. It was an excellent preparatory school for the War of the Revolution so soon to follow. It taught them the use of arms, bayonets having now been introduced for the first time. It made the country conscious of its own strength, and in other towns as well as in this the leading soldiers in the French and Indian wars became the officers of the Revolutionary Army.

It was not until many years after the War of Independence had ended that the Indians finally disappeared from our town. Roving bands often visited the scattered farmhouses, asking for a drink of cider, or perhaps a seat at the dinner table. They were much given to pilfering, but still displayed their national characteristic, and were grateful toward those who afforded them food and shelter. Months afterwards these persons who had befriended them were the recipients of numerous gifts.

A daughter of Dr. G. G. Hitchcock, of South Hadley Falls, thus describes an incident in the life of one of her ancestors, who had purchased a "shay" in the early days:

"In the first stage of his pride of ownership an Indian chief in the neighborhood came to borrow it in order to visit a chief in New York State. 'I will return it at the end of three months,' he said. The owner looked at his resplendent purchase in despair, but the Indians were too powerful to be refused. So he gave them the shay, never expecting to see it again, picturing to himself the forest paths, the rude wood roads it must traverse. He was mistaken. At the end of the three months, punctual to the day, came the old chief and his followers, bearing with them the chaise. Not a scratch marred its shining surface; not a mark of wear was on it. All the long way the tribe had made a path before it. Think of the figure that proud chief had been able to cut before his rival brother! It was at a time when the Indians committed constant depredations upon the whites, but from that day on my ancestor was exempt. His grain, vegetables and fruit grew and ripened unmolested. Under cover of the darkness game and furs were silently left at his door by his Indian friends; his rights were protected, and he was beloved by them. Up to his last days he used to say that he had been recompensed more than the cost of many shays."

Our last Indian visitor on record appears to have been the one who, about 1835, called at the house of Mr. Simeon Judd, and his carved walking stick, left by mistake, is still in possession of the family.

Several of our oldest families can claim a remote ancestry of Indian descent. In Colonial times a young man from Northampton built himself a house on the eastern side of the Connecticut, and—a rare occurrence in those days—fell in love with one of the dusky maidens who inhabited our South Hadley forests. The girl reciprocated his affection, but when the lover asked permission to marry her the tribe held a council, and forbade the ceremony. After waiting for some time, finding the verdict remained unchanged, the maiden suggested that she leave the camp by stealth, and conceal herself from her relatives until such time as they would give their consent to the union. She was secreted in Northampton, while the Indians searched the woods and streams for a trace of the missing girl. Meanwhile a close watch was kept upon the movements of the young man, who, anticipating this scrutiny, did not leave his farm, except to attend divine service. When interrogated, he would give them no information, and at last they promised if the girl would come back the ceremony might take place. She accordingly returned, and, as the fairy books say, "they lived happily ever after."

The red men have vanished from hill and glen; but even now if you stand in autumn beneath the trees that fringe the

THE DRIVE

banks of our loved Connecticut, you may still catch an echo of the old refrain:

"Dark as the frost-nipped leaves that strew the ground,
The Indian hunter here his shelter found;
Here cut his bow, and shaped his arrows true;
Here built his wigwam, and his bark canoe;
Speared the quick salmon leaping up the fall;
And slew the deer, without the rifle ball."

CHAPTER EIGHT

SOUTH HADLEY IN THE REVOLUTION

HARDLY had the last echoes of the French and Indian wars died away, when a new danger threatened our country. England had assisted us in our struggle with France, by sending us both men and money, and now determined to reimburse herself for this expense by taxing her colonies.

To this end Parliament, in March, 1765, passed a bill known as the Stamp Act, which was not to become operative until November first of that year. This enactment decreed that no deed, bond, note, or mortgage should thenceforth be valid unless it was written upon stamped paper, and some of these stamps ran as high as thirty dollars each. Also no marriage should be legal unless a certificate to that effect were made out on stamped paper.

This edict awakened the most violent opposition in our town, and one of our ministers publicly declared that it was unjust, oppressive, and subversive of every principle of freedom.

The conclusions of South Hadley were at this era a matter of some importance since there were but four larger towns in Western Massachusetts. Springfield, stood first, then Westfield; Northampton ranked next, followed by Sheffield and South Hadley. Worcester and Palmer had not then come into being, or were too small to be noticed. This census taking was a stumbling block to many of the elders in the community; they reminded their friends how King David had "numbered the people," and how severe was his punishment, and they predicted that famine and pestilence would be the result of the present action.

It is interesting to note in this connection that in one of the annual Thanksgiving sermons of that day we find our old minister mentioning as one of the great causes for gratitude the

SOUTH HADLEY IN THE REVOLUTION

good health that had pervaded the community throughout the past year.

November first, the day on which the Stamp Act was to take effect, was everywhere observed as a fast, all places of business being closed. In cities, the morning was ushered in by the tolling of church bells, and this was continued through the day. Effigies were placed in rude coffins bearing the inscription, "Liberty, aged 145 years." These were escorted to the place of interment by crowds of citizens, who stood reverently about the grave listening to the funeral oration, while the minute guns, at intervals, boomed their mournful echo.

South Hadley had no church bell to toll, but we may be sure that Moody Corner sent her drummer to lead with mufflled beats the long procession of mourners that paraded the streets. And John Lane, Junior, skilled in the use of the conch shell, may have evoked sad notes to punctuate the slow march. We may feel certain from the aftermath that all who possessed, or could borrow, black clothes fell into line, and though Rev. Mr. Woodbridge, being over sixty years of age, may not have been at their head, it is safe to presume that Rev. Simon Backus, of our eastern parish, was there.

The privations of our early settlers had taught their children as well as themselves habits of self-denial, and now it was not hard for them to follow the advice of their spiritual director and refrain from the purchase of English luxuries, which Major John Woodbridge and Deacon William Eastman were wont to deal out to them.

The resentment against the Stamp Act was so great throughout the country that in the following spring it was repealed. The news of this event reached here in July, and the town immediately appointed a day of thanksgiving. The sermon preached upon this occasion by one of our ministers has been preserved, and some brief extracts will perhaps illustrate the dawning spirit of the Revolution which had already begun to pervade the town.

His text was taken from the twelfth Psalm: "The snare

is broken and we are escaped." After reading the Proclamation, he begins:

"We are informed in general in the Proclamation that it is God's having graciously inclined the King, and both Houses of Parliament, so far to harken to the Petitions of his loyal and dutiful subjects as to consent to a total repeal of the Stamp Act. To understand the true ground of obligation to Gratitude and Thankfulness hence arising, it is necessary to take into consideration the Nature and Genius of the Act, and the fatal consequences which might reasonably have been expected, had it been enforced. * * * It was illegal and inconsistent with the Magna Charta. There are two things in which the Act appears unconstitutional; the one is the exacting money of the subject without his consent; another is depriving the subject in certain cases of the Liberty of Trial by Jury. This principle is no better than that of an absolute unlimited Right and Authority in the Ruler or Magistrate to take away the Property of the subject whenever he pleases, and to whatever degree he thinks proper. Only admit that the King or Supreme Ruling Authority has a right to tax the subjects without their consent, it will follow by undesirable consequence that he has a right to take away their whole estate, rendering them nothing but Slaves and Vassals, and reducing them to Beggary and Starvation.

"The execution of such an Act or Law must have been a very great calamity, and consequently its being surrendered must be a Very Great Mercy and Deliverance.

"It has been the declared opinion of some of considerable knowledge in Public Affairs that all the money in the country would not be sufficient to answer the annual amount of the Duties thence arising.

"One of the most obvious as well as shocking Consequences which would doubtless have ensued from a continuance of the Stamp Act is that of Civil Wars, Slaughter and Bloodshed in almost all Parts of the Land. And what Numbers would have fallen by the Sword in the High Places of the Field before the country would have been brought to submit, we cannot determine.

"Considering the Vast Disproportion and strength of this country as compared with Great Britain, it would be stupidity and madness to imagine that we would finally stand out and defend ourselves against them, by which means we should probably have been stripped of all our Privileges, Properties, and Liberties, as having forfeited them by Rebellion and Treason. * * * Therefore, with Regard to the late Merciful Dispensation of Divine Providence, we should consider that it is God indeed who hath done this great thing for us, whereof we are glad, and not ascribe it to our Wisdom, Policy, Spirited Opposition, Resolute Resistance, Humble Petitions, etc. But it behooves us to cry out with the Psalmist, 'Not unto us, not unto us, oh, Lord, but unto Thy Name be the Glory.'"

During the following year political matters seemed quieter and life moved on in its accustomed channels. Our people gathered in their new meeting houses, with their high pulpits and great, square pews, but they carried with them their loyalist Hymn Books, and as the precentor lined out the words, "And own the King the Lord hath made," the whole congregation sang them with undiminished fervor.

The English Crown had long ago claimed that it held a copyright upon the Holy Scriptures, and to the title page of the Bible had been added this clause, "Printed by the Authority of His Majesty, King George III." But before the Revolution had ended, so bitter was the hatred against their sovereign, that one of our deacons actually tore out these obnoxious words from the title page of his Bible, and others doubtless followed his example.

In 1767 fresh complications arose from England's attempt to levy a tax upon all the tea, glass and paint brought to America. In this juncture, covenants for the Non-importation of British Goods were promptly circulated and signed, both here and elsewhere, but these promises were not always kept. Building windowless houses was not to be thought of, and glass was one of the prohibited articles; for Parliament had, with cunning foresight, taxed the very things that were considered indispensable. People soon began to retaliate by eating less meat, lamb and mutton, thus increasing the number of sheep and avoiding the necessity of importing wool from England. Tradition tells us that some of the dwellers south of Mt. Holyoke, in their patriotic zeal, used the flesh of the woodchuck as a substitute for mutton.

Public opinion was plainly indexed by the action of Harvard College. Though many of the students were the sons of rich men, and possessed clothing of the finest broadcloth, and the long, silk stockings so universally worn, yet the senior class of 1768, in order to show that they could dispense with English luxuries, voted to graduate in suits of homespun, and carried their resolution into effect.

As a result of the popular indignation, the tax bill was later on rescinded; the duty upon tea, however, being still retained.

In 1770, another piece of British jurisprudence fanned into flame the smoldering embers of Colonial wrath. South Hadley had always been famous for the multiplicity of its town meetings. If there was a dispute in regard to the location of a new church, or a quarrel over the seating of the meeting house, the records show that they were willing to hold two a week if necessary, although in cold weather they were sometimes glad to adjourn to the schoolhouse or tavern for their discussions. Now they found themselves forbidden to call any town meetings unless they had first obtained the consent of the Royal Governor; even then they could hold but one meeting a year, and that simply for the election of officers. But if the Governor chose he could order another one to be held.

Then, too, our town had for fifteen years been in the habit of drawing its jurors by the same method in use at the present day. Now they were informed that by direction of the Crown, a sheriff appointed by the Governor would select his own jury.

During the following year South Hadley was ordered to hold a second town meeting, because at the first one, "the officers did not take the oath respecting other government money." Also Dr. Woodbridge and Eleazer Goodman had not been sworn into their offices.

COL. RUGGLES WOODBRIDGE

Doctor Benjamin Ruggles Woodbridge appears to have been at this time the acknowledged head of the Liberty Party. He was a man in the very prime of life, well educated, and a clever and original thinker. His keen, penetrating eyes seemed to read one's very thoughts, but his smile was gentle and winning. He was a firm disciplinarian and was made a colonel during the first few months of the war, but was never arbitrary, and kept both the respect and love of his soldiers.

In process of time a new covenant for the Non-consumption of British Goods was prepared, and Colonel Woodbridge began to hold Liberty Meetings in the towns about us. In one of these, an evening meeting at which he presided, he awakened such enthusiasm that the next morning several of the leading citizens hastily prepared a covenant, and carried it to their minister for his signature.

After reading it he told the committee that he objected to signing it because there was no recognition of God in it, the name of the Deity not occurring even once. Flushed with excitement, his parishioners said, threateningly, "We tell you plainly, that if you do not sign this paper, you will be considered and treated as an enemy of your country" (the latter phrase being the shibboleth of the Whigs, and the dread of the Tories). The parson was not a tall man, but at these words he fairly towered. "This," he cried, "is not Liberty, but Tyranny, and I doubt if King George himself would be more tyrannical." The matter was finally compromised by his writing on the paper his reason for not signing, and adding that he was a friend to the country and should aid it by every means in his power. And in coming years nobly did he redeem his promise.

Ebenezer Stoddard, one of South Hadley's soldiers, had resisted an attempt on the part of a deputy sheriff to arrest him. The following extract from the warrant shows how the minutest matters were referred to the King: "He did then and there resist, oppose and hinder the said sheriff of the due execution of his office, all which is contrary to Law, and Peace of the said Lord the King, his Crown and Dignity" * * *
"Being put to plead, he says that he will not contend with the

King, and he submits himself to the King's grace. The Court having considered of the Offense, do order that the said Ebenezer pay a Fine of twenty shillings for his Majesty's use; and cost of Prosecution, taxed at one pound, twelve shillings and two pence.''

Everybody had been taught, from their childhood up, to honor the King. If his Majesty died, funeral sermons were preached as soon as the news reached this part of the country. "God save the King!" was heard in both home and sanctuary, and it was hard for the older people to unlearn in a moment the teaching of years.

The whole trend of public opinion was now changed. In Harvard College the students had always been ranked, not according to their scholastic attainments, but in the order of their social standing. The sons of rich and influential men could have the best rooms, help themselves first at table, and sit in the highest places at chapel. Now they were to be catalogued alphabetically, and the rod of correction would pay no regard to caste, whatever might be said of the prayer which was expected to precede or follow the whipping, when profanity on the part of a student was to be punished. It was now apparent that the leveling of social distinctions had begun in earnest.

England had found her experiment of taxing the Colonies a costly one. For every dollar of revenue that she had received, she had expended more than a hundred times that amount. She had quartered her soldiers upon the citizens of Boston, with a demand that they should be supplied with "Food and lodging, cheese and rum." "Nothing to eat, drink or wear from Great Britain" had been our country's response; even the custom of wearing mourning for the dead had been in a measure abandoned, since much of the black cloth in use had been imported.

South Hadley had appointed a Committee of Inspection, whose duty it was to visit from house to house in order to forbid all use of East India tea. It had been customary here, if a neighbor called in the afternoon, to greet her with the words, "How do you do? Won't you take off your things, and stay to tea?" The word "supper" was unknown in polite vocabularies.

Substitutes for the "cup that cheers but not inebriates" must be found. Every garden had its patch of currant and gooseberry bushes, the leaves of which were dried and steeped, making a drink called "Hyperion." There was a plant named Labrador Tea, whose blossom resembled that of hard hack, and this also was in popular use as a beverage. Infusions of spearmint, pennyroyal, or sage often appeared at the evening meal, though the latter was thought to savor too much of illness.

On December 16, 1773, matters were brought to a crisis by the action of a party of young men, of whom Dr. A. J. Miller, for many years a resident physician of South Hadley, was one. At this time three ships laden with tea had entered Boston Harbor. Dr. Miller was, at this time, probably a student in Harvard College, and on that memorable night he and a score or more of his associates banded themselves together in order to throw this cargo overboard. Before starting, everyone pledged himself to the undertaking, agreeing that if any one of their number flinched he should be thrown overboard with the tea. In silence they proceeded to their work. Some of them tried to secrete a small portion of the Old Hyson to carry home with them, but as soon as this was discovered, jackknives were out and the pockets slitted open. Dr. Miller contrived to bring away a handful, which was preserved as a souvenir for over a hundred and thirty years, and then lost through the blunder of a careless servant.

After this episode, things went from bad to worse. The courts were prevented from sitting, and mobbing and rioting ensued. An old diary, written May 1, 1777, states that no courts had been held in this vicinity since September, 1773, and adds, "Lived without the exercise of law for four years, and made it do pretty well."

Our town had certainly cause to be proud of its comparative freedom from disorders, while the towns about us were rent by internal strife. There was one exception to this rule. Joseph Ashley, the hated spy and informer, avowed himself a Tory, upon which, as we learn, the people "made it so hot for him that he was obliged to flee to New York." There were others here who espoused the cause of Great Britain, but most of these chose a home in Halifax, where the King had promised them protection, and offered to each the gift of a farm. Very possibly some of them were mobbed while here, and forbidden to partake of the sacrament at communion, at all events, their social ostracism drove them to Nova Scotia.

The town was certainly making a great effort to preserve good order. A Committee of Safety had been previously appointed, and about six weeks before the Battle of Lexington a second one was chosen, composed of "sober and discreet persons, who shall suppress mobs, quiet disturbances between neighbor and neighbor, and shall give assistance to the towns about us if they shall be asked." It was also voted that if any person should be found assisting any "mobbish, tumultuous or riotous company, without first informing this committee and obtaining their approbation (which is not to be granted except in cases of extreme necessity), they should forfeit the assistance and protection of their neighbors, should it afterwards be needed, in their own defense, and they should never be considered eligible to any office of trust in this town."

It would appear from the accounts given by the old people of South Hadley, that the visits of the mob were for the purpose of insulting the Tories, rather than that of injuring their property, though in the excitement of the raid many things were done which upon sober second thought were greatly to be regretted. To the mobbings were brought horns, drums, pewter pans, anything that would make a jangle of discordant notes. But the chief musical instrument was termed a horse-fiddle. It was prepared by stringing across the top of an empty wooden box hempen cords covered with rosin. A bow was prepared in a similar manner, and the harsh grating of one upon the other, as it was played by its two performers, caused so horrible a sound that it defies description. After the din had been kept up for some hours, usually till about midnight, the rioters dispersed. There were occasions upon which the owner of the house came out with a club and drove them off, but these were rare.

SOUTH HADLEY IN THE REVOLUTION

These bitter animosities had brought dissensions into neighborhoods, and disunion into families.

Poor old Jonathan Selden! Next to our six pioneers, he had been one of the very earliest settlers south of Mt. Holyoke. He had been taught to reverence "Our Lord the King," as second only to Deity, and disobedience to his commands was in the eyes of Selden a sin. He was so pronounced in his opinions that six months after our first volunteers started for the army he was lodged in Northampton jail, where he died nearly eight months later. He must have inculcated in his children a love of country, for his son and namesake enlisted and fought as a soldier in the Revolutionary War.

A very common method of punishing Tories was by confining them to their own farms, which they were never permitted to leave except in order to attend church service and funerals. Upon these occasions they were forbidden to have any conversation with others, either before or after the exercises. This proceeding sometimes bore bitter fruit in after years. Several of our leading citizens still tell the story of their ancestor, Mr. Consider T.———, whose unjust treatment darkened his whole life. He was a devoted member of the Church of England, and came to this country simply for commercial reasons. He settled in Connecticut, purchasing a large farm. Believing as he did that the King was the head of the Established Church, rebellion seemed to him like the most wicked of conflicts. He having expressed this opinion, the selectmen ordered him not to pass the boundaries of his own land under pain of imprisonment in the county jail. Fifteen months later they released him from restraint, but he refused their offer in these words: "I am, and always was, a sincere friend of America, but if I had the same opinion of the United States that I have of this town, I should think it my duty to do my utmost to have them subdued. * * * I would further tell you I retain the same principles that I had four years ago, don't mean to hurt any man, and am content to remain in my own business, and happy in not seeing the faces of my implacable enemies. Therefore, please so use your endeavors that I may remain happy as I now am, and you will oblige your old friend—Consider T." He lived nearly forty years after this, but never went beyond the boundaries of his own farm.

During the night which preceded Wednesday, April 19, 1775, the tocsin of war was sounded upon all the church bells from Boston to Lexington, and the deep-toned cannon confirmed the alarm. No sooner did Charleston catch the warning gleam of the lantern in the belfry of the Old North Church, than mounted horsemen were sent in hot haste to warn the country. The messenger despatched to Western Massachusetts directed the people of Belchertown to send a courier to Granby and South Hadley, while he continued his journey to Amherst, Hadley and Northampton.

We can picture to ourselves the best rider and most ardent patriot of Cold Spring traversing the rough track, called the Pichawamache Road, shouting to the farmer in his field, and the housewife standing in her kitchen door, "To arms! *to arms!*" How it must have gladdened his heart when the athletic John Lane responded, "I will go."

Down the steep side of Cold Hill, now changed and leveled beyond recognition, he passed at its base the house of Deacon David Nash. Here was another volunteer, and a little beyond, John Marshall's heart warmed to the cry.

Arriving at the Center, the messenger went at once to the Woodbridge parsonage. The news was quickly made known by the beating of drums and the firing of guns, the former giving that long, loud roll that told the minute men it was a call for volunteers. South Hadley had not been caught napping.

The town had voted during the previous year that they were willing to "raise and pay men for the army." They had ordered every man to keep weapons and ammunition in his house. Cartridge boxes had been purchased and were now held in stock. The militia had been exercised on training days, but the minute men had met for an extra half day in every week, in order to learn the art of war, each one of them being paid for his time. Now, under the alert leadership of Colonel Ruggles Woodbridge, provision enough to last three days was hastily prepared, the

THE SECOND PARSONAGE

guns put in order, and on the following day, Thursday, over a hundred men from Belchertown, Granby and South Hadley set forth on their march to Lexington.

Among the volunteers from this town was Peter Pendergrass, a legacy left to us by the British army after the close of the last French and Indian War. He had come to our town, married a young woman named Abial, a church member, and they, with their only son, James, lived in a tiny dwelling on the site now occupied by the house of W. H. Jewett, on Hadley street. Life had not gone well with him, and a kind deacon who had moved from here to Granby sheltered him and his family for a year. The events of April 19 awoke the old war fever, and instead of turning back with the others, when a messenger met them with the news that they were no longer needed, he proceeded to Cambridge with Captain Moses Montague and Colonel Woodbridge, accompanied also by two or three of our minute men. Reaching Cambridge, he found a fine, large house, whose Tory owner had fled to the British camp. Here he established himself in luxurious quarters, little dreaming that twenty-five years later he would be set up at vendue as a town pauper and struck off to one of our good deacons at fifty cents per week.

Before the battle of Bunker Hill, Colonel Woodbridge and Peter had joined the camp in Roxbury. A part of their regiment fought in that memorable conflict, but though they could see the smoke and hear the cannon they were, themselves, too far away to take part in the engagement.

During the following November, word was sent here that the poor of Boston were suffering for lack of food and clothing. A town meeting was called and a committee appointed to collect donations. A requisition for blankets to be used in the army also met with quick response. The Whigs gave willingly, and often more than they could well afford to spare. If a Tory refused to produce his hidden store of new blankets this committee straightway helped themselves to those already in use.

In our northern army the long marches had so worn out both shoes and stockings that the footsteps of our men left their crimson imprint upon the Canadian ice and snow, and messengers were despatched to Massachusetts in order to make known their imperative need. Letters could not be used to diffuse information, since at this time each state had on an average but six postoffices in its whole area. The only place where the scattered population could easily be reached was at the meeting house, and the Sunday service was often interrupted by the coming of a horseman, charged with the duty of transmitting intelligence.

It was the custom of Rev. Mr. Woodbridge on every Sabbath morning to give a summary of the latest news from the army. Springfield was our recruiting station, and whoever went there on business was expected to call at the minister's house on his return and repeat all that he had learned regarding the progress of the war.

In front of the wooden desk, which at that time served as a pulpit, sat Deacon Daniel Moody and Deacon David Nash, their pew being on a raised platform, facing the congregation. It was their duty, in case the minister had "exchanged," to introduce the new preacher to the audience, and they had also been appointed to receive on every Lord's Day gifts for the soldiers.

When the clank of a horseman was heard without, Mr. Woodbridge paused in his sermon and at the entrance of the messenger said, with a courtly bow, "Brother, if you have any message for my people, say on." And when the pitiful story had been told, we may well believe that for days to come spinning wheels hummed, and knitting needles clicked in answer to this appeal.

In one of the towns reached by a courier during the morning sermon, all the women, with the consent of the minister, remained at home that afternoon in order to spin and knit for the suffering men at St. Johns. "Mercy is better than sacrifice," said the pastor, in explanation of his act.

Nor were the men less patriotic. After the close of the war it was said that, excepting the ministers, there was hardly an able-bodied man in either Granby or South Hadley who had not served in the army. This had been made possible by a rotation in enlistment. No sooner had a soldier started for camp than his neighbors assumed the responsibility of caring for his farm. In case no son was old enough to milk and "fodder," it was expected that the women of the household would attend to those duties. But at planting time, the volunteer's land must be ploughed for him before any other, and when his grass was ready for the scythe, a mowing bee was appointed, for his haying must be done before the rest began theirs. Later on the town voted that they would provide "For those women and their families whose husbands were in the continental army."

In order that those who were dependent upon the kindness of others should be as evenly distributed as possible throughout the town, when a draft of seven men was called for, South Hadley was divided into seven districts, and one man was chosen by lot from each district.

The first person south of the mountain who sacrificed his life to the cause of liberty was Lieut. Eleazer Nash. He lived in Moody Corner, a few rods east of the Granby line, and though he was already in his fifty-sixth year, enlisted at the call of Lexington and set off the next morning. He may have taken a chill from sleeping on the damp ground, for he returned with a hard cold; inflammation of the lungs set in, and within a month he had passed away. There must have been some bitter self-reproach among those overzealous Whigs who had, six weeks before, tried to bring disgrace upon his name. Some of the towns about us had been building bonfires, and feeding the flames with the military commissions issued by Governor Hutchison and General Gage some years before. Captain William Eastman, Lieutenant Eleazer Nash and Ensign Experience Smith do not appear to have shared in the wild excitement that dominated this section, and a town meeting was called on March 6, 1775, to consider their cases. At this time Lieutenant Nash, being asked to speak, replied, in answer to their questions, "I have no desire, intention, or design to act from any authority by virtue of my commission, and further I never will." "Ensign Smith declared that he acquiesced in the above declaration made by Lieutenant Nash." Captain William Eastman said that he "Would never exercise any authority of his commission until such time as the controversy subsisting between Great Britain and the colonies was settled."

For some unknown reason these answers were not considered satisfactory, but the matter seemed to have been dropped. Lieutenant Nash died, Ensign Smith left town, and Deacon William Eastman, who forty years before was the first clerk of our South Hadley church, was mobbed and called an enemy of his country. But he moved serenely on in the even tenor of his way, and a few years later Granby, recognizing his sound judgment, honesty of purpose and sincere patriotism, sent him as her delegate to assist in formulating our state constitution.

An entry in the records of Rev. Joel Hayes, our third minister, states that on June 8, 1786, he married Samuel White and Eunice Eastman. There was a curious romance connected with this item. A brother of Deacon William Eastman, called the squire, lived at Granby Five Corners, in the house now occupied by Henry Moody. Samuel White, then a youth of fifteen, called at the house one day, when Squire Eastman said, jocosely, "Samuel, if you will go to the war and return all right you may marry any one of my daughters." We quote the sequel. "Samuel White was only fifteen years of age when he enlisted, and being under the regulation height, was obliged to stand on tiptoe when measured at the mustering in. The father of the young patriot also enlisted with him. The first winter of the campaign had not passed when the elder White froze both his feet, and was obliged to return home, where his wounds failed to respond to treatment, and he died. The son went through the service without injury, and when the war cry of 1812 sounded he was among the first to respond, raising a company of which he was made captain."

Previous to the Declaration of Independence there had been in the vicinity of Springfield what the old people called a "Nest of Tories." Their secret headquarters were said to have been in West Springfield. If any continental officer of rank came home on a furlough his house was liable to be suddenly raided by men who sought his capture.

SOUTH HADLEY IN THE REVOLUTION

At West Parish Four Corners, in Granby, a little to the southeast, rises an elevation of land called Phin's Hill. At the time of the Stamp Act, Phineas, son of our pioneer, Chileab Smith, was living on the present Woodbridge street in South Hadley. Before 1775 he had built a house upon and removed to the eminence, named in his honor. He was one of those who answered "present" to the call of Lexington, and his son David, afterwards Major Smith, enlisted on his eighteenth birthday. The widow of the latter died in South Hadley in June, 1850, and the following incidents were related to the author by her. When Captain Phineas Smith joined the army in 1776 he took with him a young and very strong horse. When a colt it had always been allowed, once every day, to walk up the stone steps and enter the kitchen door in order to eat the piece of rye bread which was always saved for it. One day, Captain Phineas having been granted a short furlough, set out for home. Passing through West Springfield his horse was possibly recognized by the tories, and a party of them started in pursuit. Before he had been at home a scant half hour his wife, chancing to pass the open window of the "keeping room," saw them just fastening their horses under a large cherry tree that stood close by. Part of the tories went to the rear of the house in order to watch that side, while the others went to the front door, which was, fortunately, barred. They pounded it loudly with their fists, crying out, "Open in the name of the King! Open in the name of the King!" While his wife unbarred the door Captain Phineas leaped from the window and, jumping upon one of their horses, climbed to the top of the cherry tree, whose dense foliage screened him from any but the closest observation. The tories searched the house from garret to cellar; they pulled the feather beds to the floor and trampled upon them as they thrust their swords into the ticks of the straw beds, and, in the language of Mrs. Smith, "They even looked in the bureau drawers." After their departure Captain Smith descended from the tree, and as soon as dusk had fallen, mounted his horse and returned to camp, for he had heard them say, "He has probably stopped somewhere on the way; we will come again after dark."

Later on his wife, looking one day from a window, saw in the distance a black speck which appeared to be followed by a dark spot, the latter constantly gaining upon the former. Some intuition told her that it was her husband upon a tired horse, pursued by tories upon fresh ones. She hastily collected the guns, pushed the heavy oak shutters across the windows, then, with a sudden inspiration, ran to the kitchen door and, taking off her apron, shook it frantically. They were now all ascending the steep hill, and almost abreast of one another. By some subtle telepathy her husband caught at her idea and waved his hand reassuringly. Entering the dooryard together, two tories slipped from their horses ready to grasp the Captain as he alighted, but to their surprise he rode his horse straight up the steps into the kitchen, whose door clanged together an instant after. The house was now like a little fort and the baffled tories, fearing that the firing of guns would alarm the neighborhood, decided that "Discretion was the better part of valor," and speedily withdrew.

This was about the time when the Declaration of Independence was signed, and that event caused many of the tories to seek other homes for themselves upon English soil.

Early in the year Rev. Mr. Woodbridge had read from the pulpit a proclamation sent by the General Court at Boston, which asserted that we owed no obedience to Parliament nor to the royal governors, who had abrogated our charter, but it entreated all officers, from judge to tithing-man, to suppress all disorders and immoralities, and directed the congregations to be faithful in their attendance at divine service. This proclamation omitted the customary "God save the King," and substituted "God save the people." It was also read at our annual town meeting.

A second proclamation called for a meeting to be held for the sake of obtaining our "Concurrence in declaring the Independence of the Colonies." This was called for June 20, 1776, and South Hadley at that time "voted in the affirmative by a great majority." Five days later their sincerity was put to the test, for an order came from the General Court that twelve men should go from our town to reinforce the troops in Canada, and each man must carry with him provisions for the journey, a blanket, and other accouterments. There were at this time about eighty families living here, and before the close of the war each had, upon an average, sent two of its members into the army.

During the succeeding year the call for volunteers grew more and more imperative, but the response came promptly and cheerfully. One of these recruits was Josiah Draper, our Fall Woods schoolmaster, to whom reference has been made in preceding chapters. He was in the habit of keeping a daily journal of his doings, and this diary now enjoys the rare distinction of being, so far as is known, the only one still in existence, that was kept by a private of the Revolutionary Army. A messenger had come asking for men to aid in opposing the march of Burgoyne, and if possible to attack his army in the rear. For this service, Josiah Draper and others in the town volunteered. Some extracts here and there from his journal may prove to be of interest; and though his orthography might have made poor old Lindley Murray blush for him, yet he was for those times an unusually clever man.

"Sept. 12, 1777. Set out from South Hadley at two o'clock, the day of enlistment. Stayed over night at S. Judds." "Sept. 13. Had a breakfast of coffee, rost pig, punkin pie, cheese, and butter. Sold my Snuff Bottel." "Sept. 19. Paid a man six shillings for carrying my pack to Ruperts." "Sept. 20. Yesterday wrote a letter to send home. Sent it to-day. Had a fine chicken stew, eat hearty. The old wolf (Burgoyne) is gone."

Sept. 26, he reached Ticonderoga and was put upon guard duty, the countersign being 'America.'

"Oct. 18. I wrote a letter to Captain Clark. One of ye Deserters Court-Marsheled." "Oct. 19. The man was whipt, belongs to Col. Brewers Regiment, thirty lashes for Desertion." "Sunday, Oct. 20. Mr. Throop preached from 'What is Man?'"

"Nov. 26. Dismissed to open my school. Sold my Brass Buckles for five shillings. Set out for Home."

He walked one hundred and fifty-six miles in eight days on his way back.

"Dec. 4. Got Home. Sold my quart tin cup for fifty cents, which was just half what it cost me. The Place I left the Bible Class was the Psalter Class, Psalm 78:26."
The 28th verse chanced to be, "And he let it fall in the midst of their camp."

When Josiah Draper "Reckoned with my book," he found that he had not only spent up all his wages, but a good deal more, owing, perhaps, to such entries as these:

"Wednesday, October 23. Bought Mutton taller.
"Bought sugar and Rum. Bought a barrel of Beer.
"Feel very weak and poor. Bought a gill of Brandy at night."

But he was a true patriot, for only a week after his return he was taking his savings of former years in order to equip three more of our townsmen for the army, one of whom lived in Pearl City.

A few weeks before Josiah Draper's enlistment there had been an emergency call from Vermont for immediate help. It was known as the Call of Bennington. Dr. A. J. Miller, who helped to throw the tea overboard, was now a surgeon in the army. His brother, Leonard, the ancestor of Mrs. C. A. Gridley, had enlisted during the preceding March, and was now stationed near the point of danger. Their younger brother, Joseph, father of the late Mr. Daniel Miller (more familiarly known to the old residents of South Hadley as "Uncle Daniel"), was very desirous of joining the rescue party. He had no suit of clothes befitting such a journey, through tangled woods and thorny swamps. Only two days had been allowed the recruits for preparation, and something must be done. Something *was* done, for two sheep, one black and the other white, were hastily led into the water and their fleeces washed. The shearing of the pair was soon completed; then everyone, even the children, was set to work picking the wool apart, beating it with sticks, and tossing it into the air. The older women, their hands thoroughly greased, mixed the white and black wool together in order to make the "pepper and salt" cloth, which was, at that era, in universal use. They had only hand cards with which to

LAKE NONOTUCK, SOUTH HADLEY

SOUTH HADLEY IN THE REVOLUTION

form it into rolls, and the women took turns during the first night in sitting up to prepare it for spinning. Next morning these rolls were twisted and drawn out on the spinning wheel until fine enough to be called yarn. It was then wound on a spindle and quilled. Twelve hours were spent in weaving the five yards of cloth which were needed. The second night and the next morning were fully occupied in cutting out and making, by hand, the coat and knee breeches which composed the suit.

The news of Burgoyne's surrender was received at Hadley on Sunday, October 20, 1777, and the good tidings were doubtless sent at once to the assembled congregations at South Hadley and Granby. The joy must have been great indeed, for Colonel Woodbridge and his men had been in Ticonderoga at the time of its evacuation, and there were many others from these two towns still at the front.

One of the soldiers present on the occasion of Burgoyne's surrender never forgot the scene. A grandson and namesake of our pioneer, William Montague, had been apprenticed to Lieutenant Reuben Judd, of South Hadley, in order to learn the carpenter's trade.

During the summer of 1777 Lieutenant Judd was drafted to joint the northern army. He had already seen as much of military service as he desired, and young Montague offered to go as his substitute. His parents at first objected, but Colonel Woodbridge obtained their consent by taking the youth as a kind of aide-de-camp, under his own personal care. At the time when Burgoyne delivered up his sword to General Gates, William Montague, being at that hour off duty, established himself upon a gate post whence he could witness the ceremony. Burgoyne's sword, which was immediately returned to him, is now in Hadley, he having presented it to Colonel Porter on his way home.

After the American victory at Bennington, finding that they possessed no adequate means of keeping the captured Hessians confined in that place, numbers of them were sent to this and neighboring towns to be "farmed out among the inhabitants, who had the use of them in return for furnishing board, lodging and safe keeping." Some of them found such pleasant homes and were so happy that when an opportunity was given them of returning to the Fatherland they chose to remain. Others were less contented; the records in Boston show that one of these who had been located in our town, having heard that the British had captured an American soldier, wrote a letter asking to be exchanged for the new prisoner. Had he but known it, there were still tories in West Springfield, who would have given him shelter and concealment could he have escaped, but such precautions were taken, and their treatment was so kind that few desired to leave this region.

While these events were taking place the officials of our town had not been idle, and on February 11, 1777, a meeting of the selectmen was held at the house of Captain Moses Montague, "to prevent monopoly and high prices."

Horses were, at that time, in greater demand than ever before. There were frequent journeys to Springfield, partly in order to obtain the latest news, and partly to carry the generous contributions which were sent to the soldiers,—stockings and shoes, clothing and food. We find one entry in our town records —"Voted to provide 3460 waite of Beef for the Continental Army;" and three months later,—"Voted to have by Feb. 6, 8000 pounds of Beef, our quota for the army."

Then, too, Springfield was the mustering point for Central and Western Massachusetts; Colonel Woodbridge was the muster master for that section, and Major Josiah White and other leading citizens of South Hadley assisted him. In addition to this, some who could not go to the war themselves lent their horses to be used in the army. Taking all these things into consideration, our Town-fathers said, "The price of horse travel shall be two and one-fourth pence a mile."

Men's long stockings, knit from the best of wool, could be charged for at the rate of six shillings "a pare," but common shoes must be sold for eight shillings. Cheese was to be sixpence and butter eight pence per pound, while rum was listed at nine shillings a gallon. A mug of the best flip was to be sold for a shilling, but for a "good meal of vittles" our innkeepers could charge only ten pence, and lodging must not exceed three pence per night.

The most important matter left to the decision of this meeting was in regard to the amount of wages which should be paid for labor, especially during haying and harvesting. If the rate were fixed at too high a figure then South Hadley might be complained of at the General Court by the surrounding towns. If it were too low, help would be hard to obtain. In the early days strikes and labor troubles were a thing unknown, for the state, taking matters into its own hands, had empowered town officials to "impress men for mowing, reaping of corn, and inning thereof." This law directed the husbandman who needed more help during the ingathering of crops, to request the constable to procure it for him. The latter was told to go to the "artificers and handy craftsmen" and order them to take their place in the field, "unless necessarily attending to like business of their own." The shoemaker who refused to lay down his last, or the carpenter who continued the use of hammer and plane, and the weaver who remained at his loom, disregarding such a summons, must each pay double the day's wages to the poor of the town, and if the constable forgot or neglected to notify the artisans, then he must himself pay the forfeit in their place.

The final decision of our selectmen was to double the wage rate established by the legislature of a century before, and give the farm laborer three shillings a day.

So rapidly did the paper currency depreciate that two years later it was voted, in South Hadley, "Town bills shall be doubled twenty-four times for payment." The same year, when a call came for six months' men, our town offered a bounty for enlistment. One thousand dollars in continental bills, or twenty silver dollars at the close of the service. Most of the volunteers wisely chose the latter alternative.

Few people can rightly estimate the cost of our independence. Aside from the sufferings of the wounded, who could command so little medical skill for the alleviation of pain; aside from the ever-present loneliness of the home that had been made desolate by the hand of death, there were other troubles to be encountered. The laws which permitted imprisonment for debt were still in force. Despite the kindness of neighbors, there were some soldiers in this region who felt compelled to mortgage their farms in order to support their families during their long absences at the front. At the close of the war they received payment in continental bills, which became almost valueless, so that they were obliged to sell their farms and begin life anew.

This was not the case with Deacon David Nash, who had slaves enough to till his land when he was absent. And David Mitchell, who lived on the old Hyde place, sent his slave Cæsar into service for the country, while himself remaining here in order to promote the work of collecting food and clothing for the army. Cæsar enlisted early in the war, at a time when the soldiers were still paid in silver. He saved his wages and purchased his own freedom, and thereafter it is doubtful whether a prouder man than he ever entered our meeting house. His very name, Cæsar Cambridge, was classical, though his comrades from South Hadley and Granby, Peter Pendergras, Selor Sword, Lorin Larkin and Jonas Jackson, could boast that theirs were no less alliterative.

Barry, in his History of Massachusetts, states that the grievance which induced South Hadley to join in the Revolution was the refusal of Great Britain to permit the erection of slitting mills in this country. So many buildings were constantly going up that there was frequently a shortage of hand-made nails, and these mills were able to convert iron bars into nail rods. During the first half of the last century old people used to describe the process of nail making as they had seen it done in our town.

On a cold winter's evening, when plenty of wood had been heaped upon the flames in the big, old fireplace, the boys took turns in holding the long nail rod in the coals till the end was red hot. Then the father, with a stout hammer and many quick blows, shaped this end into a point. Taking his chisel, he cut off a piece of the rod, a little longer than the steel mold, or bore, as it was called, into which he forced the bit of hot iron. Upon the part which projected beyond the mold he struck heavily until

SOUTH HADLEY IN THE REVOLUTION 159

he had flattened it into a head. When sufficiently cooled, the nail was withdrawn from the mold, which could then be used over again.

Some families became very expert at casting bullets, though the melted lead oftentimes came from the sacrifice of their cherished pewter. There was a call for ammunition at home as well as abroad, for the very animals in the forest seemed to know by intuition the defenseless state of many homes, and we read in an old diary, kept by one of our ancestors, that the wild hogs, with which the woods were filled, "Infested my garden." Another entry runs thus—"To-day a wolf killed a young goat for me in the pasture east of the house." The owner, hearing the outcry, came with a loaded gun, but the wolf fled to a swamp, where he concealed himself. The neighboring men were called together, but Sir Lupus had escaped, and the record ends with—"Drove the swamp and nothing got."

It will be no matter of surprise that the pastures and gardens south of Mt. Holyoke were less carefully guarded when we remember that Granby and South Hadley together sent two hundred and fifty fearless and faithful soldiers into the army. Since they were all of them born previous to 1768, at which time the East Parish was set off as a separate town, South Hadley may be forgiven for claiming their nativity as something of which it might justly be proud. A part of these volunteers were at West Point at the time when Washington first learned of the treachery of Benedict Arnold. It was a season of deep discouragement throughout the country. The regiment to which these men belonged had served its time and was waiting to be discharged. The commander-in-chief desired to retain them longer, but they were naturally impatient to return home. Levi Taylor, who had enlisted at the age of sixteen, was among them. Often in later years did he repeat to the wondering children the story of what followed this appeal—General Washington told them of his difficulties, and of the dangers that threatened their common cause, and asked them if, as a personal favor to himself, they would consent to stay a little longer. "Let every man who will promise me to remain a month longer poise his gun!" said the commander. And the old soldier's voice rang out triumphantly on his closing sentence—"And every man of us pized his piece."

Fifty years after the Revolution one of these old soldiers remarked that he had seen as hard fighting in the streets of South Hadley between whigs and tories, as any he had witnessed while in camp. Stones and brickbats, however, though dangerous missiles, did not, so far as we know, inflict any mortal wounds. As time went on toryism disappeared from the town. Its leaders selling their farms, or leaving them to be confiscated, retired to other lands on a pension from the King. Some who had been, perhaps, unjustly suspected of being British sympathizers, removed to neighboring states. One family of Smiths emigrated to Vermont. After the battle of Bennington they opened their house to our wounded soldiers, whom they nursed tenderly back into health.

A very pretty story might be written concerning the South Hadley man who was consigned by the surgeon to the care of a family named Smith, and found to their mutual surprise that he was in the hands of his old neighbors.

Among the many incidents of the Revolution handed down to us by our forefathers is the story of Mrs. Philips, the great-grandmother of Granby's historian, A. W. Fisk. A party of Revolutionary soldiers, recently discharged from service, and returning to Chesterfield, New Hampshire, lost their way in the woods and wandered for days, having only a few mouthfuls of food to be shared between them. When at last they reached the house of Mrs. Philips they were in a starving condition, and begged piteously for something to eat. "If you will promise to follow my directions implicitly, I will feed you," answered the astute matron, and to this they agreed. A large kettle, filled with hot water, was swinging from the crane in the big fireplace. She stirred in Indian meal until it had attained the right consistency for gruel and gave each of them a cupful to drink. They clamored eagerly for more. "No," she said firmly. "You promised to obey me, you must wait." Later on they had another cupful. Little by little she nourished them till they were able to partake of solid food, and the verdict of the doctor was that her resolution and good sense had saved their lives.

Owing to the limits of the present chapter, many interesting details in regard to the war must be omitted. We know in brief that whenever our army met with defeat a day of fasting and prayer was appointed by our minister, and neighboring pastors often preached for him upon these occasions. But when a victory occurred all was joy and gladness. We learn from the old orderly books that a great triumph was heralded by remitting the punishment of those who had been sentenced to the whipping post, and a gill of rum was allowed to every soldier in honor of the event. Our minister always appointed a day of special thanksgiving, and bonfires were lighted to express the universal joy.

A brother of one of our deacons, who lived north of Mt. Holyoke, one day met two youths rolling an empty tar barrel before them. "Whither away, boys?" he asked. They answered him respectfully, "We are going to the mountain, sir, to celebrate the victory of which we have just heard." "And is that the way to praise God for his goodness? Back to yonder building," pointing to the meeting house, "and let us there thank God as we ought." So saying he drove the reluctant youths before him, and kneeling in the sacred edifice, with a boy upon either side of him, made a long prayer.

Soldiers returning from camp brought back to us many new songs, which were soon heard in both kitchen and field, and even upon the very steps of the sanctuary. One of the favorites, sung to the tune of Chester, ran thus:

> "Let tyrants shake their iron rod,
> And slavery clank her galling chains;
> We'll fear them not; we'll trust in God,
> New England's God forever reigns.
> The foe comes on with haughty stride,
> Our troops advance with martial noise;
> Their veterans flee before our arms,
> And generals yield to beardless boys."

The surrender of Cornwallis on October 19, 1781, must have seemed a complete fulfillment of this prophecy. The news of that event did not reach South Hadley until the following December, at which time the Granby minister promptly appointed a day of thanksgiving. We find by old records that the pastors of Belchertown and Granby always acted in unison with Mr. Woodbridge in such matters, so we must have had a service of praise. The Granby minister is said to have preached from the text, "Thou has done great things for us, whereof we are glad."

Among the ensigns of Colonel Woodbridge's regiment was a person of fine appearance and pleasing address, who fought in the battle of Bunker Hill. This man was Daniel Shays, the leader and instigator of the insurrection called Shay's Rebellion. The history of this uprising is too familiar to need repetition; but the flight of his soldiers from Springfield to Amherst gave to many of our townsmen a night of terror.

On the 27th of January, 1787, Jonathan Burnett. a veteran of the Revolutionary War, was absent from home. He lived on College street, in the house now owned by G. F. Canney. It was a very cold day, and the snow lay thick upon the ground. As the darkness deepened his children gathered before the open fire. Strange sounds were heard in the street, and before the little one in the trundle bed was sound asleep their uncle hastily entered the house. He briefly informed them that Shay's men had seized two barrels of rum in the tavern a little south of them and were already so intoxicated that they were breaking windows, furniture, and anything that came in their way. He begged the mother to hide herself and the children without delay. A stairway led from the kitchen to a large cellar where the cider barrels were kept. Adjoining this, but separated from it by a thick wall, was a small excavation known as the root cellar, access to which could be obtained from the southeast front room, through a small recess that might easily be mistaken for a cupboard. Hardly were the family concealed in the root cellar when the troopers raided the house. They went from room to room, punctuating their march with frequent libations, oaths and empty boasts of what they would do in the future. The frightened children did not utter a sound, and remained undiscovered.

Meanwhile, one of their officers outside the house shot a comrade by mistake, supposing him to be one of their pursuers. This fact, however, did not stop the rioting. Captain Noah Goodman, who lived in the house next to Judson Hall, was a prominent government official. He had been for years a member of the legislature, and was one of the committee who formulated our state constitution. His house was attacked and plundered, also that of Colonel Woodbridge, and many others.

Tradition tells us that some of our men gathered at the parsonage, but were too few in number to go out and engage in battle. At the turn of the road, where the Amherst highway leaves Woodbridge street, a majority of Shays' men started toward the Notch. A few kept on through Pearl City, and one of the latter stopped at the old "Heman White place," for warmth and rest. Upon departing he handed the host his horse-pistol with the words, "Keep this till I call for it." It has never been reclaimed.

Deacon Daniel Moody was ill that night, and the fire had not been banked as usual. Some of Shays' followers, seeing the ruddy glow upon the window pane, knocked at the door. A servant girl admitted them to the kitchen, where the deacon was sleeping upon one of the rude folding beds of that day. The loud voices of the men awoke him. Starting up in indignant surprise, he called out, "How came those villains in my house? Begone instantly, every one of you." A drunken soldier advanced with his weapons, ready to kill the doughty deacon, but the servant girl interposed. "La, now!" she said, soothingly, "don't mind him. He is only a doited old man, and not worth noticing."

The insurrection found but few adherents in this immediate vicinity. When its discomfited volunteers returned, those of them who were church members found themselves debarred from partaking of the bread and wine at communion. But later, after they had taken anew the oath of allegiance, and had avowed their penitence, they were again received into fellowship with the church.

Upon each recurring Fourth of July we are reminded of the war which gave us independence. It was not until 1783 that this day became a national holiday. Previous to that year, March 5 had been observed in commemoration of the Boston massacre. But after peace had been established, it was thought best to adopt in its place the Fourth of July as the date for annual celebration. In the beginning the day was filled, not simply with noisy demonstrations, but with sermons, orations, and patriotic songs, which were followed by an ample collation for the whole town. It was intended to recall to everyone's memory the brave deeds and heroic suffering of our soldiers.

The price paid for our independence cannot be measured by the standards of to-day. The nameless graves on distant battlefields, and the sacred dust that beneath the bronze marker reposes in our old-fashioned churchyards, prove the truth of the poet's description—

"They left the plough share in the mould,
Their flocks and herds without a fold,
The sickle in the unshorn grain,
The corn, half garnered, on the plain
And mustered in their simple dress,
For wrongs to seek a stern redress,
To right those wrongs, come weal, come woe,
To perish or o'ercome the foe."

THE GROVE

CHAPTER NINE

SOUTH HADLEY AFTER THE REVOLUTION

IN 1800 female missionary societies were first instituted in Boston. Later, spinning, weaving, and knitting societies were formed for the purpose of sending the Gospel to the heathen, and cent societies and mite societies sprang up as if by magic.

In those days it was customary for the women to retain the money received from the sale of eggs and butter, with which they were expected to defray their own personal expenses, including their contributions toward benevolent objects. The story of their introduction here may be learned from the following extracts, taken from the letters written by one of our old residents:

"South Hadley, September 27, 1803. I have lately seen a plan of a Female Charitable Association, for the purchase and distribution of the Bible and other good books among the needy inhabitants at the West. This plan is transmitted to the ministers' wives throughout the country. In Longmeadow I hear that there are a hundred subscribers. I do not know the number in South Hadley." . . . . "We are attempting to form a society to assist the Cherokee Mission by furnishing clothing for the children in that school. Twenty-four have given their names as members, and there will probably be enough to make thirty, who come very cheerfully, and for conscience's sake. Some others will probably fall in reluctantly and for fashion's sake, and many will keep back for covetousness' sake. They will ask:

" 'What constitutes a member of this society?'

" 'Fifty cents annually, and the privilege of giving as much more as you choose.'

" 'What! Fifty cents every year?'

" 'That constitutes a member, but I presume the ladies generally will esteem it a privilege to give more.'

"'What! More than half a dollar every year? How much to the other societies?'

"'Fifty cents to the Cent Society, and twenty-five to the Dorcas.'

"'Fifty and fifty make a dollar, and twenty-five makes 7/6, seven and sixpence a year given away for nothing. And who knows what becomes ont? I don't spose a bit ont ever gits where they pretend to send it, and if it did I don't know as 'twould do any good. I have a large family of my own to support and carnt do half as well by them as I wanter.'"

From a subsequent letter by the same writer, we glean this account of our first Sabbath School:

"South Hadley, August 2, 1819.

"Our Sunday School flourishes; we have 120 scholars. We use Cumming's Catechism, with Psalms and Hymns and the Sacred Scriptures. I have a class of young ladies from sixteen to nineteen years old who were themselves teachers when the school commenced.

"I generally select the lessons, and recommend it to them to read Scott or some other expositor, on the portion which they commit. They usually get fifty answers in Cummings, and from fifty to sixty verses of Scripture each week. Sister Harriet, E. Whitney, Mr. P. and E. White have classes, and many others. We think six enough for a class."

The first superintendent was Deacon Josiah White, who was assisted by Mr. Joseph Strong. In 1826 to its other attractions was added a Sunday School Library. After the opening of Mt. Holyoke Seminary some of its most gifted members became teachers in our Sabbath School, two nieces of Mary Lyon being among the number.

More than sixty years ago an infant class was started, with a membership of forty, and has ever since remained a marked feature of the school.

Soon after 1830 Sunday School concerts began to be held. These were attended only by adults, and were observed as a season of prayer for the conversion of the pupils. About the middle of the century children were admitted to these concerts, and even allowed to join in the singing. After a few years the young were asked to recite verses from the Bible, and so little by little it became almost wholly a children's meeting. Its inception and continued success may have resulted in some measure from Josiah Draper's Psalter Class, in which, as his diary shows, he felt a vital interest.

Colonial laws permitted the enslavement of Indians taken captive in war. But, skilled as they were in woodcraft, it was almost impossible to prevent their escape. They were accordingly exchanged for negroes from the West Indies, nearly six thousand of whose descendants were, at the time of the Stamp Act, held as slaves in the State of Massachusetts. Some of this number were owned in our town, though their servitude was of so mild a type that it could hardly be called bondage. If no guests were present they sat at the same table with their master and his family, and partook of the same food.

If the child of Cæsar or Phillip died our minister entered the fact on the church record with as much precision as if he had been the son of an archbishop.

The state line between Massachusetts and Connecticut was near enough to us so that an escaping fugitive could easily cross the border, but so kindly were the slaves treated that we find no case of a runaway here who did not return of his own accord. There was an unwritten law in this vicinity that any slave who had been cruelly and unjustly beaten by his master should be given food and concealment if he asked for it. The truth of the following incident is fully vouched for:

Two brothers, both of them having families, lived near here, but several miles apart. The elder had an undisciplined temper, which was easily aroused, while the younger was of a gentle disposition. The former had, in a fit of anger, punished one of his slaves so severely that the negro ran away. He soon found his way to the house of the younger brother and asked for his protection. Here he remained, working faithfully, until on a certain day word was hastily brought that the owner was approaching, determined to reclaim his property, and vowing that vengeance should be taken on the culprit. The "Live Moor," as negroes were then called, was quickly hidden beneath an empty hogshead in the cellar, and the host went forth to meet the quondam master with a placid smile. In respose to an impatient demand for the bondman, he said that he would search for the slave if the owner would promise upon the Bible not to whip the fugitive. This offer met with a prompt and decided refusal. "Look for him yourself then," said the younger brother, in an unmoved tone. Look he did, but to no avail. At last, finding that threats, bribes and prayers were wholly unheeded, he gave the required promise, and thereafter treated the runaway so well that he never again attempted to escape.

The slaveholder was often a man of religious as well as social prominence, and ministers sometimes found this ownership their leading title to aristocracy. The list of masters in this town included the names of—Deacon David Nash, Deacon William Eastman, Squire Benjamine Eastman, David Mitchell, etc. The road from the house of the latter to the present homestead of John Graves was designated for years as Slave street.

After the Revolution it had become evident that the climate of Massachusetts was too severe for a race reared in the warm latitudes of the Antilles, and slavery was an unprofitable investment. It died away in this region quietly, and without the exercise of law. One of the stones in the old burying ground bore this inscription: "William McGee, Died Mar. 2, 1861, AE 101." This marked the grave of the last slave born before the war of independence, who was buried in our cemetery.

"Bill McGee," as he was always called, had been owned in youth by a man in New Jersey, who was not always kind to him. One day he was sent to pick huckleberries in a swamp infested with wild animals, and was not permitted to carry even a stick with which to defend himself. His pail was nearly full when he saw a large bear advancing leisurly toward him, snipping at the bushes on either side of the path. "I knew jest what kind of a huckleberry dat bar was after, and I started to run, and never stopped running till I got to Massachusetts," was his explanation to his South Hadley neighbors. In extreme old age it was his delight to gather a group of children about him and tell them stories of the Revolution. His fame as a centenarian annoyed him, and if anyone questioned him in regard to his age his answer was, "I am so old that I am ashamed to be alive." He was held in such universal respect that everyone was ready to contribute to his headstone.

Even before the passage of the Fugitive Slave Bill, South Hadley became one of the earliest stations on the underground railroad. Runaway slaves who reached Springfield were sent to a Mr. Bullens, at Chicopee; he forwarded them to our town, whence they were transported across the mountain to South Amherst, where, feeling themselves comparatively safe, a part of them remained, while others pressed on to Canada. A parallel line ran upon the other side of the Connecticut River. Slaves were sent from Springfield to be concealed in the house of Rev. Thomas Rand, who was or had been one of the first Baptist ministers in Holyoke, and were sent from there to Northampton. These journeys were usually made under cover of the darkness, in the middle of the night. Among those who received hospitality here were Lewis and Milton Clark, the former being the original George Harris of Mrs. Stowe's "Uncle Tom's Cabin." The story of all these escapes would fill a volume.

Few events have produced so great a change in our town as the Temperance Reformation. It was a common saying here that cider was as plentiful as water. Some of our old inventories state that the deceased had "a decent supply of furniture," but the list usually includes a hand-press for the grinding of apples. Soldiers returning from war sometimes brought back an appetite for something stronger than cider. Rum had been served as a part of their rations when there had been unusual exposure, or on occasions of great rejoicing, and statistics show that twenty-five years after the Revolution the average consumption of intoxicating liquor was three times as large as it had been when the Declaration of Independence was signed.

At the settlement of the town there had been a law that no one should drink liquor after nine o'clock in the evening, but this appears to have become a dead letter. The moderate drinker had always the example of the parson to plead in his own defense. Rev. Joseph Condit, who was settled here in 1835, was the first one of our ministers who refused the glass of cider, brandy, or the spiced elderberry wine, which his parishioners delighted to offer him, and when he made his pastoral calls, cake and cheese soon took the place of the former hospitable toddy.

It was not considered a heinous offense for young men to get together for a convivial time, in the long winter evenings. It was looked upon as a great joke to give one of their number a surprise, and ask for spirituous liquor till they had exhausted his store and he was compelled to refuse them. The last of these gatherings was at the house of Mr. J.——, on Hadley street. This host was himself a professional joker, and was looked upon as a fair butt for their fun. Fortunately for him, he had five minutes' warning before the company arrived, and filled the shelves of his cupboard with empty bottles of dark glass. As he opened the last of the full ones, he swung back the door of the cupboard, and pointing to the row of bottles, said cheerily, "Don't stop yet! We must go through all those." His visitors, much chagrined, soon departed, and when later they found out the truth, this custom of "drinking a man dry" was dropped.

The faithful sermons of Mr. Condit against the use of ardent spirits had prepared the way for a Temperance Crusade. The Washingtonian Movement, which was said to have reformed 150,000 persons, had begun in Northampton, and conventions were held there. To these went delegates from South Hadley, and the following incident was related to the author as being the first total abstinence story ever told in this town:

One of the farmers, who, like all others of his ilk, kept sheep, was in the habit of taking a glass of bitters every morning before breakfast. Two of his sons did the same, but the third, too young to drink spirituous liquors, had only the sugar at the bottom of the glasses. The father, much impressed by what he had heard at the Temperance Convention, and feeling that he might have given his children a better preparation for the duties of life than teaching them to drink ardent spirits, promised that if his two sons would for a specified time give up their morning dram, he would present each of them with a fine sheep. They

SOUTH HADLEY IN 1850

assented to this proposal, upon which the small boy asked, "What will you give me if I will go without the sugar at the bottom of the glass?" "You," returned the parent promptly, "shall have a lamb." Next morning the three sons were sitting at table while the father mixed his usual dram. Suddenly the youngest said, in a perfectly respectful tone: "Father, hadn't you better take a sheep, too?" His conscience was touched, and, throwing the contents of his glass from the window, he signed the pledge, and was ever after a total abstainer from strong drink.

The pledge, which was signed by nearly all the children in our town, ran thus:

"This little band do with our hand
The pledge now sign, to drink no wine,
Nor whiskey hot, which makes the sot,
Nor fiery rum, to turn our home
Into a hell where none can dwell.
So now we pledge perpetual hate
To all that can intoxicate."

A portion of these rhymes, with an appropriate picture, was printed upon pieces of thick satin ribbon and given to the children to wear as badges at South Hadley's great temperance picnic, which the oldest inhabitants still delight to recall.

The contagion of example spread, and the successive years in which our town voted no-license may have been a part of the aftermath from these early reforms.

The annual observance of Visiting Day was retained here until after the middle of the nineteenth century. On a certain day in each year, appointed by the minister, all the inhabitants of the village were expected to be at home, the men freshly shaven, and the women and children in clean dresses and aprons. The family Bible was placed ready at hand upon the candle stand. The deacons, in their Sunday best, and assisted by some of the leading church members, sallied forth two and two in order to visit every family in the neighborhood. They began their call by inquiring of everyone in regard to the state of his or her soul. "Have you been converted?" "Do you spend some portion of each day in secret prayer?" "Have you the full assurance of faith?" "Do you maintain family worship every morning and evening?" etc. After a time one visitor read aloud a chapter from the Bible. Then all knelt while the other offered a long prayer. This custom appears to have been a survival of the old times when five tithing men were chosen at our town meeting to look after the moral and spiritual welfare of families and see to it that the children were taught to repeat the catechism.

During the Revolution so many of our men were absent in camp that, as in other towns, women and girls learned to care for the fields and gardens. One of the South Hadley matrons thus describes life in 1785:

"It was not uncommon for young ladies of the first families to spend some hours in a day in weeding their gardens. They were dressed in a coarse wrapper, with a slat sunbonnet completely covering the face, and gloves from the shoulders to the middle of the fingers, leaving the ends bare to pull the weeds. Thus they set an example of humility and diligence to their inferiors, which had a very desirable effect."

We are indebted to the same writer for the following picture of our old church, with its square pews, when the August sun streamed through the windows, all of which were guiltless of blinds.

"You would almost laugh to look into our meeting house on the Sabbath, to see the young men in the galleries, all in their shirt sleeves, and the girls and women with their bonnets untied, and all looking as if they had been making hay."

The discomfort of the summer heat was, however, but trifling when compared with the suffering occasioned by the winter's cold. The severity of the climate was simply mitigated, not tempered, by the use of small foot stoves. The supply of these was so limited that only the aged, the infirm, and children were expected to use them. Stoves of the old-fashioned box kind appeared in our meeting house but a short time previous to 1840. We find the parish in 1838 voting to "make such alterations in fitting up stoves to warm the house, as they (the committee) shall deem expedient." They also voted to "take away partition to give room for stoves."

During the long time before the introduction of artificial heat into the meeting house, people had become accustomed to a cold church, and there was now some opposition to the purchase of stoves. Their warmth, it was argued, would promote drowsiness, and the words of the preacher would fail of effect. This sinful indulgence of the body would also tend toward weakness of soul. The amount of heat diffused was at first so little that the old folks became reconciled, and even came to church a half an hour before time for the service to begin in order to stand together around the fire while they warmed their cold hands and exchanged the news of the day.

For a short time previous to 1830 "cook stoves" were advertised for sale at Bardwell's store in the Canal Village, as South Hadley Falls was then called. The following description of the first one actually in use here is from the pen of Mr. Byron Smith, and will be of interest to those who do not understand how so long a time could have intervened before the cooking range superseded the old-fashioned fireplace in domestic affairs.

"The first cooking stove was brought into South Hadley by E. T. Smith in the fall of 1835. The name of it was the Doctor Mott (or Nott) stove, after the man who invented it. It was made of cast iron and was so heavy that four men were needed to carry it into the ell part of the old Woodbridge house in which Mrs. Hollingsworth now lives, where it was set up. The stove was made after the style of an old iron fire frame. There were two holes for kettles, and above them a broad top, or shelf, which had to be lifted up when the kettles were taken off the stove. There was no oven in this first stove; it would take in a stick of wood two feet long. Improvements were made so rapidly that this crude affair was abandoned after two years." He adds: "E. T. Smith also brought into town the first load of wheat flour in barrels. He had moved here from Rochester, New York, where the Kempshal flour was manufactured, and had purchased twenty barrels, which were sent East by the Erie Canal to New York, then up the Connecticut River to Middletown. The river at this place was frozen over, so two teams were sent down from here, driven by Deacon Sedgwick White and G. M. Smith, who brought up the flour. The people were wild with interest, and thought it a great extravagance. Previously, wheat flour had been used sparingly, and as a great luxury."

The coming of the cook stove in South Hadley was antedated in 1821 by the introduction into the pulpit at the meeting house of an oblong iron box in which a fire might be kindled. This was done at the request of the pastor, Rev. Joel Hayes, who had preached here for nearly forty years, without losing a single service on account of illness. He was now an old man approaching seventy, and suffered keenly from the frigid atmosphere of the building.

There being no chimney, some outlet must be provided for the escape of smoke. A pane of glass was probably removed from the leaded window near by, thus making an opening through which the end of the pipe could be conveyed into the open air. The pew next this stove had always been accounted one of the most honorable seats in the meeting house, having been occupied by the leading widows of the town. It now became also one of the most comfortable. The old records were careful to state that this stove was not presented to the minister, but would remain the property of the town.

It had been customary in the winter for all the members of the congregation to spend the intermission between the morning and afternoon services either in their own homes or at the friendly Noon Houses, which every Sunday opened hospitable doors to the shivering worshipers. After the benediction had been pronounced, each person remained standing in perfect silence while the minister descended the eight stairs leading from the pulpit. As he reached the outer door, all hastened to leave the cold meeting house, the parsonage receiving its full quota of visitors. The children, with their mothers, walked across the common to the tavern of Deacon Joseph White, which

SOUTH HADLEY AFTER THE REVOLUTION

stood upon the western slope, and was later known as the Old Chandler House. Here they were received by a portly, fine looking man, and his sweet-faced little wife, whose gentleness won all hearts.

There were no furniture stores near here at that time, and in this town the chairs were made by the skilled hands of Sylvester Higgins, who pegged them together so stoutly that they are still able to defy the ravages of time.

There were not enough chairs for the children, who were bidden to seat themselves upon the little footstoves, which were now entirely cold. Then Deacon White brought in an immense pan of nut cakes, and his wife followed with a towering plate of cheese. In suppressed tones the women related to one another the events of the week, but at the first stroke of the bell, which Colonel Woodbridge had given, Deacon Joseph raked out the glowing embers from the big fireplace, emptied the iron boxes which had been taken out of the little footstoves, and filled them with live coals, placing a layer of hot ashes upon the top in order to conserve the heat. Then the little procession started back beneath the bare limbs of the cherry and pear trees that overhung their path, bringing memories of summer fruits.

Invalids, very old people and distinguished guests were expected to spend their noonings at the house of Dr. Dwight, which was afterwards removed in order to yield its site to the College Art Building. It was a spacious dwelling, a portion of which has been fitted up as an infirmary. The name of Dr. Elihu Dwight was constantly spoken of as the synonym of hospitality. In his large central hall there was always kept a table and chairs, and he had one undeviating rule for his household: "Let no person ever enter my door without finding in this hall, cake, and, in its season, fruit, awaiting him." Ably seconded by his wife, their house was usually thronged with visitors.

Dr. Dwight's kindness was not limited to his guests. Believing that the early inhabitants of Hockanum found it a hard struggle to subdue the rocky soil, he offered to give them his medical services in return for his annual supply of pumpkins.

They agreed to this, and when ill sent for him. Every autumn he might be seen on a certain day driving home a cart piled high with his yellow prizes. He was the dentist as well as the physician of the town, and his kind heart suffered at the pain he was compelled to inflict in this branch of his profession.

The late Mr. Nash, of Moody Corner, used to tell how, when he was a lad, he went down to Dr. Dwight to have an ulcerated tooth extracted. The dentist had no forceps, and only a cruel, iron turnkey with which to twist it out. The instant Dr. Dwight looked at the tooth he saw that it could not be taken out without giving the youth a moment of supreme agony. "How much will it cost to have it pulled?" asked Erastus. "Well," returned the medical man, "if I give you much pain I shall have to charge you twenty-five cents, but if I don't hurt you, it will not cost you anything." After he had finished and the boy was ready to return home, the latter produced his two ninepences. "How much is it?" he inquired. "Did I hurt you?" queried the Doctor. "N-no, sir," replied the plucky lad. "Then you owe me nothing," said the dentist, and the boy departed homeward, the coins jingling merrily in his pockets.

It is hard at this epoch to realize the fortitude required of our forefathers, and the patient industry needed at a time when the present common necessities of life were often deemed luxuries. We find among the old papers of a former South Hadley merchant this label: "Roberts, Pin and Needle Maker to Her Royal Highness, the Dutchess of Clarence. Roberts' Royal Improv'd Pins." In the early part of the nineteenth century, these London pins were sometimes a dollar a paper, and very small papers at that. So costly was this article that brides were given as a part of their dowry a sum sufficient for their purchase, which was called their Pin Money. About the time of the Revolution, people began to manufacture them in this country, but it was said that without a division of labor it would require several hours to make a single one. Some of these old pins still remain in the town. They were formed by cutting off a piece of brass wire of the required length, one end of which was carefully sharpened to a point upon a grindstone. The

DOCTOR DWIGHT'S HOUSE

SOUTH HADLEY AFTER THE REVOLUTION

head was prepared by winding a finer and more delicate wire into spirals of exactly the same size as the body of the pin. Two or three of these coils were cut off, slipped over the point, and pushed to the other extremity of the bit of brass wire, where it was riveted, thus forming the head of the pin. These proved to be clumsy and expensive affairs.

When Stephen White set up his carding mill here, the rolls of wool were sent home carefully wrapped in coarse tow cloth, but the scarcity of these brass pins was so great that he paid the boys a certain sum per thousand for thorns to be used in their stead. Eyelets through which linen twine could be passed were used as fastenings upon many articles of dress, and a bodkin was sure to be found in the work-basket of every family.

One of the most pressing needs in the olden households was to find some easy method of kindling fires. In the scattered houses of our more remote districts it was often necessary in winter for members of the family to sit up in turn through the night in order to keep the fire alive. The great back log must be banked at the close of the evening, or it would be burned out before morning, and if, on the other hand, it was covered too deeply with ashes, it would be smothered. In places where there were several houses near together one could take risks, for the men of South Hadley, who knew (as we have had ocular proof) how to make their own ploughs and pitchforks, also constructed small iron boxes, with handles two or three feet long, intended for the borrowing of live coals from a neighbor's fire. And the first smoke rising from a friend's chimney was a signal that help was to be had there.

After the close of the Revolutionary War, some of our soldiers, returning with their flint locks, resorted to a new expedient for procuring a flame. The screw at the end of the ramrod was twisted into a mass of refuse tow, then drawn out and rammed into the barrel of the gun. A pinch of powder was deposited in the flash pan, and a percussion cap put into place. When the latter had been exploded, splinters of pitch pine were thrust into the burning tow, which had been ignited, and from these sticks a blaze could be quickly started in the old fireplace. This method, however, was used sparingly, many families objecting to so noisy a process for kindling a fire.

The earliest form of matches introduced into this country found its way into South Hadley, but apparently met with scanty favor, only one of its time-worn boxes remaining here to tell the tale. It consisted of a number of small bits of wood tipped with sulphur, and a bottle of phosphorus, all incased in a small box bearing upon one side a piece of flint. The wooden matches were to be dipped, one by one, as they were needed, into the phosphorus and then drawn across the piece of flint. The flame thus obtained was of so evanescent a character that a bit of wood whose end had been dipped in turpentine must be kept at hand in order to be immediately lighted. They were sometimes dangerous when left within the reach of children, for a drop of the phosphorus would instantly burn a hole through woolen cloth.

Tradition tells us that one of these boxes of matches was carried to school by a thoughtless pupil; all the other girls must needs examine it, and the result was so disastrous to their woolen dresses that the new invention was banished from our town.

The first patent upon friction matches issued by the United States was given to Alonzo D. Phillips of Springfield, Mass.. in the autumn of 1836, and he began their manufacture in that city. He formed a paste by mixing glue, chalk, sulphur and phosphorus, and into this the end of each match was dipped. Two years later, Stephen Merchant of South Hadley, who lived in the house now occupied by Emil Burnette, made matches six inches long, which he sold for a cent apiece. They were in cards which he had sawed out by hand, and with every box there went a folded piece of sandpaper. Someone, probably Phillips, accused him of infringing upon another man's patent, and compelled him to close up his business.

Other household conveniences had been gradually coming into use. Sanded floors had been on the whole rather troublesome. The first carpet made in the town was woven by Mrs.

Jerusha Powers, and after nearly a century of wear its colors are almost as soft and harmonious to-day as when it first came from the loom. The first ingrain carpet was purchased by Mr. Robert Brainard of Falls Woods. This was deemed such an unheard-of extravagance that six of his Methodist brethren, including the deacons, came in a body to remonstrate with him, but he defended his course with such ability that they departed, half convinced that he was in the right. His wisdom has been demonstrated by the fact that seventy years later it is now still in use, and its brilliant hues were long the pride of the neighborhood.

To-day clocks are looked upon as an essential part of the household plenishing. But when the early settlers migrated to the south of the mountain, we find no trace of these useful articles in their inventories. Their first town timepiece was a large rock at Taylor's Notch, situated on the new road to the Summit House upon Mt. Holyoke. This boulder was close to the ridge where Hadley ends and South Hadley begins. In fair weather the haymaker who thrust his pitchfork into the ground knew that when its shadow pointed to Taylor's Rock the sun must have just reached its meridian, and without the winding of the dinner horn laid down his scythe.

The oldest clock in town was made with wooden wheels and but one pointer, the hour hand. The space between the figures on the dial was divided into quarters, so that one could learn from its face the approximate time. It had no case, but was intended to be hung upon the wall.

It was not until after Shays' Rebellion that the old "Grandfather's Clock" appeared. This also was destitute of covering, and its works were nailed to the wall. One of the first of these was purchased by Gardner Preston, Senior, and he determined that his clock should have a case. He accordingly carried the works to Auraunah Collins, who lived in Fall Woods, offering to give him a cow if the latter would make a cherry case. Runy did so, and it was so handsomely carved by hand that Mr. Preston gave him "the best cow in his barn."

About 1800 a town clock was installed, the payment for

which did not appear to be forthcoming. Two years later someone devised a plan by which this expense could be met. College street had been laid out ten rods wide, and it had been the custom to build houses with the front doorstep lying exactly upon the edge of the highway. But it was now the fashion to have a yard in front of the dwelling, so a strip of land was sold upon each side of the street, wide enough for a pretty lawn, and the clock was paid for. On Woodbridge street a strip thirty-three feet wide was sold from the eastern side of the highway, while the western was left as before.

The early part of the nineteenth century was a period of transition. There were changes in dress, a fleeting glimpse of which is given in a brief extract from an old letter of a South Hadley girl, dated January 29, 1806.

"The dresses here are for the outside Pelisses, Shag Bonnets, and Woolen Tippets. The most fashionable color for the latter is scarlet. They are made of common stocking yarn, netted like the trimming of your white cloak, about a quarter of a yard broad, and a yard and a half long; they look a little like a skein of yarn tied around the neck.

"Ornamental hair combs are also fashionable. They have them from seven to ten dollars apiece."

A most welcome change in dress occurred here about 1800. It was the introduction of what were called "Top Boots." The stout buckle shoes then in common use had proven to be an insufficient protection while wading through wintry snows, and most of the yeomanry had provided themselves with leggings made of deerskin. But gentlemen like Colonel Woodbridge, who reveled in white silk stockings, needed, as they walked or rode on our sandy streets, some kind of covering as a protection against dust and rain. These coverings were called "spatterdashes," and in summertime were usually made of white linen, being fastened under the foot and extending upward nearly to the knee, and sometimes beyond it. In the winter they were generally made of broadcloth, and often handsomely embroidered.

COLLEGE STREET

SOUTH HADLEY AFTER THE REVOLUTION

The coming of the boot sounded the death knell of the smallclothes, which now gave way to the pantaloon.

Though this town had sent more than its quota of soldiers during the Revolution, it wholly disapproved of the War of 1812. A meeting was called and delegates sent to Northampton with instructions to oppose to the uttermost what they deemed a needless warfare.

At the breaking out of the Civil War, however, the patriotism of the town was unquestioned. Many of our finest young men enlisted, encouraged thereto by the inspiring words of Mr. G. Morgan Smith.

Although debarred from personal service in the army by reason of lameness, he did most effective work in the securing of volunteers.

One incident of these times appears to have escaped the notice of historians. About the time that the term "Copperhead" began to be applied to Southern sympathizers, a Mr. Henry rented the house now owned by Mrs. Thomas White. From the beginning it was said there was something mysterious connected with his coming. He lived alone and his food was sent in from outside. Callers were rarely invited to enter the house. He wrote and received an astonishing number of letters, his daily mail being greater than that of any other person in South Hadley. In the barn were stored several heavy boxes, the covers of which were carefully nailed down. A story was started that the boxes contained munitions of war awaiting shipment to the Confederacy. The excitement increased day by day, until the more impulsive among the villagers determined to mob him. The appointed evening found his yard filled with angry, clamorous men. Then Mr. Emerson Bates, with two others of a like rare courage, placed themselves in front of the doorway. "You will reach this man only over our dead bodies!" they said, firmly. At this moment the door opened and Mr. Henry appeared. "Walk in, gentlemen," he said blandly. "What is it that you wish to say to me?"

In some confusion they stammered their desire to examine the boxes. "Certainly," he said, "let hammers and chisels be brought at once." With these they proceeded to the barn, and began to unpack the boxes. They found them filled to the very bottom with scientific books, many of them being works relating to chess. Then they adjourned to the house, where Mr. Henry invited them to examine his daily mail. This revealed the fact that by means of letters he was conducting games of chess with other experts all over the country, and thus the mystery was solved.

Until after the country had gained its independence, South Hadley had but small opportunity for intellectual growth. It is stated that in 1783 there was not a public library in the whole United States, nor a permanent newspaper published in Western Massachusetts. The establishment of the Hampshire Gazette in Northampton three years later gave a new impulse to the diffusion of intelligence in this section. Our town having no postal service, a horseman went through the principal streets, his saddle bags filled with Gazettes. His coming was announced by ringing a bell in front of every house, when some member of the family was expected to go out and receive the paper. In 1802 Oliver Taylor distributed newspapers in the southern part of the town, while one of the Lymans usually covered the northern route.

Ours was certainly one of the banner towns in the establishment of libraries. In 1802 was commenced "Ye Social Library of South Hadley." This organization was kept up for forty years. In the beginning several Granby families, including the Smiths, joined in the enterprise. A meeting of the association was held once in three months: upon the third Tuesday in March, June, September, and December, at "Three of the clock." The last meeting of the year was, on account of the short days, to be at "One of the clock." A few of the titles will give some idea of the class of reading.

No. 68 was fifty-four sermons bound together.

No. 101—Seneca's Writings.

No. 113—Sermons preached after the Revolution, one of them being delivered July 29, 1784, on "Thanksgiving Day, at

SOUTH HADLEY AFTER THE REVOLUTION

the close of the American War,'' from the text—''Many times did he deliver them.''
No. 145—Military Journal of the Revolution.
No. 57—Volume of Sermons.
No. 227—View of the World.

We find among the old books a collection of Hymns written in 1759, during the French and Indian War. We cull a single stanza:

>"Deserter, to the camp return,
>Resume your former post,
>Bewail your crime, your baseness mourn,
>For yet you are not lost."

The book was republished nine times, and the tenth edition, printed after we had won our independence, bore upon its title page this exultant verse of Scripture: "Oh, sing unto the Lord a new song. . . . . His right hand and His holy arm hath gotten Him the victory."

During the first twenty years this society appears to have sold at intervals one hundred and eighty volumes, which led to a renumbering. The library was kept at the house of Mr. Jonathan Burnett, this being a convenient place for Falls Woods people; and here, as one of its patrons expressed it,

>"Four times each year these savants met
>And drew their treasures from the shelves:
>Auctioned the books that each might get
>His rights; and all might suit themselves."

The auctioning was not a sale of books, but he who bid highest upon any given volume could have the first loan of it. Weem's Life of Washington was the leading favorite, followed by the Biographies by Jared Sparks, Baxter's Saints Rest, Bunyan's Pilgrim's Progress, and a multitude of Missionary Heralds kept up the religious tone of the association.

Next in succession came the "Publick Libra," of which number 202 was published in 1812, and was entitled "A Treatise of Religious Experiences."

The "Smith Library Association" was here in 1840. Books

were taken out on the first Saturday of each month, between the hours of two and four o'clock. It was considerately added, "Books may be drawn at any other time by paying to the librarian one cent for each volume." This was in District Number One.

Time would fail to describe all of our libraries, including the Farmers, the Atheneum, and the Agricultural, most of whose books were destroyed by the burning of our fourth church, they having been stored in its basement.

The Sabbath School Library, established in 1826, has been previously alluded to.

Perhaps these helps toward a broader charity came at just the right moment. In 1802 the constable had been ordered to warn eight people, with "Their children and others under their care," to leave South Hadley within fifteen days, they having settled here without first obtaining the consent of the inhabitants. This was done in order to prevent their becoming a charge upon the town.

Yet, if any of its own citizens, through sickness or some other misfortune, had become destitute, both church and town showed a generous sympathy. In the note book of an old deacon, we find these entries:

"Minutes of the committee meeting of South Hadley Church. Voted to send Abigail a quart of wine on Communion Sunday, May 1st."

"Voted to send Abigail a pint and a half of wine next Communion Day, July third."

"Abigail" was a chronic invalid, unable to attend divine service and with but a scanty pittance of her own. The minister was expected to take one of the deacons with him and occasionally administer the sacrament of the Lord's Supper at her bedside. There were other quaint entries:

"To-day Enos Woodbridge forgot to bring his ninepence to church; Josiah Snow paid it, and he is to pay Josiah Snow's at the next contribution."

The case of Anne Hillyer would surprise a present-day overseer of the poor, Her grandfather, Timothy Hillyer, had been

FOURTH MEETING HOUSE, DESTROYED BY FIRE, 1895

SOUTH HADLEY AFTER THE REVOLUTION

one of the early settlers and had built a small, three-roomed house a few rods east of the present residence of A. P. Kjoller. He was a warm friend of Rev. Grindall Rawson, and when the latter was forcibly dismissed, showed his disapproval by absenting himself from communion for more than a year. His descendants were poor, and seventy years later the house began to show signs of decay. In 1807 the town sent its selectmen and assessors to examine the house, "And if they find it not worth repairing, they are empowered to build a new one in the same place." It was put into such good order that it lasted thirty years longer. Then David, the last of the Hillyers, took his own life, and the house was torn down by David Chandler, who inherited the place by will, the town making no claim for past expenses.

After the Revolution came the fashion of giving children what was called a double Christian name. Before that we had Comfort Smith, Bitterne Selden, Ivory Witt, Cotton White, Preserved Wood, Aristobolus Lyman, and Resolve Tuller, all these being men.

Of girls there were Philopheta Ferry, Esmereniana Preston, Sapplina Judd, Comfort Domo, and Spiddy Ferry. But during the Nineteenth Century, modern names were substituted.

CHAPTER TEN

IN THE CHIMNEY CORNER

A CENTURY ago, any South Hadley family who could secure the services of Granny Murray for the week preceding Thanksgiving Day was accounted fortunate indeed. She was received with as much state as if she were a duchess, and the best seat in the chimney corner was reserved for her during the long evenings.

The merely mechanical work of cookery was distasteful to her, and the young folks were required to chop the meat and pare the apples for the mince pies, and do what she termed the drudgery. They found her a strict disciplinarian. If the youth tired of the persistent chopping, and inquired in a plaintive tone if it were not fine enough, a high-pitched, mocking voice was sure to reply: "If you chop it too fine it will be rank pizen."

But when the day's work was ended and the household sat 'round the big fireplace, Granny Murray would tell stories of the olden time, legends that sometimes held the children spellbound at their vivid recital. She could repeat to them the story of the old witch who lived on the Belchertown Road. How one day a man, against whom the witch held a grudge, was driving to South Hadley with his ox-team. As he was nearing her house, a green frog suddenly leaped upon the neap of his cart, and on the instant the oxen stopped. Vainly the owner urged them on with voice and whip; they remained immovable. Suddenly alighting, he struck the frog a swift blow across the mouth, when it disappeared, and the team jogged along as before. Soon they passed the house of the witch, who stood at the well, washing a bloody mark from her face. "I was climbing the fence, and I fell off," she exclaimed, but he knew now from whence came the green frog.

There were stories about Enos Woodbridge, a son of the town's second minister. His baptismal name was Aeneas, and some of his oddities of speech were recorded in Holland's History of Western Massachusetts. "Uncle Enos," as he was familiarly called, had been a shrewd lad, kindly disposed, but sensitive to an unusual degree. At one time his parents, supposing that he was persisting in a falsehood, when he was actually telling the truth, administered a severe chastisement, and it may be that in order to make the impression of his punishment permanent, they followed the example of other South Hadley families, and left the culprit for part of the day in the garret, with a pitcher of water, a slice of bread, and the Bible, bidding him read while there the future doom of the wicked. From that day on the boy was changed. Only once again in his life did he ever say "yes" or "no." "Pretty likely 'tis," "Pretty likely 'tisn't," were his favorite substitutes. But many stories were told about him in the chimney corner, for he lived to be nearly eighty years old. One of the children's favorites was the following: Uncle Enos was an expert swimmer, and very fond of the water. He often strolled down to the canal village, and was always ready to lend a hand, if needed, in order to man a boat. One day after the fishing season was over, and the beach nearly deserted, some young men who saw him coming down the road agreed to play a trick upon him. Taking him into their boat they went a short distance upstream, and then informed him that unless he would say "yes" or "no," they were going to throw him overboard. When asked if he would promise to do this, he gave his tormentors to understand that it was pretty likely he would not. They lifted him up and threatened to toss him into the swirling waters. He maintained a stubborn silence. "Say yes or no," they repeated, and receiving no reply they threw him into the river. Then they waited for him to rise to the surface, when they intended to take him into the boat, if he complied with their demand. But though they waited long, they saw no signs of his reappearance. At last, in some trepidation, they called his name, telling him they were only joking and entreating him to return. Finally they became alarmed lest he had been seized with cramp; they tried to examine the bed of the river, but the turbid waters made the attempt useless. At length, with blanched faces and quivering lips, they went back to the boat-house. Meanwhile a most unusual thing had taken place, the gentle Enos had lost his temper, and, as he plunged into the water, determined to give his assailants the punishment that he felt they deserved. According to the printed statements of former years, he had been known to swim under water half way across the river. He now swam rapidly till he had reached one of the artificial islands that had been made in the river in order to be used as fishing wharves. Climbing up through the dwarf willows and coarse sedge, he concealed himself, peering through the bushes at his late companions. He heard their entreating cries for him to return, but remained in hiding till they were out of sight on their way to the landing. Then he swam to the shore and began his wet walk uptown. Near the brickyard he passed the tavern kept by the Widow Mary Pomeroy, and seeing the horse of his brother, Colonel Ruggles Woodbridge, fastened in the yard, he turned and stole around to the kitchen door. The widow immediately ushered him into a small room, and after a brief search returned with a handful of towels and a suit of clothes which had belonged to her late husband, Major Pomeroy; this she bade him wear while his own dripping garments were hung to dry in front of the kitchen fireplace. Hardly had the change been effected, when his late companions were seen coming slowly up the road. They, too, had observed the horse of Colonel Woodbridge, and approaching the front door, asked to see him. Enos again retired into the little room, and his brother, having previously heard the whole story, met them in the hall, determined to give them a lesson they would never forget. They knew that in those times the death penalty awaited murderers, and there were few of the modern methods of evading it. Trembling in every limb, the young men confessed their guilt and begged for clemency. But their eyes quailed before the stern glance of Colonel Woodbridge, as he answered, "The law must take its course. My brother was an inoffensive man, who had never harmed you, and it is clearly my duty to deliver you up to the officers of justice." Their prayers and protestations that they were only in fun melted the kind heart of Uncle Enos. The door of the little room had been left ajar. It was now pushed

FERRY AT THE FOOT OF MOUNT HOLYOKE

open, and a familiar voice said: "Pretty likely somebody'll stretch a rope." The repentant young men said afterward that "Pretty likely" were the sweetest words they ever heard, and thenceforth treated him with grateful respect.

A new generation, however, arose who showed him less consideration. His evenings were generally spent at the tavern of Deacon Joseph White, this being the usual rallying point for those who, like Enos, were good church members. Moreover, he and Jack White were inseparable friends. One day the latter came to him saying that a party of travelers had just engaged lodging for the night. Some of the youths who had annoyed Enos laid a wager with the guests that they would bring in a man who could be neither bribed, coaxed, nor forced into saying either "yes" or "no." The stakes had been placed in competent hands. "And now, Uncle Enos, "continued Jack, "you can get even with those young men by just this once saying "yes" and "no" in answer to their questions, and if they lose their money, they will perhaps in future let you alone." The event justified this prediction, and the discomfited young folks afterwards gave Enos a wide berth.

Our town has its "Dolly Woodbridge Chapter of the Daughters of the American Revolution," and the name keeps in mind one who was for many years a leading lady in this place. Little Dorothy, always known as Dolly, was born May 2, 1763, just at the close of a long and desolate French and Indian war, in which her father, Lieutenant John Woodbridge, had spent years of active service. He was the tenth of that name in direct succession, but the nine who preceded him had all been ministers of the Gospel, and he would doubtless have followed their example had not the exegencies of the war called him into the field. His was a true patriotism; for he entered the lowest rank of the soldiery; but his ability and worth were soon apparent, and his promotion rapid, eventually reaching the position of major.

After the completion of the town's second meeting house, he appears to have purchased the old one, which he moved a short distance to the north, and turned at right angles to its former position. As the meeting house had never had a chimney, the removal was accomplished with little difficulty, and the street had been laid out of such great width that the site of Judson Hall was then a part of the highway. The building was remodeled, and its two tenements were occupied, one by Lieutenant Woodbridge and the other by John Chandler. Here little Dolly was born; but her father soon sold the dwelling and moved to the Rawson parsonage, where he spent the next nineteen years. At his death, Dolly, now a young woman nearly twenty years of age, seems to have taken into her special love and care her little seven-year-old brother, named Benjamin Ruggles in honor of her uncle, Coloned Woodbridge. He became a minister, but at the last came back to South Hadley, where he died at nearly the same time as his sister Dolly. There was a double funeral, and brother and sister were buried side by side in one wide grave. Dolly Woodbridge certainly combined in herself the leading traits of her ancestors. The patrician pride of the Earl of Dudley reappeared in her delicate gowns, for she was in summertime constantly habited in white when she entered the big square pew on the minister's right hand on Sunday mornings. And her dress was edged at the neck and wrists with fine embroidery, or feathery lace, all the work of her own hands. Her bonnet, a Dunstable straw, and still preserved in the historical room, was also trimmed with white, and in very warm weather she changed her dress during the noon intermission, appearing at the afternoon service in dainty, fresh attire. "She was aristocratic to the very tips of her fingers," said an old person in describing her, "but she was never haughty and repellent in her manners, and was always kind to the poor. She had all the dignity of her grandfather, the minister, and was never known to exhibit any signs of ill temper." She was a descendant of the famous John Elliott, and had inherited the same earnest spirit of religious devotion. No storm kept her from her place in the sanctuary. "The minister, the deacon, and Dolly Woodbridge are sure to be at church," was a common remark. She was not addicted to housework, and her fair, white hands and

THE FIRST MEETING HOUSE, NOW USED AS A DWELLING

good eyesight enabled her to do fine needlework even to extreme old age. She died in May, 1844.

About ten years before this event a strange episode had taken place in the religious life of the community. Mormonism had sent some of its advance guard to South Hadley, with an evident intention of proselyting the inhabitants of the town. They did not call themselves Mormons, but Perfectionists, claiming that they had attained sinless perfection. They did not openly avow the doctrine of polygamy, but were believed to practice it. They baptized only in the name of Jesus, the rest of the Trinity being rarely spoken of in their meetings. The large woman who led the singing was named Polly, and was known in town as Polly Jesus. Their preacher was accused by our own church of being an excommunicated minister from a Congregational pastorate.

In 1818, Israel Lyman had built a brick house near Rock Ferry, and its kitchen furnished a commodious place for the Sunday services of the Mormonites, who soon gathered adherents all the way from South Hadley Falls to Hockanum. A prayer meeting was held one afternoon in each week, and did much toward spreading their influence in this vicinity.

From the late R. O. Dwight's account of their Sabbath Day services, we quote the following: "The large room, on week days a kitchen, was now arranged with rows of chairs on three sides, leaving a large space vacant in the center." . . . . "There was the brooding stillness of a Quaker meeting. At last the very large woman arose, stepped into the vacant space and began a solemn march. Others joined in the silent promenade around the floor until all who felt moved to take part had done so. Then the men and women formed lines facing one another, and in Shaker style began a shuffling dance toward each other, singing, under lead of the large woman's clear and powerful voice, strange psalms to stirring tunes. Gradually the dance grew faster, forward and then back again, and the singing louder, until those who came to look on were drawn by the exciting scenes to join this strange people, and dance and sing with the best of them. This performance was continued so long as strength and breath remained, and then the Mormon meeting abruptly ended."

As this sect gained in numbers, it was proposed that a church should be formed and a building erected for public worship. Subscriptions were solicited and obtained for the furtherance of this plan. Upon this our own church became alive to its responsibilities. Rev. Mr. Boies, assisted by Rev. B. R. Woodbridge (the brother of Dolly Woodbridge) engaged in an active campaign against Mormonism. Eight members of our church were excommunicated, and others were persuaded to forsake the new sect. The Perfectionist leaders, and a part of their disciples, left town. One of the latter returned, saying that she had received a revelation directing her to go home. She married happily, and in her old age used to say that she had never regretted coming back.

Later on others were excommunicated from our church on account of their change in religious belief, and for persistently absenting themselves from communion.

A spirited warfare of words was carried on, an example of which is subjoined.

In his letter, Rev. Mr. Boies accuses the Mormonites of reviling their fellow church members, and calling them "Children of the Devil," also of despising the House of God, denying the Sabbath to be Holy time, and pretending to be endowed with the power of working miracles. He denounces their belief as "The doctrines of the devil," and concludes his letter in these words: "Think, oh, think of the dreadful apostasy you have commenced! But should you disregard this friendly admonition the church has but one duty to perform, awful as it is. It is to cut you off from the congregation of the Lord, and leave you in the hand of that God whom you have deeply dishonored, and before whom you must soon stand to answer for the deeds done here in the body. In behalf of the Church, A. Boies, Pastor."

In reply to this letter Miss A.——— wrote back: "You say you have one more duty to perform, 'awful as it is,' that is, to cut us off. It is not at all awful to *us*. I cut myself off months ago, and have no longer any fellowship with the unfruitful works of darkness. And if I must tell you the truth, I care nothing what steps you take, for I feel the fire of God's love burning in my soul, while writing Glory! Glory!! When I turn my eyes towards you, it looks like midnight darkness, while the candle of the Lord shines upon *us*."

Hardly had the Mormon heresies ceased to disturb, when a new cause of disquietude arose. The Millerites, in order to disseminate their principles, were holding meetings all over the country. Their leader, after careful study of the Old Testament prophesies, believed that the time for their fulfillment had arrived, and that the end of the world was near. There is still preserved in town one of the tiny slips of paper distributed here at that time. Upon it is printed this inscription:

"How long shall be the vision? Unto 2,300 days. Then shall the sanctuary be cleansed. * * * Dan. VIII 13, 14. Began B. C. 457, ends in 1843."

In a private journal, one of our citizens thus records his own experiences:

"In 1843 began the great Millerite excitement. Everybody was talking about the destruction of the world which William Miller was predicting would happen that year. This beautiful world was surely going to be burned up, and the Judgment Day would soon be here. Miller was going to preach at Chicopee Falls, and I, with other South Hadley people, went down to hear him. He preached in a large tent, which was full of hearers, and as it was a hot day, he preached in his shirt sleeves. He was a large, stout man, and of course felt the heat. I do not remember many particulars of his discourse, but it was exciting. 'Many believed on him there.' A collection was taken to pay expenses, and 'for the good of the cause.' People were urged to give something if they had no money—I saw rings, earrings, and other articles contributed. Before the meeting groups of men could be seen discussing the subject, quoting from the Bible, and scaring us youngsters. All that year and afterwards, I could not see the sky red without fearing the end of the world was at hand. Once I drove two seminary girls to visit in Brimfield. When we reached Ludlow, it was red in the south, and a shower came up, and, oh! how frightened we were. We stopped at a farm house and begged to be allowed to stay over night. The next morning we started early; the clouds in the east were red, and my scare continued. The girls were older than I and probably had a little more sense. We arrived safely at Brimfield, stayed a day or two, and got back to South Hadley, with the world still on top." * * * The record closes with these words: "They had been taught by the Bible and the preachers that the world was surely going to be burned up sometime, and they did not know but it might be then. It is not strange that some ceased trying to lay up treasures on earth, stopped sowing and reaping, gave their lands away, and made their ascension robes."

The events referred to in the last paragraph made some changes in the town. Several of its citizens, in order to prove the sincerity of their belief in Millerism, sold their farms for a few dollars, and were afterwards compelled to become day laborers in order to support themselves and their families. Finally a part of them went West, where it was said land was so cheap it was almost to be had for the asking, and they thus succeeded in retrieving their fortunes.

During the summer of 1843, whenever the setting sun went down in a flood of crimson light, people were wont to assemble in the Old Cemetery, with the thought that they would be found upon consecrated ground. Some brought their ascension robes with them. These were usually white, and were made long like a riding skirt. One South Hadley girl confided to her schoolmates the fact that, unknown to her mother, she had run a gathering string through the hem of her ascension robe, so that when she was taken up through the air she could draw it closely beneath her feet.

Evening meetings for prayer and discussion of the subject were held from house to house, though the prank of two mischievous boys made a slight interruption. One of the brethren usually had much to say about Gabriel's trumpet which would announce the dissolution of all things. One night a roguish boy climbed to the apex of the roof, and standing close

THE FIRST MOUNTAIN HOUSE ON MOUNT HOLYOKE

to the chimney of the house where the meeting was to be held, stood waiting ready to blow a tin horn when the signal should be given. Round his wrist was tied one end of a long cord, the other end being in the hand of his accomplice, who lurked below. After a time, nothing having been said in regard to the Angel Gabriel, one man, in loud exhortation, told his auditors that "The end of the world draweth nigh." An instant after the blast of the horn was heard, and the men sprang to their feet, while the women screamed. In the confusion that ensued the boys escaped without discovery.

The influence of this doctrine remained in town for years. Clouds flaming with scarlet hues would send the frightened children home from berrying excursions. But after a time tranquillity was again restored, and matters went on in the old way.

In 1825 the old soldiers of the Revolution (many of whom still remembered the battle of Bunker Hill) were made thrice welcome in every chimney corner. For the Marquis de Lafayette, who was then on a visit to this country, had been invited to lay the cornerstone of the monument which now marks the site of that memorable battle.

It was learned that the French General, on his way from Albany to Boston, would pass through Northampton and South Hadley. His progress through the state was a triumphal march, towns and cities vying with each other in the splendor of their ovations. No courier having been sent in advance to announce his coming, there was in South Hadley but brief time for preparation. It was known that in order to reach Boston on the 16th of June, he must be in Belchertown by the evening of the 14th. Therefore everyone knew that on Tuesday, at the latest, the Friend of America would honor this town by passing through it. Young and old were up at dawn, luncheon baskets were packed, flower beds despoiled of their choicest treasures, and the address of welcome prepared for the occasion was rehearsed for the last time. Before noon a motley procession was en route for Rock Ferry. In the van were ox carts with layers of clean straw, upon which the children were huddled, while the father and mother were enthroned upon the driver's seat. At intervals came the long farm wagon, drawn by a span of horses, and filled with young people, who flaunted showy banners of welcome. The elite of the town started a little later in their chaises and high-topped narrow carriages, one of which had formerly belonged to a Governor of Massachusetts.

Four years earlier the men of this vicinity had determined that a house should be placed on the summit of Mt. Holyoke, and for this purpose they planned to have a Building Bee on the anniversary of the Battle of Bunker Hill. In 1821, the 17th of June came on Sunday, and they were accordingly obliged to postpone the matter until the following day. On Monday morning, therefore, they appeared with boards, nails, and the necessary tools. The corner posts and larger timbers of the house were then cut down and hewn near the site previously selected. This first house could be approached only by persons on horseback or on foot. The horses trained to mountain climbing could thread the narrow pathway as far as the last steep ascent. From here people must pull themselves up by catching hold of the branches of trees, or the young saplings that bordered the path. It was decided to escort Lafayette to the Mountain House, in order to show him the beautiful valley of the Connecticut, which lay like a panorama below. Mrs. Abby Wright Allen of South Hadley had written seven verses commencing:

"Great Friend of Mankind,
Honored Guest of the Nation,"

and this poem was to be recited by a number of little boys while the General partook of refreshments. He could choose from the following list:

'Choice Jamaica Spirits.
"St. Croix Rum.
"Cogniac Brandy.
"Holland Gin.
"Cherry Rum.
"Brandy.
"Spanish Segars, with other refreshments generally desired."

"THE OLD SLEIGH"

At two o'clock in the afternoon Lafayette left Northampton attended by a military escort from that place. Reaching the Connecticut River, he crossed at Rock Ferry, and when his carriage drove from the boat he found the townspeople waiting to strew flowers along his pathway. They saw before them a pair of eloquent brown eyes, that seemed to look you through and through, while above them was not the silvery locks of old age, but a wig of dark hair. His long and slender hands were still delicate, though his face was that of a man in health and strength. The grace and courtesy of his manners while bowing from right to left, as the carriage passed, won for him a lasting place in the memory of those who saw him.

At the turn of the road a committee of reception were watching his approach in order to extend to him an invitation to visit the mountain. But it was now nearly the middle of the afternoon, and young girls dressed in white were already lined up on the Belchertown Common awaiting his arrival; there was no time left for even a short excursion.

An eye witness in describing the scene ended with the sorrowful words: "The General's carriage turned south and was soon lost to view."

For many years after this all needful supplies for the little Mountain House were conveyed up the narrow bridle path by a single horse. The water was brought up in india rubber sacks, each one holding five gallons; these were placed in canvas panniers and fastened across the back of the horse. In 1851 a wagon road was constructed up to the summit and a new two-story house erected a little north of the former one. The timbers for this building were drawn up by teams, and it sometimes needed two yoke of oxen and a pair of stout horses in order to carry a load up the steep pitches. Three years later a single track railroad was built up the last ascent; it had a "length of 600 feet and a rise of 365." The car used on this track was made from the bodies of two sleighs, fitted together to form its main part. "This was propped up in a horizontal position at an angle to the car truck, which ran parallel to the rails. A single rope was attached to the upper end, and a horse beneath the house furnished the motive power." As this was a new idea (being probably the first railway of its kind in the world), there were crowds of visitors, even from great distances. When the car rolled up the steep ridge, not far from the summit, a view of surpassing beauty met the eye. Finally "the car and its occupants came up through an opening in the base of the Mountain House and stopped just when the body of the old sleigh was even with the floor."

Near the foot of Mount Holyoke, but a little farther south, lay one of the town's first ferries, which was established by the County Court in 1755. Its landing was close to the palisades in Hockanum, and from this fact it derived its name "Rock Ferry." J. G. Holland, who in his youth was for a time assistant ferryman, has described the view from the summit of Holyoke in these words:
"At my feet

> The ferry boat, diminished to a toy,
> With automatic diligence conveyed
> Its puppet passengers between the shores
> That hemmed its enterprise; and one low barge
> With white, square sail, bore northward languidly,
> The slow and scanty commerce of the stream."

A. M. Lyman, a grandson of Israel Lyman, the ferryman, states in his letter that the latter "carried on quite a business in connection with a large farm, including the running of the ferry, a broom and shoe shop, tannery, still, etc. Situated beside the river were about forty acres of fine meadow land, which has since been washed away. The road from Rock Ferry to Hockanum was called Gate Hill. In old times there was a fence on the town line in order to keep the cattle, that everyone in Hadley turned loose to pasture, from straying over the line. A gate was kept near the Hockanum burying ground, and everyone that passed that way must open and close it. On Sundays and holidays, boys tended this gate."

Across the present highway there existed at this time a barrier of rocks called the mountain wall, which made even a

PASS OF THERMOPYLAE

THE FRANKLIN STOVE

IN THE CHIMNEY CORNER 199

rude cart track impossible. The road was thus compelled to make a wide circuit, running northwest of Eugene Lyman's house. Israel Lyman determined to remedy this evil. The letter continues: "Grandfather and his boys, with the help of the neighbors, cut the road through the rocks. It was done for the most part by building fires upon the surface of the rock, and when well heated, pouring on cold water, thus taking off a little at a time." This opening, then wide enough for a wagon to pass through, was a favorite resort of the seminary girls, who named it the Pass of Thermopylæ. It was then described as having "a high rock ledge on one side, and a good-sized cliff on the other." But our town fathers have long ago sacrificed beauty to utility; dynamite and blasting powder have done their work well, and now only memory or a vivid imagination can replace the former romantic grandeur of the spot.

In the front rank of those who climbed Mt. Holyoke on the day when General Lafayette passed through South Hadley was doubtless the President of the Lazy Men's Court. This was a society which had its beginning on Hadley street, then known only as "Lubber's Hole." It was not the object of this organization to inculcate habits of industry, but quite the reverse. All members who were guilty of any unnecessary exertion were punished by fines, and each was expected to report any case of this kind that might come under his own observation. A single instance of the method of conducting their sessions will suffice. One of the members was accused of having run violently down the hill leading from the park to the house of Samuel Judd, now owned by F. A. Loomer. The point of the story is lost in the telling, for the steep pitch which at that time led from the village is unrecognizable in the graded hill of to-day. After the testimony of the witnesses had been taken, the judge asked the offender in a stern voice what excuse he could offer why judgment should not be pronounced against him. He replied that the facts as stated were true, but he found it was harder to stop than to keep on running, and so carried out the principles of the society. His discharge was immediately ordered. The next culprit, having attempted on a warm summer's day to jump across the brook near-by, missed the farther bank and fell back into the water. When permitted by the judge to speak in his own defense he asserted that he had broken none of the rules of the order. "It was a sultry day and I wanted to sit in the water in order to keep cool. It is my privilege to choose such a place for myself if I find it contributes to my comfort, and no man has a right to interfere." "True, true," murmured the judge, "let his fine be remitted."

Aged people frowned upon these frivolities, and shook their heads at the attempt to introduce the burning of charcoal as a means of heating the South Hadley houses. They said it was not much like the olden days; then every week a horse dragged into the kitchen a big backlog, so heavy that they could hardly roll it into the fireplace. But the dear old grandmother, sitting in the chimney corner, whispered softly to herself, "Old times are always best."

Used by Permission of Silver, Burdett & Co., Publishers
DRAWING IN THE BACK-LOG

CHAPTER ELEVENTH

SOUTH HADLEY FALLS

HISTORIANS tell us that the first navigable canal in the United States was situated in that part of South Hadley originally called Taylor's Field. It was begun during the first decade after the Revolution, and soon impressed its name upon the thriving little settlement at its base, which was for nearly half a century known as the Canal Village. It was looked upon as a wonder, being between two and three miles in length, and a portion of it is still visible from the Head Road, a highway so named because it skirted the head of the canal.

Visitors flocked from far and near to see this new method of diverting a part of the river for the purpose of conveying boats past the rapids. The well-to-do farmers came on horseback, their wives sitting on pillions behind them, while the poor yeomanry rode in ox carts. At rare intervals a two-wheeled chaise appeared, from which looked forth the serious face of some neighboring minister, but the proudest equipage of all was the long wagon with paneled sides, wherein the young people disported themselves. It was called a Thoroughbrace, and had no springs, the body being suspended by leather straps. It jolted over the rough roads most unmercifully, but little cared they.

All found it a most attractive spot. The towpath beside the canal was fringed with lofty sycamores, and towering maples, dotted here and there with hemlock green. Their lower branches were festooned with sprays of wild clematis, and the clinging tendrils of the frost grape. In every crevice where they could find a foothold, red and yellow honeysuckles were nodding to the ferns, while above them, later on, the bittersweet would do its best to replace their lively hues.

It was easy work towing through the canal, requiring but a single horse and its driver, while in order to bring boats up the river from Willimansett to the foot of the South Hadley Falls, it was necessary to use in addition several pairs of oxen.

Freshets and other leveling processes of nature have already filled up a great part of the canal.

For more than half a century before the establishment of this new waterway, boards, lumber, and sometimes produce, had been brought down from Northampton and Hadley upon rafts, or freight boats, and were landed at the mouth of Stony Brook. From here they were carted across the fields to a point just below the free bridge.

This trespass upon private lands aroused violent opposition on the part of the owners, who perhaps failed to consider that if the circuitous highways already laid out were followed it would lead them through South Hadley Center, thus more than doubling the distance. From this cause arose the most bitter animosities between neighbors. One of the first innkeepers in Falls Woods, a bustling, energetic man, combined the three offices of captain, landlord and teamster.

One day in December, 1744, wishing to drive across the field of an impetuous young man, who owned a large section of land in this region, the Captain began taking down the fence in order to obtain an entrance. This action being seen by the owner, he was promptly ordered to desist. An exciting contest ensued, a contest which was not wholly confined to words. The matter was carried before the Church, the usual tribunal for adjusting such cases.

Public opinion seemed to favor the land owner, and it was expected that the Captain would make a public confession, but nothing was farther from his intentions. He was recorded as having been "Guilty of a breach of gospel rule, in his violently pulling down, or attempting to pull down, the fence in order to force his way through with his team."

The matter was kept in abeyance until the following June, when the Captain called an ex-parte council at his own expense. The ministers came in the afternoon and were ready to begin work at about six o'clock the next morning. Notice of this meeting had been given out on the previous Sabbath, and all members of the church were invited to be present. This being the

THE CANAL VILLAGE

very busiest season of the year, there was likely to be but a meager attendance.

The shrewdness of the Captain was now made manifest, for the famous Jonathan Edwards, of Northampton, was a member of the council. He had always been a firm friend of the Rev. Grindall Rawson, while the land owner was one of the young men who about three years before had forcibly dragged our first minister from his pulpit—possibly the celebrated divine was not allowed to forget this fact, for certain it is that the verdict of the council said decidedly that the church had no right to require a public acknowledgment from the Captain. The church was compelled to acquiesce in this decision. The Captain was once more allowed to partake of the Lord's Supper, and afterwards it was made one of our by-laws that "If any man communed with another, knowing of unchristian conduct on his part, he could not afterward complain of him."

Ten years later we find the Captain obtaining permission by vote of the town to make an agreement "with several persons to cross their lands with lumber in the Falls Field and Taylor's Field."

Within a few years after these events South Hadley was asked by some of the towns north of us to lay out a new road through Falls Woods, but little attention was paid to this request.

In 1766 the selectmen offered to give William Taylor three pounds if he would make and maintain a good cart bridge over Buttery Brook, near its mouth, he agreeing to keep the same in good repair for ten years.

It is claimed that North Main street was the first highway laid out in that part of the town, and for nearly a century it was known as the Carrying Way, because it was the one used for the transportation of lumber.

In the early times the leading industry of South Hadley Falls was the fisheries. Every spring thousands upon thousands of shad, salmon and bass came up from the ocean and ascended the Connecticut River, sometimes as far as Vermont. Shad were at first so plentiful they were either sold at a cent apiece or thrown back into the river, and eating them was looked upon as the badge of poverty.

An old gentleman once told the author that when he was a boy his family used them as an article of food and sometimes sent him out to catch them, but he was so much ashamed of his errand that if he saw anyone coming he hid the shad among the bushes. There was one place, however, where they were most certainly welcome.

During the Revolutionary War our town sent to the army its full quota of beef and pork, and we are told that during their season hundreds of shad were barreled and forwarded to an appreciative soldiery.

Salmon were looked upon as a more valuable species of fish, and we find from the account book of one of our old school teachers that in 1762 he paid for them at the rate of two pence per pound.

Since there was always a dearth of fresh meat in the summer time, every man was expected to have in his cellar one barrel of salt pork, two of corned beef, and a keg of salt salmon.

The shad and salmon were caught in what were called sweep nets, which often were three or four hundred feet in length. These meshes were usually five inches square in order that the small fishes might escape. The method of using this net is thus described by an old fisherman:

"Swinging out from the bank in their boat, the four men who drew the net went straight out for about twenty rods, then turning almost at right angles they went down stream about ten rods more, and then swung again toward shore.

"All this time the hurrying current was carrying along the net, and the fish, which had been seeking the upper waters of the river, found themselves suddenly fenced in. Shouting to the shoreman to keep his end of the net steady, the men in the boat set toward the shore until the net took on the shape of the letter 'U.'

"The men in their hurry to haul in jumped into the shallow water near the bank, and holding down the lead line as well as they could, grasped the dripping network with its living freight and pulled it ashore."

During the late springtime one of the favorite evening amusements at the Canal Village was going eeling. The lampreys came up the river with the salmon and shad, but they could ascend the rapids more easily than other kinds of fish. They would dart suddenly forward, then by means of their curiously-shaped mouths and power of suction, attach themselves to a rock, where they remained suspended until sufficiently rested for a second effort. This process being several times repeated brought them to the head of the falls. They were deemed unwelcome intruders, for their clinging mouths made them a menace to other fishes larger than themselves. As an article of food they were generally despised in South Hadley, though in towns away from the river they were sometimes valued.

A brief description of one of these excursions through the rapids at South Hadley Falls will perhaps give some idea of its difficulties. Landlord Smith had offered to take one of his guests eeling with him.

"All was ready at last and Smith, having placed his lantern upon a box for a beacon, pushed off the boat. A sudden curve of the river at this point formed quite an eddy, where the still water contrasted strangely with the rushing current in the channel. Into this current they pushed the boat, heading it carefully up the stream and keeping as near the shore as possible. Then began the struggle. With poles in hand they stood opposite one another, the landlord being on the river side, and pushed with might and main. The noise of rushing water allowed no conversation had the labor of poling given time, but Davis now and then heard his companion shouting some unintelligible words of caution or encouragement.

"After a time they came under a steep bank which rose fifteen or twenty feet from the water. Passing this in their toilsome course, they reached at length a large rock which sloped to the water's edge and glistened in the moonlight. Just north of this rose another, higher and steeper, which projected into the river. The boat was pushed into the little eddy below this rock and their goal was reached.

"The tavernkeeper having fastened the boat, said: 'There, Mr. Davis, is what I call my pork barrel. The Simsbury and Suffield folks swap pork even for them, barrel for barrel. If you want to see something to surprise you, look here!' and he pointed with proud satisfaction to the lower side of the rock. Davis looked as desired, and at first could make nothing of the strange spectacle.

"On the surface of the rock, along its whole circuit, brown and white streamers, one or two feet in length, were fastened by one end to the rock. Not one dozen nor dozens, but hundreds of them, so thick together that no pressure could crowd them closer.

"The tavernkeeper having enjoyed for a moment his guest's astonishment, said, with proud significance, 'Them's lampers.' 'But what are they doing there?' asked Davis. 'Why, they are laying up for the night, gone to bed and asleep like other honest folks. You see, they have been following the shad around all day, sucking up the spawn where it is laid in the soft sand, and at night they just catch hold of a rock and go to sleep; this appears to be a favorite place for them.'

"By this time Smith had thrown off his coat, rolled up his sleeves, and put on a pair of coarse mittens. Kneeling in the bottom of the boat, he reached over both hands and, grasping an eel in each, threw them behind him into the boat. * * *

"The boat having been loaded and loosened, was brought close under the rock and the order given to push off. Davis' vigorous push sent them well into the stream before the current seized them. * * * But the most skillful will sometimes slip, and it is not therefore to be wondered at that when the boat was swiftly approaching the head of the island nearest the shore, as Mr. Smith stepped hastily to one side his foot slipped and threw him into the river with his cargo in close company. When, like an ancient river god, he had risen from his watery bed, he found that he had been swept around immediately in front of the fish house. His pole came thump against him, and, with its assistance, he waded ashore. As he reached land he saw Davis drawing the boat up on the beach, and made his way through the coarse grass and willows to the spot."

The lampreys continued to reach the upper level above the falls until about the middle of the last century. Being such expert climbers, they were able to ascend the new fishway, a feat impossible for shad, as was discovered later on.

As late as 1848, parties of men from Connecticut came annually to the Canal Village, boarding at the house of the Widow Judd, and remaining sometimes two weeks or more for the purpose of eeling.

Early in the nineteenth century numberless sturgeons decided to spend the summer in Vermont or Massachusetts, and passed this town in their ascent of the Connecticut River. They were a large, coarse fish, often eight or ten feet in length, and so tough they were considered unfit for food. But we read that in 1809 Tom Chandler, an eccentric and independent person, "took home some sturgeon to eat, being the first man among those acquainted with the circumstances who ever tried the experiment."

Later the fashion penetrated to the Canal Village, and a fish pound, or sturgeon coop, was installed. When the water in the river was low a semi-circular wall of stones was built with an opening left at the center for the entrance of the fish. A line of upright timbers was placed at intervals across this opening, leaving room for the sturgeon to enter between them. This huge trap was baited with their favorite kinds of food, and when once within its enclosure the fish were apt to swim around and around without noticing the means of escape.

A well-known lawyer, whose boyhood and youth were spent in South Hadley Falls, used to tell how one Sunday morning word was brought that a school of sturgeon had entered the pound. People flocked to the shore and the fishermen decided that since they had come in on the Lord's Day, they should be given to the villagers. Reverence for the Sabbath would not permit them to be taken out until the following day. In the meantime there was some danger of their escape, but the minister bade them trust in the Lord and He would give them the desire of their hearts, and the next morning found his words verified, for the fish had remained in the pound.

About 1800 a society was organized and christened the United Enterprise Fishing Company. After a time, however, it was said that many of the members did not live up to their name. It was charged that in the morning they were usually late at the wharves, and that after each haul they took a long rest, on the plea that they must wait for the fish to collect in the eddies. This led some facetious individual to recall the words of Solomon, "Go to the ant, thou sluggard, consider her ways and be wise," and he named them the Old Sluggard Company, a title which clung to it throughout the rest of its existence, yet its members were not inactive, the most energetic one being appointed salesman and occupying a box upon the beach.

No sooner were the fish landed than they were disposed of to the crowd of waiting purchasers. Salmon were in great demand, the supply being far less plentiful than during the preceding century. Shad also had increased in price, being sold in 1816 at ten cents apiece. They so greatly outnumbered all other kinds of fish it was made a rule that if a man purchased a twelve-pound salmon he must also buy twelve shad, or the bargain would not be closed.

Another sluggard, who was considered a good accountant, was placed in charge of the bar at the old fish house. The latter was an unpainted, one-roomed structure, standing near the junction of the Beach Road and the highway leading to Granby. Across the beams within this old fish house were placed oars, poles and boat hooks, while one side of the room was piled with nets and other fishing gear. Upon the opposite side stood the bar, a rough wooden counter stretched across the corner. Ready at hand were toddy stick and flip iron, with mug, bowl, pitcher and glass to be used when needed. The wall behind the counter served as day book and ledger, for upon it was written daily each man's account. The fishermen were not paid until the end of the season, but at that time all indebtedness would be canceled.

Sometimes the sluggards, between the hauls of their long sweep net, manned a boat in order to ascend the rapids with their scoop nets. This was somewhat dangerous, but was generally attended with success, and the boat returned well laden. At the close of the day's work the last boatload was retained for the use of the sluggards, the division of which was effected in the following manner: One of their number was blindfolded and the fish were placed in as many piles as there were men to share them. The blindfolded man was then led to each pile and named the person to whom it should be assigned. This was looked upon as a very honest and impartial method of division.

As Hartford and the towns lower down established fisheries of their own, the number of shad and salmon that ascended the river to the Canal Village became less, and it was thought best to build fishing wharves near the present site of the Free Bridge. These wharves, some half dozen in number, were artificial islands made of timbers and huge stones; they were wedge-shaped, a hundred feet in length, and were placed one hundred feet apart, and parallel to the shore. The freshets soon gave them a coating of soil sufficient to sustain a scanty vegetation, coarse grass and stunted willows. From these points of vantage the old sluggards, armed probably with long poles, frightened back the fish that were seeking to enter the rapids, thus making them an easy prey to the men below.

Portions of these old wharves are still visible near the bridge in low water.

In apple-blossom time, the Canal Village was a busy spot with throngs of people passing to and fro, but in winter the spirit of repose seemed to have fallen upon the little hamlet. When the Connecticut was well fettered with ice and snow, ox teams from Hadley would call at some house near the landing to inquire if it were safe to cross the river with a load on their way to Springfield. The housekeeper could always give a prompt reply to this question. A basin of milk was kept in front of the buttery window, and until that became solid to the very bottom of the dish the ice bridge was looked upon as unsafe.

The long winter evenings were spent by the men of the village round the big fireplaces in the taverns. Here they related to one another their experiences in hunting and fishing, and a vivid imagination must have stood sponsor for some of these tales. Or perhaps they told stories about witches and ghosts, incited thereto by reports of a new Witch Hole discovered in the Slipe, a hole so deep that the longest pole could not touch the bottom, but would be drawn down by some invisible power till it disappeared from sight. Geological kettles and quicksands were not at that time as well understood as they now are.

Among the chaos of tales that have survived the years, one ghost story was deemed more authentic than any other of its kind. It was thus told by an old resident:

"You see, just after old Elder Pendleton gave the burying ground to the Baptists, there was a fellow with a mighty fine horse put up one night at Colonel Lambie's tavern. Before he had finished his supper, along comes the High Sheriff, and claps onto him for horse stealing. Well, it was too late to take him off to Northampton jail that night, so they waited until morning. But before morning he had taken poison and died. So he was the first person that was buried there. Some fellows who have been along the river dark nights have seen him streaking along the bank on horseback, looking over his shoulder as if he was followed. When he gets to Catamount Hollow, he puts up the brook into the woods. I never seen him myself."

At the outset the fishermen's tales generally had some foundation in fact. An old sluggard would describe the manner in which a salmon ascended the dam. At the first trial it failed. Then it went down stream and came back for a fresh attempt, which would almost enable it to accomplish the feat. But failing in this, it went still further back, and swimming rapidly up stream, with the momentum thus acquired, it leaped upward, clearing the dam by several feet, and calmly proceeded on its way northward.*

As the evening waned, the stories grew more and more improbable, till the climax was reached when some ancient fisherman told how his grandfather said that in Revolutionary days the shad were so thick in the river during the month of May that one day, wishing to cross to the island, and not being able to find a boat, he borrowed a pair of snow shoes and walked safely over upon the backs of the fishes.

Nor were the fabled exploits of our hunters less marvelous. The cornfields of South Hadley had been devastated by crows and blackbirds. The former, instead of migrating, spent their winters on the south side of Mount Tom, and were invariably present at the first planting. They bade open defiance to the ragged effigies that had added to the English vocabulary the word "scarecrow," and continued to ravage the crops till the town in despair offered as bounty a certain fixed sum for the old crows and a smaller amount for the younger ones. This gave rise to so much controversy in regard to the dividing line between the two classes that a committee was appointed in order to settle these claims.

The favorite boast of the hunters was that upon one occasion a young man saw twelve of these thieves sitting side by side on the branch of a large tree. Taking careful aim, he sent a charge of shot which split the bark of the branch lengthwise. The concussion widened the cleft for an instant, just long enough for the startled birds to spread their wings for flight, but closing quickly enough to make them prisoners, their toes being held firmly in the bark of the tree. The storyteller probably closed with the same statement as a former narrator, that he had not himself witnessed the sight.

---

*The salmon has the power of swimming with great velocity; of stemming rapid rivers, and of jumping over dams and waterfalls of considerable height. It has been known to spring fourteen feet out of water, and to describe a curve of at least twenty feet in order to surmount a cascade. If not successful at first, it perseveres until it succeeds, unless the obstruction is insurmountable.".
—Appleton's Condensed Encyclopedia, page 520.

About 1830 a company was organized, and steamboats built, for the navigation of the Connecticut. These boats were from sixty to ninety feet in length, and were capable of carrying a hundred persons, though they seldom had that number of passengers. They were towed through the canal at South Hadley Falls, on their way to and from Greenfield.* They were very narrow, being on the average but fifteen feet wide; this led a facetious passenger to remark that he always kept on the middle of the deck lest the boat should tip over. The cabin might have been fitted up for Tom Thumb, it was so small, but the little turkey-red curtains hanging loosely at the windows gave the one touch of brightness to the dingy place. The engines were crude affairs and not to be relied upon in these primitive steamboats; they had neither steam nor water gauges, and the safety valves often proved uncertain. The engineers sometimes patronized the bar, which was to be found in every boat. Only one accident is reported as having taken place in our waters. A steamboat near Smith's Ferry, whose safety valve had been tied down, exploded its boiler, killing three men. The boats were painted white and are said to have always been kept spick and span. Charles Dickens, in his American Notes, writes of them as being "Half a pony power." Yet in going from Springfield to Hartford, they sometimes reached the latter place in half the time consumed by the stage coach. They had no coal for their engines, but yellow pine wood was cut into lengths of three feet each, and piled at intervals near the shore, where the steam-

---

*Mr. George Lamb of South Hadley Falls writes: "These boats were of the stern-wheel type, which so disturbed the water as to wash and damage the canal bank. To overcome this difficulty, there were numerous inventions, which, however, did not prove practical.

"Luther Alvord, a resident of Falls Woods, contrived a very ingenious device for a canal boat propeller, having a small model that he operated at the mouth of Stony Brook. It was considered very ingenious, but too complicated to be adopted.

"Another model was built by a man named Durkins, of the 'New City' (now Holyoke). He had a device for propellers opening and spreading against the water, backward and forward, like the feet of a duck. The trial of this boat did not prove a success, and it was finally towed back into the canal, not being able to make progress against the current, and being in imminent danger of going over the dam.

"The swing ferry at the Falls was considered the most prosperous on the river, not only in regard to the immense traffic, but also the rapid trips and the ease of operation made possible by the strong current."

boats could load it easily. These boats began running early in spring, sometimes even in February, and continued in service till the following winter. The last steamboat that ever passed through the canal entered it on Thanksgiving day, 1847. George Lamb and another boy had gone down intending to skate near the head of the canal. As they were testing the strength of the ice with their spike poles, they heard a grinding, cracking sound behind them, and looked back to see a boat crushing a path down the narrow waterway. It forced its way through the canal, but never returned, for the Hadley Falls Company bought the water privilege, and the next year built the great dam, whose sorry fate is too well known to need repetition.

The coming of "Lection Day" was, a century ago, a great event in South Hadley Falls. Even the glories of Independence Day paled before the delights of this annual carnival. The scene upon the beach was thus described by a resident of the Canal Village:

"On this day at Springfield, Northampton, and the other larger towns, the militia were out for their annual training, but take the county through, nowhere could be found a larger crowd, or more that was worth seeing, than at the Canal Village. Here were no end of sunburned farmers, wearing knee breeches, long waistcoats of homespun, and stout, buckled shoes. Hats, low-crowned and broad of brim, shaded their clean-shaven faces, and their long queues. The hot sun forced them to carry on their arms their short-waisted coats, with broad lapels and tremendous swallowtails. Here and there a man appeared in his farmyard dress, a long brown frock of undyed tow cloth. Rivermen and others who now and then visited Hartford were distinguishable by a change in dress. To be sure, it was only a lengthening of knee breeches, so as to button at the ankles; but what an absurd name this garment had—'Pantaloon!' Those who wore these pantaloons had a strange way of fastening their shoes with strings instead of buckles. How Frenchified everything was getting! But if the men were comical in their new style of dress, what should be said of the women? Just look at those dashing young people from Northampton, who set the fashions for the country round. They were very lively in that two-horse wagon, with its brace of double-chair seats. How the good wives and daughters from the hill towns, looking out from the recesses of their gig-topped calashes, wondered at the little helmet-shaped bonnets, or the straw caps with visors, which perched upon the frizzled heads of the young women. But those criticizing girls from the hills, poor things, probably had nothing but little bits of looking-glasses at home that did not show their red or butternut-colored flannel gowns, tied about the waists with black ribbons, and gathered at the necks with green ones. There were others in the great concourse besides farmer folks, rivermen and dolls of fashion. It was only on Election Day at Canal Village that so many curious characters were to be seen.

"Here was a man on horseback with a load of strange-looking articles behind him, which he was trying to sell. 'Only fourpence for a corn broom that will out-sweep and out-last all the birch brooms and split brooms in creation. You farmer folks had better go home and plant broom corn. I tell you the time is coming when the corn broom business will be a bigger thing than all your fishing, potashes, and what not. You folks had better buy two brooms apiece, and take one home to use and the other to keep, so as to remember the first time you ever saw a corn broom.'

"Farther on an indigo peddler, stained with his own wares, was supplying housewives with provision for their dye tubs. Beyond him was a Scotch-Irishman from Pelham, opening his pack to exhibit the beautiful linen cloth and thread for which his townswomen were unrivaled. Now came tin peddlers from Berlin,* very keen for a trade.

"Next came another Connecticut man, offering funny little

---

*President Dwight of Yale College tells us that tinware was first manufactured in this country at Berlin, Conn., by William Pattison, in 1740. After the Revolution, the business was carried on by young men who had learned the art from Mr. Pattison. For many years the only method used by peddlers for conveying tinware to distant towns was by means of a horse with two baskets balanced, one upon each side. After the war carts and wagons began to be used for this purpose.

THE PRESENT MILLION-DOLLAR DAM

wooden clocks, without cases, and intended to be hung against the wall; wonderfully cheap, only twenty-five dollars, and the peddler would take anything in trade.

"Such were some of the characters that added zest to this rare break in the dull uniformity of country life.

"As fishing had been suspended for the rest of the day, some exciting substitute was needed, and arrangements had been made for trials of strength and skill. The ground selected was at the upper end of the beach. * * * When every preliminary had been settled, and all boys removed from within the lines, official announcement was made of the various prizes.

"The quoits of rounded stone were first produced, and after a long contest, Springfield and Northampton were beaten by Hadley. Next came the shooting. A piece of white paper five inches square was fastened to a tree for a mark. The marksmen took their stand fifty yards away. Selden and Smith of Hadley, Birge and Alexander of Northampton, and young Moody of Granby, all famous hunters, exhibited their skill amid great applause. * * * Then came the wrestling match. Time will not allow a full account of the 'Indian hug' with which Dunham* mastered all opponents, or his discomfiture in the running jump by a slim youth from Skipmuck.

"Next came the lifting. Robinson of Granville was promptly on hand when the trial was called. While he rolled up his sleeves, stories of his great strength circulated through the crowd, but no one came forward to meet him. He glanced scornfully over the assemblage, and called for the man who dared try him. A group of men were urging a companion who towered a good head above them: 'Go in, Capen, you can whip two of him!' 'I guess I can,' answered the Captain, with a mellow laugh. Accordingly the good-natured man took himself into the ring, to the great delight of the crowd, for all dwellers by the river knew what Captain Henry Strong could do.

---

*Years before Mr. Dunham had been misled into joining in Shay's Insurrection. Later on he reinstated himself in the respect of his fellow townsmen by saving the life of Enos Woodbridge (the son of our second minister) on the evening when the scattered troops of Daniel Shay raided the town of South Hadley.

Among the piles of merchandise lay some barrels of cider. Robinson rolled one of these to the side of a box about four feet high, and seizing the barrel at each end, lifted it by sheer strength onto the box. The applause which greeted this feat gave him time to recover his breath before lifting the barrel down again. 'There's your stunt,' said he, wiping the perspiration from his face. 'We rivermen generally take toll on such things,' replied the Captain; loosening the bung with a stone and placing it upon a clean tuft of grass, the boatman easily lifted the barrel to his mouth and took a hearty drink. 'Perhaps you'll take a pull,' remarked the Captain, depositing the barrel at Robinson's feet. The Granville champion was bound to accept the challenge, and fairly earned his drink before he succeeded in getting it. In the meantime Captain Strong was arranging for another trial. Two strong planks were leaned against a pile of timbers; his friends rolled forward a hogshead of molasses, and it lay ready at the foot of the plank. 'We've had boy's play, and now we'll try some grown men's work,' said the Captain. He bared his arms and rolled the hogshead, hand over hand, to the top of the incline. There he held it for a moment, while all wondered whether he could possibly jump aside in time to escape being crushed when he let go of it. But their fears were needless, for he rolled it easily back to the ground, and courteously stepped aside to make way for Robinson. The champion, however, declined the trial, saying he was no boatman to go rolling things round; what he wanted was a clean lift. 'Well,' returned Captain Strong, 'you gave me a fair stunt, and I done it. Then I stumped you, and you—well, we'll allow you done it. And then I stumped you again, and you daresent try; that's all I've got to say now.' At this moment word came that Captain Strong's boat was about to enter the canal, and he was soon on his way, amid the hearty cheers of the crowd." * * *

"I don't see as there is any great call for girls to spin," said a middle-aged visitor, whose white shirt told that he was no Hampshire County man. "Down in Rhode Island an Englishman has a big mill where he uses water to spin with. Land near

THE CAREW MILL

the waterfalls that you could have bought five years ago for a hundred dollars an acre is now worth fifteen hundred." "My sakes!" exclaimed Smith, "perhaps if they knew of these falls, they'd try here. There's water enough, I guess, for the two saw mills don't near use it all." "There is a considerable powerful fall here," allowed the other. "but this is too far west, too far from Boston. This will always be a lumbering and fishing river, I guess. I am not afraid to say there will never be such a thing as a cotton mill so far back in the country."

With the expression of these and kindred sentiments, the company left the beach, which had faintly imaged a county fair, and in the crowded taverns a good supper and the evening dance rounded out the festivities of the day.

In process of time the number of outside guests at the Canal Village lessened, though Election Day was still esteemed a gala occasion, and the journey up to South Hadley Center, which was then the only polling place, was sometimes a thing worthy of note.

In 1840 a spirited contest arose between the whigs and the locofocos, as the Democrats were then called. William Henry Harrison was the whig candidate for the presidency, and was known as Tippecanoe, on account of his having won the battle of that name in the war with the Indians. The old refrain, "Tippecanoe and Tyler, too," was borne upon every wind that swept through the gap in the mountains, and the Falls people decided to let the uptown locos see what they could do. Accordingly, a short time before election, the men at the Canal Village built a long platform, which was placed upon wheels. Upon this was erected a log cabin, modeled after the old one at North Bend. Through the stove pipe, which did duty for a chimney, issued a fine column of smoke, as, with ten yoke of oxen to draw it, they started for the Center.

The log cabin was eight feet long, and above its open door one could read, "Tippecanoe's door, whose latch string is never pulled in." Above the heads of the leading pair of oxen was framed a large banner, and the most radical among the whigs carried pocket handkerchiefs more than two feet square, upon which were imprinted pictures of General Harrison on horseback, the Capitol at Washington, the log house, etc. Concealed in one corner of the cabin, as the procession of voters marched up the road, was a keg of cider and a huge bag of crackers. There was to be an address in the interests of Harrison, and his adherents left their cortege east of the meeting house and seated themselves in the church, ready to listen to the speaker.

Under the able leadership of Dexter Ingraham there was first an interval of patriotic music that stirred the pulse of every whig, but hardly was the address well begun when the locos stole softly out of the house.

Political feeling at this time ran high at the Center, as was shown by an incident that occurred here during this campaign. "Uncle Sim" and "Uncle Joel," as they were familiarly called, were near neighbors, the former being an ardent whig and the latter a decided Democrat. One day Uncle Sim, on his way to Northampton, overtook his neighbor, also on the road to the Meadow City, and invited him to ride. Unfortunately the conversation took a political turn, and after two or three miles both men became so excited that Uncle Sim stopped his horse and asked his companion to alight. Uncle Joel begged to stay in, promising that he would not mention the name of Harrison again. "No," replied the other firmly, "my horse is just as good a whig as I am, and he refuses to carry you a step farther." So Uncle Joel plodded slowly on to Northampton. His fellow politicians, however, did not allow this slight to pass unavenged, for after the exercises in the church were finished on that memorable day, when the whigs repaired to the log cabin for refreshment, they found the keg of cider empty, and of the crackers only a few crumbs remained.

But upon the day of Harrison's inauguration, the victorious whigs had their innings. A brass cannon was brought up from Chicopee and stationed upon the beach. A feast was prepared in the old tavern near the present site of the Glasgow Mill, and a series of signals with flags was arranged so that the gunner might know when to fire. Captain Calvin Goodman was requested to give a toast. He rose gravely and said: "The locofoco party: a wheel without a single spoke in it." Then the cannon boomed, and the thunders of applause, it is said, shook the house to its very lowest foundations.

After the close of the Revolution, it was said that every family in the Canal Village owned either a horse or a yoke of oxen, which on Sunday gave them conveyance to the church uptown. But as years went on, mills were erected and many of the new inhabitants were compelled to walk the long, circuitous road through Falls Woods, there being at that time no other highway between South Hadley Center and the Falls. Perhaps the most welcome of these new industries was the salt mill. Previous to this, every family must own an iron mortar and pestle, wherein the hard crystals of salt could be pounded to a powder. This was wearisome work for the young people, and they hailed with delight the "salt house" of Josiah Bardwell, which was working in 1824. Here were ground the great lumps of salt brought from Nantucket. The late R. O. Dwight, whose value as a historian only those who have studied carefully the archives of our town can fully understand, says that at first "It was sold in bulk, being weighed out to purchasers as sugar is now." Later on a new firm "Introduced an improvement by selling their salt in cloth bags, each holding a specified weight . . . . The novelty took at once, and spread from South Hadley Falls all over the country."

About this time Rev. Joel Hayes resigned his pastorate at South Hadley, and a call was extended to Rev. Artemus Boies, with the proviso that as often as every third Sunday he should preach at the Canal Village, taking his congregation with him. This seemed to him like having the care of two parishes, and being in delicate health, he refused to accept upon such conditions. He was then invited to become our pastor, but to preach only at the Center, and to this call he sent an affirmative reply. The dwellers by the river now concluded that it was high time for them to start a new organization of their own. They were already in the habit of holding prayer meetings in the Canal Village, and in 1784 they had asked to have the control of their own school money, and it had been granted. The Baptists had commenced a preaching service years before. In 1785 Rev. John Pendleton officiated, and four years later Rev. Mr. Dodge started a Baptist church. Before 1805 this had been merged in the Holyoke church, for at that time South Hadley voted "To excuse the Baptists from paying a minister's tax." The assessors accordingly sent a portion of that year's taxes to Elder Rand.

In 1824 Rev. Eli Moody began preaching in what was called the Brick Chapel. He writes concerning this: "My audience room was in the second story, the stairs leading up to it being on the outside of the house, and all the accommodation for sittings was rough plank or slat seats, without any backs to them. This room had previously been loaned to the people of the village for religious meetings. In this room I preached three months."

At the expiration of that time the place was arranged with "Comfortable pews and a neat and pleasant pulpit."

At the installation of Rev. William Tyler, in 1832, some fears were expressed lest the floor of the Brick Chapel would not be strong enough to sustain the weight of the crowd who would be present, and the exercises were held in the Ames Paper Mill, which was then in the course of erection.

The first church edifice was built in 1835, and became the home of the South Evangelical Society, which had been organized eleven years before, and whose original membership of nineteen had been much increased.

From one of their later ministers, we quote the following: "I was your pastor during the Civil War, and am inevitably carried back to those eventful times; the thrilling scenes we witnessed in this meeting house, when one after another of our young men, the flower of our families, came forward and signed their names to the roll of volunteers for their country's service. I call to mind the gathering of the citizens around the liberty-pole on South Hadley Green, when the town clerk read the oath, and, with uplifted hands, we all renewed our allegiance to the Constitution and Government of the United States; the camp at Greenfield, where I was requested to present a sword to Lieut.

DECORATION DAY AT SOUTH HADLEY FALLS

Williams (of South Hadley); the mustering of the young soldiers in the east gallery of this house on the Sabbath before their departure, and the words of farewell and Godspeed from the balcony of the hotel.''

These words revive the memory of earlier conflicts, the French and Indian wars, and the Revolution, when there was neither newspaper nor telegraph here, and, only at rare intervals, a letter to bring news from the battlefield.

The flight of years has wrought great changes in our town. The deathknell of the old-fashioned fireplace was sounded, when, in every room save one in that first seminary building, Mary Lyon installed a little Franklin stove, which had already begun to supersede the big back log.

Many interesting incidents have been related to the writer of the fraternal friendships which existed in families at that time. There was the story of the two Smith brothers, who owned separate farms, both of which were very large. Every morning at sunrise each went to the top of a hill near his home, and the elder gave three long blasts upon a horn, which told his listening brother that all was well. The younger brother returned his answer in like fashion. The custom was continued for years, and at any failure of this signal a messenger instantly was dispatched to the house of the other.

> Now camlet cloak and homespun suit
> No longer flit from door to door.
> Yet patient years have borne their fruit,
> In school, and home, and church of yore.
> Those days remote, long, long are past.
> The empty nest has left the bough,
> A plaything of the whirling blast;
> And moss-grown stones confront us now.
> We reap the harvest of their deeds
> In rustling fields along the lea;
> The fruitage of immortal seeds,
> The golden sheaves of liberty.
> We pray you, birds, sing sweetly there,
> We bid you, flower-grown meads, to show
> At spring's return a bloom so fair
> That our unwilling hearts may know,
> 'Tis time that stays, 'tis *we* who go.

INDEX

	PAGE
Angel of Hadley, The	4-6
Apple Trees	12, 97
Arithmetic	50, 55, 60
Bears	18
Bees, Chopping, etc.	18, 35-37, 196
Bees, Honey	33
Bible, The	26, 71, 95, 118, 139, 154
Bricks	16
Brick Oven	110
Brooms	214
Buttery Brook	9, 203
Canal, The	201, 213
Carpets	178
Census, The	136
Chairs	87, 175
Children	25-27
Children Catechising	172
Churches, South Hadley Falls	220
Clocks	179, 215
Condit, Rev. Joseph	62, 119, 170
Copy Books	61
Courtship	16, 23
Crows	211
Dame School	51
Deacons	112, 114, 148
Draper, Josiah	44, 55-57, 153
Dress	180
Dwight, Dr. Elihu	175
Eeling	205-207
Election Day	213, 217
Emergency Call, An	154
Examination Day	63
Fires, Kindling of	177
Fisheries	202, 203
Fish House	206, 208
Forks	22
Funeral Customs	29-33
Geography	50, 51
Goffe, General	4-6
Halfway Covenant, The	3, 101, 105
Harrison's Campaign	217
Harvard College	140, 142
Hanks, Rev. Roswell	79, 91
Hessians, Farming of	155

	PAGE
Highways	14, 180, 203
Hilliard's Knob	50, 184
Holland, J. G.	24, 198
Home Lots	8-11
Houses	11, 15-17, 81
Hungry March, The	127
Ice Houses	40, 41
Independence of the United States	152, 164
Indians, The	121
Informers, The	55, 66, 143
Ink	49
Labor Troubles	157
Lafayette, Marquis de	195-197
Land, Divisions of	7-15
Land Grants	7, 13
Lexington, Call of	146
Libraries	182-184
Lubbers' Hole	8, 199
Lyon, Mary	75-93
Matches	178
Meeting Houses	94, 95, 114, 115, 119
Meeting Houses, Seating of	98, 111
Mighill, Samuel	53-57
Millerites	193-195
Missionary Societies	165
Mobbing	104, 144
Montague, Peter, Houses of	11, 16, 19, 81
Mormonism	191-193
Mountain House, The	196
Mourning	142
Nails, Making of	158
Names	158, 185
Noonhouses	174
Pantaloons	181, 213
Parsonages	78, 96, 109
Pass of Thermopylæ	199
Pendergrass, Peter	147
Peperidge Tree	21
Pins	176, 177
Pioneers	6, 7, 12
Post Office	41, 148

	PAGE		PAGE
Potatoes	54, 97	Stoves	98, 172-174
Pouting Pen	114, 117	Sturgeon	207
Preston, John	15, 33	Sunday Schools	166
Punishments	52-69	Superstitions	30-33, 101
Rate Day	111	Taxes	139
Rattlesnakes	17	Tea	140-143
Rawson, Rev. Grindall	95-103, 105-107	Tea Parties	21
		Temperance	169
Rock Ferry	191, 195, 198	Texts	13, 118, 119, 183
Salt Mill	219	Tinware	214
Schools	48-69	Tories	143, 145, 147, 150, 160
Seminary Mt. Holyoke	79-92	Tunnel, The	49
Seminary Receptions	89	Underground Railroad	169
Shad and Salmon	203-205, 208-210	Visiting Day	171
Shay's Rebellion	70, 162	Wages	43, 65, 156, 158
Sickness	112	Warrant, The	141
Singing	43-47, 82	Washing Day	21
Slaves	158, 167-169	Weddings	28, 101
Sleep, Hours of	24	Witches and Ghosts	186, 210
Sluggard Company	208, 209	Wood Day	109
Smith, Chileab	102-105	Woodbridge, Dorothy	189
Spelling Schools	64, 65	Woodbridge, Enos	186-189, 215
Spatterdashes	180	Woodbridge, Rev. John	107-112, 137, 148
Spinning	19, 20		
Spinning, on Sunday	148	Woodbridge, Col. Ruggles	70-72, 117, 141, 146, 155, 162
Stamp Act	136		
Steamboat	211-213	Wright, Abby	72-75

EVERY NAME INDEX

----, Abigail 184 Esther K 27 Horace 42 Jerusha 71 Mary N 58 Polly 191 Polly Jesus 191 Uncle Joel 218 Uncle Sim 218
ALEXANDER, 215
ALLEN, Abby Wright 79 196 Capt 79 Mrs 75 79 Peter 74 78
ALVORD, Job 132-133 Luther 212
ARNOLD, Benedict 159
ASHLEY, Joseph 55 143
BACKUS, Simon 137
BAGG, Hiram 66
BAKER, Henry 121
BARBER, 42
BARDWELL, Johnathan 99 Josiah 219
BARRY, 158
BATES, Emerson 181
BIRCH, Dr 61
BIRGE, 215
BOIES, A 192 Artemas 79 Artemus 219 Rev Mr 192
BRAINARD, Robert 179
BREWERS, Col 153
BROCKWAY, Sheriff 12
BRUIN, Sir 9 17
BULLENS, Mr 169
BURGOYNE, 155
BURNETT, Jonathan 162 183
BURNETTE, Emil 178
BURR, Nancy 49
CAMBRIDGE, Caesar 158
CANNEY, G F 162
CARTER, Mr 64
CHANDLER, David 185

CHANDLER (Cont.) John 190 Tom 207
CHAPEL, Mary Lyon 32
CHAPIN, Mary W 91 Miss 91-92
CHARLES I, King of England 4
CHAUNCEY, Dorothy 100-101 Isaac 94 100
CHOATE, David 81
CLARENCE, Dutchess of 176
CLARK, 102 C 116 Lewis 169 Milton 169 Mr 116 Totty 67
COLLINS, Auraunah 179
CONDIT, Joseph 170 Joseph D 119 Mr 62-63 119 170 Mrs 119 Rev Mr 78
CORNWALLIS, 162
COTTON, John 1
COWLS, John 99
DAVIS, 205 207 Mr 206
DAY, I N 8
DEWITT, 114
DICKENS, Charles 212
DICKINSON, Nathaniel 4-5
DODGE, Rev Mr 220
DOMO, Comfort 185 Peter 13
DRAPER, Josiah 44-45 55 57 153-154 167 Master 56
DUDLEY, Earl of 107 190 Thom 107
DUNHAM, Mr 215
DUNKLEE, Mrs 12
DUNLAP, 109
DURKINS, 212
DWIGHT, Clarissa 20 Dr 36 175-176 Elihu 78-79 175 John 46 88 Mrs 73 Pres 214 R O 191 219

EASTMAN, Benjamin 126
  Benjamine 168 Eunice 150 Joseph
  41 124 126 Miss 96 Squire 126 150
  William 126 137 149-150 168
EDWARDS, Johnathan 99 Jonathan
  77 105 203
ELIOT, John 107
ELLIOTT, John 190
ELY, Samuel 70
EMERSON, 90
FAIRFIELD, Walter 99
FERRY, Philopheta 185 Spiddy 185
FISK, A W 160
FISKE, Fidelia 82
GAGE, Gen 149
GATES, Gen 155
GEORGE, King 141
GEORGE III, King 104 139
GOFFE, Gen 4-5
GOLDTHWAIT, Albert 11
GOODALE, Nat 26 113
GOODMAN, Calvin 218 Eleazer 140
  Mr 73 Noah 163 Titus 31
GOODWIN, Elder 3 Mr 2-3 Wm 1-2
GRAVES, John 168
GRIDLEY, C A 154 Mrs 154 Rev Mr
  73
HARRIS, George 169
HARRISON, 218 Gen 218 William
  Henry 217
HARVEY, Saml 103 Simeon 102-103
HASTINGS, Deacon 46
HAWKS, Mr 79-80 86 91 Roswell 79-80 91
HAYES, Joel 66 73 78 116 150 174
  219 Julia 20 Mr 116-117 Mrs 73
HENRY, Mr 181-182
HERRICK, Cynthia Wright 82
HIGGINS, Sylvester 175
HILLYER, Anne 184 David 185
  Joseph 38 Timothy 50 184
HIRST, Sam 95
HITCHCOCK, G G 133
HOLLAND, 186 J G 9 24 198
HOLLINGSWORTH, Mrs 9 70 173
HOOKER, Mr 2-3 Thomas 1-2
HUTCHISON, Gov 149

INDIAN, King Philip 4 Old Zuba 127
  Phillip 127
INGRAHAM, Dexter 46 82 218
INGRAM, Nathaniel 8
JACKSON, Andrew 63 Jonas 158
JEWETT, W H 147
JUDD, Andrew 92 Levi 114 Lt 155
  Reuben 155 Samuel 199 Sapplina
  185 Simeon 134 Sylvester 4 Widow
  207
KELLOGG, 16 Widow 112
KINNEY, A S 9
KJOLLER, A P 185
KRUG, 14
LAFAYETTE, 197 Gen 199 Marquis
  de 195
LAMB, George 212-213
LAMBIE, Col 210
LANE, John 38 146 John Jr 137
LARKIN, Lorin 158
LAUD, Archbishop 1
LEMON, Elizabeth 43
LESTER, Mrs 20 78
LOOMER, F A 199 Fred 16
LUCAS, G W 45
LYMAN, A M 198 Aristobolus 185
  Eugene 199 Israel 191 198-199
  Miss 74
LYON, Mary 70 75-76 78-80 82-87
  90-91 102 105 109 117 166 221
  Miss 75 77-92 118 Mr 76
MARKHAM, William 9
MARSH, Eb 12 Ebenezer 6 12 16
MARSHALL, John 146
MCGEE, Bill 168 William 168
MCGREGOR, 46
MERCHANT, Stephen 178
MIGHILL, Master 53-54 Saml 53 57
MILLER, A J 143 154 Daniel 154 Dr
  143 Joseph 154 Leonard 154
  William 193
MITCHELL, David 158 168
MONTAGUE, Abigail 133 Clara 62
  John 131 Josiah 131 133 Luke 6
  11 16 112 Moses 79 147 156 Mrs
  112 Peter 11-12 16 19 131 133
  Peter Jr 10 Samuel 103

INDEX

MONTAGUE (Cont.) William 13 112 131 155
MONTCALM, 132
MOODY, 215 Daniel 31 148 163 Deacon 104 Ebenezer 101 103 Eli 220 Eliphaz 31 Henry 126 150 Irene 62 Sarah 103
MOORE, Miss 85
MOTT, Dr 173
MURRAY, Granny 186 Lindley 153 William 10
NASH, Daniel Jr 16 David 36 53 146 148 158 168 Eleazer 149 Ephraim 38-39 50 Jno 33 Lt 149-150 Mr 176 Timothy 4
NOTT, Dr 173
PAINE, Daniel 63 Master 63 Squire 63
PATTISON, Mr 214 William 214
PENDERGRASS, Abial 147 James 147 Peter 147 158
PENDLETON, Elder 210 John 220
PERSTON, Jerusha 29 John 6
PHELPS, 99 Charles 55
PHILIPS, Mrs 160
PHILLIPS, 178 Alonzo D 178
PIERCE, Josiah 54 Master 54-55
PIPER, Sally 35-36
POMEROY, Maj 188 Mary 188
PORTER, Col 155 Samuel 10
POWERS, Jerusha 29 179 John 29
PRENTISS, Elizabeth 92
PRESTON, 10 15 Calvin 11 Dr 48 Esmereniana 185 Gardner Sr 179 J S 8 John 12 15 32-33 81 John Sr 6 Leftenant 29 Mr 179 Norman 46
PYNCHON, Maj 127
RAND, Elder 220 Thomas 169
RAWSON, 98 190 Grindall 48 95-96 98-99 102-103 109 185 203 Madam 105 Mr 96 99-101 103 105-108 Rev Mr 105
ROBERTS, 176
ROBINSON, 215-216
ROOT, Mr 17
RUNY, 179
RUSSELL, John 3-4 Mr 5

SCOTT, 166
SELDEN, 145 215 Bitterne 185 Jonathan 145
SEWALL, Judge 95
SHAY, 70 162 215 Daniel 215
SHAYS, 163 Daniel 162
SKINNER, J A 9 81
SLAVE, Caesar 158
SMEAD, Molly 129-130
SMITH, 10 14 16 103 108 160 182 215 217 221 Byron 88 173 Capt 151 Chileab 11-12 15 102-105 109 151 Chileab III 103 Chileab Jr 6 Chileab Sr 7 Comfort 185 David 25 151 Deacon 30 E T 79 173 Ensign 149-150 Experience 149 G M 174 G Morgan 181 Harry 66 James 102 Jno 33 John 54 109 112-113 Jonathan 109 Landlord 205 Maj 151 Mr 206 Mrs 151 Mrs Chileab 104 Phineas 131 151 Rebekah 133 Samuel 4 Sarah 103 Selah 114 Silas 114 Totty 67 William 46 109
SNOW, Josiah 184
SPARKS, Jared 183
STEBBINS, Dr 31 73 Mrs 73
STICKNEY, John 43-44
STODDARD, Ebenezer 141 Solomon 101
STONE, Rev Mr 2-3 Samuel 1-2 38
STOWE, Mrs 169
STRONG, Capt 216 Henry 215 Joseph 166
SWORD, Selor 158
TALBOT, H C 103
TALCOTT, 128 Maj 127-128
TAYLOR, 16 Frank 54 Levi 159 Oliver 182 William 203
THROOP, Mr 153
TILTON, Peter 4 126
TODD, Mr 82
TUCK, Irene 62 J W 61 Mr 61-62
TULLER, Resolve 185
TYLER, William 220
WAITE, J W 14
WASHINGTON, 159 Gen 159
WATTS, Dr 24 Isaac 47

WEBSTER, John 9 Noah 7
WELLS, Jonathan 103
WHALLEY, Gen 4
WHITE, 9 Cotton 185 Cyrus 79
   Deacon 175 E 166 Enoch 114
   Ezekiel 44 Heman 163 Jack 189
   John 4 Joseph 31 73 174 189
   Josiah 156 166 Moses 121 Mrs
   Joseph 73 Mrs Thomas 181
   Nathaniel 44 P 166 Sally 20
   Samuel 150 Sedgwick 174 Stephen
   177
WHITMAN, Miss 85 91
WHITNEY, Harriet E 166
WILLIAM, Peter 6
WILLIAMS, John 125 Lt 221

WITT, Ivory 185
WOLFE, 132
WOLFINGER, Leslie 13
WOOD, Preserved 185
WOODBRIDGE, Aeneas 186 B R 192
   Benjamin Ruggles 141 190 Col 70-
   73 117 141 147 155-156 162-163
   175 180 188 190 Dolly 189-190 192
   Dorothy 189 Dr 140 Enos 184 186
   188-189 215 John 107 132 137 189
   Lt 190 Madam 110 112 Mr 108-
   109 111 115 148 162 Parson 38
   Rev Mr 108 116 137 148 152
   Ruggles 31 70 146 188 Uncle Enos
   187
WRIGHT, Abby 72 Miss 72 74

www.ingramcontent.com/pod-product-compliance
Lightning Source LLC
Chambersburg PA
CBHW052051230426
43671CB00011B/1870